VICTORIAN WOMEN WRITERS AND THE WOMAN QUESTION

Women writers dominated the vast novel market in Victorian England, yet twentieth-century criticism has, until now, been chiefly concerned with a small number of canonical novelists. This collection of essays by leading scholars from Britain, the USA, and Canada opens up the limited landscape of Victorian novels by focusing attention on some of the women writers popular in their own time but forgotten or neglected by literary history. Spanning the entire Victorian period, this study investigates particularly the role and treatment of "the woman question" in the second half of the century. There are discussions of marriage, matriarchy, and divorce, satire, suffragette writing, writing for children, and links between literature and art. Moving from Margaret Oliphant and Charlotte Mary Yonge to Mary Ward, Marie Corelli, "Ouida," and E. Nesbit, this book illuminates the complex cultural and literary roles, and the engaging contributions, of Victorian women writers.

NICOLA DIANE THOMPSON is Senior Lecturer in English at Kingston University, England. She is the author of *Reviewing Sex: Gender and the Reception of Victorian Novels* (1996) and a number of articles on Victorian literature and culture.

CAMBRIDGE STUDIES IN NINETEENTH-CENTURY
LITERATURE AND CULTURE 21

VICTORIAN WOMEN WRITERS AND THE WOMAN QUESTION

CAMBRIDGE STUDIES IN NINETEENTH-CENTURY
LITERATURE AND CULTURE

Nineteenth-century British literature and culture have been rich fields for interdisciplinary studies. Since the turn of the twentieth century, scholars and critics have tracked the intersections and tensions between Victorian literature and the visual arts, politics, social organization, economic life, technical innovations, scientific thought – in short, culture in its broadest sense. In recent years, theoretical challenges and historiographical shifts have unsettled the assumptions of previous scholarly syntheses and called into question the terms of older debates. Whereas the tendency in much past literary critical interpretation was to use the metaphor of culture as "background," feminist, Foucauldian, and other analyses have employed more dynamic models that raise questions of power and of circulation. Such developments have reanimated the field.

This series aims to accommodate and promote the most interesting work being undertaken on the frontiers of the field of nineteenth-century literary studies: work which intersects fruitfully with other fields of study such as history, or literary theory, or the history of science. Comparative as well as interdisciplinary approaches are welcomed.

A complete list of titles published will be found at the end of the book.

VICTORIAN WOMEN WRITERS AND THE WOMAN QUESTION

EDITED BY

NICOLA DIANE THOMPSON

CAMBRIDGE
UNIVERSITY PRESS

CAMBRIDGE UNIVERSITY PRESS
Cambridge, New York, Melbourne, Madrid, Cape Town,
Singapore, São Paulo, Delhi, Tokyo, Mexico City

Cambridge University Press
The Edinburgh Building, Cambridge CB2 8RU, UK

Published in the United States of America by Cambridge University Press, New York

www.cambridge.org
Information on this title: www.cambridge.org/9781107404151

First published 1999
Reprinted 2000
First paperback edition 2011

A catalogue record for this publication is available from the British Library

Library of Congress Cataloguing in Publication Data
Victorian Women writers and the woman question / edited by Nicola Diane
Thompson.
p.   cm. – (Cambridge studies in nineteenth-century literature
and culture; 21)
Includes bibliographical references and index.
ISBN 0 521 64102 0 (hardback)
1. English fiction – 19th century – History and criticism.
2. Feminism and literature – Great Britain – History – 19th century.
3. Women and literature – Great Britain – History – 19th century.
4. Popular literature – Great Britain – History and criticism.
5. English fiction – Women authors – History and criticism.
6. Women's rights – Great Britain – History – 19th century. 7. Women's
rights in literature. 8. Sex role in literature. I. Thompson,
Nicola Diane, 1961–   . II. Series.
PR878.F45W66   1999
823'.8099287 – dc21   98–35820
CIP

ISBN 978-0-521-64102-9 Hardback
ISBN 978-1-107-40415-1 Paperback

Contents

Illustrations

Notes on contributors

ANN ARDIS, Associate Professor of English at the University of Delaware, is the author of *New Women, New Novels: Feminism and Early Modernism* (1990). She has written numerous articles on late nineteenth-century and early twentieth-century novels by women writers and is currently working on a book entitled *Modernism, Modernity, Mass Culture: The "Rise" of English Studies and Modernist Aesthetics, 1880–1920.*

ALISON CHAPMAN is Lecturer in English at the University of Dundee, Scotland, and is the author of *Christina Rossetti and the Aesthetics Of The Feminine* (1998). She has written several articles on Victorian women poets and is currently working on a new study of the uncanny.

MONICA COHEN is Assistant Professor of English at the California Institute of Technology. She is the author of *Home Inc: Domestic Work and Professional Culture in the Victorian Novel* (1998), as well as a number of articles on Victorian fiction.

DENNIS DENISOFF has recently completed a postdoctoral fellowship at Princeton University and is currently Assistant Professor of English at the University of Waterloo, Canada. He has recently co-edited a collection of essays entitled *Perennial Decay: New Essays on the Politics and Poetics of Decadence* (1998) and is completing two book-length projects, *Misleading Strangeness: Aestheticism, Sexual Identity, and Satire* and *Ekphrastic Passion: Identity, Portraiture, and Gender.*

ALEXIS EASLEY is Instructor of English at the University of Alaska Southeast. Her publications include "Wandering Women: Dorothy Wordsworth and the Discourse on Female Vagrancy" (*Women's Writing* 3.1 [1996]); "Victorian Women Writers and the Periodical Press: The Case of Harriet Martineau" (*Nineteenth-Century Prose* 24.1 [1997]);

"Authorship, Gender and Identity: George Eliot in the 1850s" (*Women's Writing* 3.2 [1997]); and "Harriet Martineau and the Victorian Periodical Press," in Laurel Brake, William Bell, and David Finkelstein (eds.), *Defining Centres: Nineteenth-Century Media and the Construction of Identities* (forthcoming, 1999).

ANNETTE R. FEDERICO is Associate Professor of English at James Madison University, Virginia, where she teaches Victorian literature and Women's Studies. She is the author of *Masculine Identity in Hardy and Gissing* (1991) and numerous articles on Victorian literature and culture.

PAMELA GILBERT is Assistant Professor of English at the University of Florida and 1996–97 Fellow at the Center for Twentieth-Century Studies at the University of Wisconsin, Milwaukee. She is the author of *Disease, Desire and the Body in Victorian Women's Popular Novels* (1997).

ANNE HUMPHERYS is Professor of English at The Graduate School and University Center, the City University of New York. She is the author of *Travels into the Poor Man's Country: The Work of Henry Mayhew* (1977) and chapters, articles, and reviews on Tennyson, G. W. M. Reynolds, Charles Dickens, Victorian popular culture and the press. She is currently writing a book on the impact of the 1857 divorce legislation on novels by Victorian women.

LYN PYKETT is Professor of English and Head of Department at the University of Wales, Aberystwyth. She has published widely on nineteenth-century fiction and on turn-of-the-century culture. Her books include *The "Improper" Feminine: the Women's Sensation Novel and the New Woman Writing* (1992), *Engendering Fictions: The English Novel in the Early Twentieth Century* (1995), and an edited collection, *Reading Fin de Siècle Fictions* (1996).

AMELIA A. RUTLEDGE is Associate Professor of English at George Mason University, Virginia. She has published articles on the science fiction of Olaf Stapledon, on the figure of Merlin, on philosophy in the works of Italo Calvino, and most recently an article on the use of Darwin in late nineteenth-century music criticism. Her current research centers on children's literature and women's poetry of the nineteenth century.

VALERIE SANDERS is Senior Lecturer at the University of Sunderland, England, and the author of several books and articles on Victorian literature. Her publications include *Eve's Renegades: Victorian Anti-Feminist Women Novelists* (1996), *The Private Lives of Victorian Women: Autobiography in Nineteenth-Century England* (1989), and *Reason Over Passion: Harriet Martineau and the Victorian Novel* (1986). She is the editor of *Harriet Martineau: Selected Letters* (1990).

JUNE STURROCK is Professor in the English Department at Simon Fraser University near Vancouver, British Columbia. Her monograph, *"Heaven and Home": Charlotte M. Yonge's Domestic Fiction and the Victorian Debate Over Women*, was published in 1995; other publications include articles on Christina Rossetti and Charlotte Yonge. She is currently working on an edition of *Mansfield Park* for the Broadview Press.

BETH SUTTON-RAMSPECK is Assistant Professor of English at The Ohio State University, Lima, where she specializes in Victorian literature. Her current research interests focus on Victorian women writers and feminism, with particular concentration on Mary Ward.

NICOLA DIANE THOMPSON is Senior Lecturer in the English Department at Kingston University, England. She is the author of *Reviewing Sex: Gender and the Reception of Victorian Novels* (1996) and has published a number of articles on gender and literature in Victorian and twentieth-century England. She is currently working on a book entitled *Reading Victorian Women Writers*, as well as researching Victorian children's literature and gender issues.

CHAPTER I

Responding to the woman questions: rereading noncanonical Victorian women novelists

Nicola Diane Thompson

"She fought for Women: yet with women fought." In this extract from his obituary of conservative Victorian novelist Eliza Lynn Linton (*Queen*, July 23, 1898), Walter Besant encapsulates profound contradictions in the lives and careers of Victorian women novelists regarding what the Victorians called the "woman question," the ongoing Victorian discussion about woman's nature and societal role. This same duality is now evident among contemporary feminist critics working to reclaim forgotten Victorian female novelists. In effect fighting both for and with Victorian women writers, they often instead actually hinder their entrance into the canon.

Women writers dominated the vast novel market in Victorian England. Yet from the hundreds of women novelists popularly and critically admired in the nineteenth century, twentieth-century critical conversations have revolved around the canonical few: George Eliot, Emily and Charlotte Brontë, and, more recently, Elizabeth Gaskell. Here I argue that Victorian women novelists' inherently complicated and conflicted positions on the "woman question," in conjunction with the evolving horizon of expectations toward what we now call feminism, are responsible for their noncanonical status. By recognizing unconscious prejudices, we may now give renewed and sustained critical attention to neglected novels by Victorian women.

We might expect Victorian novels by women to benefit from the interest of feminist critics in the Victorian period in general and Victorian women in particular. Studies by critics such as Nancy Armstrong and Mary Poovey have provided important perspectives on conventionally acclaimed women novelists such as the Brontës. Nevertheless, when one ponders the ambivalence and the relative scarcity of contemporary writing on noncanonical Victorian novels by women, it becomes evident that the ideological agendas of twentieth-century feminism are incompatible with the unstable, fluid, and fundamentally *different* posi-

tions of Victorian women writers on the woman question. Very often,
the heroines of these popular novels, created against the backdrop of
shifting nineteenth-century debates about the woman question, stub-
bornly resist appropriation by twentieth-century critics as subversive
role models for women. While feminist criticism makes it possible in
principle to recover forgotten women novelists, its ideological basis has
limitations: what, for example, do you say about a conservative woman
novelist like Charlotte Yonge once you've discovered her?

In the classic work on Victorian woman writers, *A Literature of Their Own*,
Elaine Showalter argues that women's literary history has been deprived of the enormously diverse range of Victorian women novelists
because of the traditional insistence upon the greatness of the elite few.[1]
Before Showalter's reassessment, noncanonical Victorian women
writers were largely ignored. More surprisingly, however, feminist
critics have since continued to overlook or examine cursorily the work of
most Victorian women novelists. In the last few years, a small number of
books have emerged that begin to address noncanonical Victorian
women writers in more depth. However, none provides an overview of
the spectrum from conservative to radical women novelists, and no
studies focus on how the novelists' positions on feminism have in turn
influenced critical attention. While no work yet exists that focuses on
both conservative and radical Victorian women novelists, critics have
recently begun to write a few studies or biographies of individual women
writers; occasionally, criticism directs attention to women writers as a
group.[2] Most of the (still relatively few) studies that exist look at New
Woman or sensation novels, those genres most apparently compatible
with feminist readings, thus revealing how our own "woman questions"
shape current interpretation and evaluation. And New Woman and
sensation novelists, whilst they have received the most critical attention,
are still inadequately represented in literary studies.

Given the prominence of discourse and discord on the woman
question in Victorian England, Victorian women novelists were central-
ly concerned with the developing debates over women's proper role and
status in society. Throughout the second half of the nineteenth century
there was passionate discussion and agitation on matters such as marriage and divorce laws, women's property and custody rights, and
educational and employment opportunities for women, as well as a
vocal debate on female suffrage, which gained intensity later in the
century. To name simply a few of the dramatic events forming the

material for lively debate on women's issues, one could cite the 1857 Divorce Act, the foundation of the Society for the Promotion of the Employment of Women in 1859, the opening of Cheltenham Ladies College in 1856, of Girton College in 1869, John Stuart Mill's *The Subjection of Women* in 1869, and the apocalyptic fears and apparent ideological threat of the New Woman in the 1890s. It was impossible for educated people not to be aware of such developments and not to form opinions and take a stance. In fact, the complexity and multifariousness of the debates about women's nature, role, and literary status, in Victorian and twentieth-century discussions, make it more appropriate to pluralize the term "woman question," changing it to "woman questions."

Harriet Martineau, Geraldine Jewsbury, and Elizabeth Gaskell were among many who signed activist Barbara Bodichon's petition to support the Married Woman's Property Bill in 1854. Most women novelists, while stating their approval of single women's financial independence, or the usefulness of education for women, made sure that they differentiated themselves clearly from the excesses of the "shrieking Sisterhood," as Eliza Lynn Linton called them, or from the personal extremes and unconventionality of activists such as Mary Wollstonecraft. Harriet Martineau asserts in her *Autobiography*: "The Wollstonecraft order . . . do infinite mischief; and for my part, I do not wish to have anything to do with them."[3] In her chapter for this book, "Gendered observations: Harriet Martineau and the woman question," Alexis Easley argues that Martineau attempted in fact to gain credibility and to distance herself from stereotypes of "public women" by developing narrative strategies intended to create an omniscient but politicized perspective.

Twentieth-century critics have tended to label women novelists as feminist or antifeminist, even classifying whole genres or subgenres according to their position on the woman question; a closer examination of Victorian novels demonstrates divisions and tensions concerning women that make such judgments simplistic. The lives and the fictions of Victorian women writers reveal endlessly contradictory perspectives on the woman question. All Victorian women novelists, whether we now label them radical or conservative, were fundamentally conflicted in their own beliefs about women's proper role, and I believe that the critical reception of their novels from Victorian times to the present has been filtered through the ambivalence of the novelists themselves as well as their critics on the complex of issues which constitute the woman question.

Novels by Victorian women writers tend to be melting-pots of ideological conflict and exploration of attitudes toward women's nature and role, full of the dialogic interplay of voices that Bakhtin identifies as central to the novel genre. Traditionally and currently, we nevertheless tend to classify Victorian women's novels as either radical or conservative. For example, the domestic novel written by writers such as Charlotte Yonge is often disparaged as conservative and antifeminist, whereas the sensation novel by writers such as Mrs. Henry Wood and Mary Elizabeth Braddon is celebrated as explosively radical; the New Woman novel of the end of the nineteenth century is reputedly the most apocalyptically feminist type of all. All of these definitions are essentially labeling the novelists according to our perception of their ideological position and the labels unfortunately serve to distort the complexity of the historically specific discourses and contexts in which the novels are embedded. To some extent such categories are inherited unquestioningly from our Victorian critical predecessors, but I hope in the following brief exploration of some representative novelists to show how misleading such distinctions can be.

Whatever the ostensible ideological position of novels by Victorian women, a dialogic interplay of competing voices can be glimpsed below the surface of the plot. Novelists such as Margaret Oliphant and Charlotte Yonge, for example, have been labeled as antifeminist, even though, beneath the overt conservatism of their plot-lines, their novels reveal distinctly empathetic identification with the limitations women faced in Victorian society. Monica Cohen's contribution to this volume, "Maximizing Oliphant: begging the question and the politics of satire," argues that a close examination of Oliphant's "rhetorical caginess" and stylized syntax in her treatment of the woman question reveals an ironic questioning of conservative authority.

Charlotte Yonge's *The Clever Woman of the Family* (1865) is another case in point: the novel shows sympathy for the protagonist, Rachel, desperate for an outlet for her energies and intelligence: "I have pottered about cottages and taught at schools in the dilettante way of the young lady who thinks it her duty to be charitable; and I am told that it is my duty, and that I may be satisfied."[4] Rachel's hubristic attempts at independent action end in near-apocalyptic tragedy, however, when a child dies under her care. The novel ends with Rachel's reform as she becomes engaged to a military man who promises to make her "a thorough wife and mother"[5] and to whom she confesses that she was never "a Clever Woman" after all; "'I never thought you one', he quietly returned."[6]

While the plot does on one level clearly indicate disapproval of Rachel's ambitions, a substantial part of the book is devoted to exploring Rachel's aspirations in a sympathetic way, as is apparent from the first quotation above. And simply the novel's title itself raises subversive expectations on the part of the Victorian or contemporary reader about Rachel's distinctive intelligence, juxtaposing "clever" with "woman." (Yonge's perspectives on marriage and woman's work are explored further in Valerie Sanders' and June Sturrock's contributions to this book.)

Though apparently inimically opposed to the radical sensation novel genre of the 1860s and 1870s, Yonge's novel can be viewed, from one point of view, as analogous. Mary Elizabeth Braddon's *Lady Audley's Secret* (1862) and Mrs. Henry Wood's *East Lynne* (1861) also explore transgressive actions on the part of their heroines, albeit more dramatically than Yonge.[7] Lady Audley is bigamous, pushes her first husband down a well, thinks about poisoning her second husband, and deserts her child, among other things. Lady Isabel Vane in *East Lynne* leaves her husband, and runs away with her lover, who then deserts her. After she is disfigured in a train accident, she returns as governess to nurse her own children unrecognized. While the nature of the transgression and punishment differs, the structure of Yonge's plot is similar to that of Braddon and Wood: in all three novels the heroine rebels from convention and in each case the behavior is dramatically condemned, though Yonge's novel ends finally with the heroine's marriage, which could be viewed as punishment or reward. Both Braddon and Wood thoroughly punish their heroines for their subversively willful actions and conventional order is restored at the end of all three stories, with stern admonitions by Wood to readers never to leave their husbands regardless of the provocation.[8] Problematics of divorce and marriage play complex roles in society and in literature throughout the Victorian period; Anne Humpherys' interesting exploration of the early Victorian divorce novel in this volume considers *East Lynne* among other novels, examining the effect of the introduction of divorce into the conventional marriage plot.

Just as Yonge's novel can be seen as parallel in some ways to the sensation novel's flirtation with women's independence and power, with similar moralizing conclusions, so can we view other apparently conservative productions like Eliza Lynn Linton's *The Rebel of the Family* (1880) as more confused and transgressive than meets the eye.[9] Linton is famous for her ardently antifeminist essays collected in *The Girl of the*

Period (1869) and certainly *The Rebel* purports to be a satirical expose of the evils of the woman's movement, epitomized by the sinister figure of Bell Blount, Lady President of the West Hill Society for Women's Rights. While Linton is consistently negative toward Mrs. Blount, whom she compares to "the Prince of Darkness clad as an Angel of Light . . . the cloven hoof well covered by the shining garments,"[10] she is more sympathetic to Perdita's independent thinking and desire to get a job at the Post Office. Perdita, the heroine, is "murderously direct in thought and daring to give an opinion on matters whereon young women of properly constituted minds have no opinions at all – she crowned her iniquities by taking an interest in politics and having views of her own."[11] And in fact *The Rebel of the Family* reveals a definite sympathy with Perdita's failures to fit in to the conventional marriage-obsessed mindset of her family, a sympathy which subverts the ostensibly conservative didactic message of the story. Linton herself in her youth was the rebel of her own family: her father threatened to disinherit her when she told him of her plan to leave home and go to work in London as an authoress. Her later conservatism seems to have been fueled in passion and intensity by her own earlier radical tendencies.[12]

My final example of the limitations of clear-cut classification according to ideology involves a New Woman novel, the late-century genre usually considered most radically feminist. Sarah Grand's *Ideala* (1889) tells the story of Ideala, an unusual woman who eventually leaves her abusive and adulterous husband and falls passionately in love with Lorrimer, a man she considers her soul-mate: "You have been the one thing wanting to me my whole life long. I believe that no soul is perfect alone, and that each of us must have a partner-soul somewhere, kept apart from us – by false marriages, perhaps, or distance, or death, but still to be ours."[13] Despite idealizing the depth of Ideala's and Lorrimer's mutual devotion, the novel takes a conventional turn: the male narrator, a close friend of Ideala's, convinces her not to live adulterously with Lorrimer as this would be socially wrong: "You would have society turned topsy-turvy, and all for what? Why, simply to make a wrong thing right for yourself! . . . There must be moral laws, and it is inevitable that they should press hardly on individuals occasionally, but it is clearly the duty of individuals to sacrifice themselves for the good of the community at large."[14] Ideala finally devotes herself to the moral improvement of fallen or "useless" women, agreeing with her friend Claudia that "an unwomanly woman is such a dreadful creature."[15] Thus, even a reputedly radical genre provides a typically conformist resolution. And of course the genre itself contains a spectrum of perspectives on the woman question, as Ann Ardis and Lyn Pykett discuss in their contributions to this volume on New Woman novelists.

Consistently, Victorian and modern critics tend to label works by women novelists according to their apparent position on the woman question, creating such categories as domestic novels, sensation novels, and New Woman novels. If we look briefly at Victorian reaction to these three genres, we can see how Victorian critics focus on the treatment of the woman question, praising writers like Yonge for their didactic and uplifting portrayal of women, while attacking sensation and New Woman novels for the dangerously debauching effects they might have on female readers.[16]

Despite the existence of a critical double standard, discussed elsewhere,[17] Victorian readers read, reviewed, enjoyed, and gave critical acclamation to works we now consider noncanonical alongside those we now consider great. George Eliot was frequently reviewed with and compared to Dinah Mulock Craik and Mrs. Oliphant, though she herself objected to such connections. G. H. Lewes reviewed and related Geraldine Jewsbury, George Eliot, and Charlotte Brontë, while Jewsbury reviewed Craik with Eliot. A diary survives of a Victorian reader who admitted to liking *Jane Eyre* but preferring Gaskell and Martineau, with her favorite author being Oliphant. Sally Mitchell describes the popularity of Ouida's *Moths* in 1880 with "serious young women" who "spoke of it in the same breath with *Villette* or *Ruth*."[18] A French critic apparently preferred Rhoda Broughton's novels to Ouida's and George Eliot's, believing her heroines "much truer to nature than Ouida's and more impassioned than Eliot's."[19] Later in the century, Mrs. Humphry Ward was taken extremely seriously, described as "the greatest living English writer" by Tolstoy and seen as Eliot's natural successor, while popular spiritualist writer Marie Corelli was told by the Prince of Wales that "you are the only woman writer of genius we have."[20] Beth Sutton-Ramspeck's "Shot out of the canon: Mary Ward and the claims of conflicting feminism" and Annette Federico's "An 'old-fashioned' young woman: Marie Corelli and the New Woman" (both in this book) explore the multilayered issues involved in the Victorian popularity and subsequent invisibility of Mrs. Humphry Ward and Marie Corelli.

As Tricia Lootens states in her recent work on Victorian women poets and the canonization process, "attention to canonization, widely conceived, can open up new understandings of specific conflicts over literary and cultural value."[21] In order to account for the status of

Victorian women writers, we need to examine trends and elements in both nineteenth- and twentieth-century criticism and culture. Some of the principal factors at work during the Victorian period which contributed to the eventual exclusion of women writers from the canon include the increasing distinctions being made between popular and serious novels, the view that works by women are subjective and biased, especially in terms of their position on the woman question, and the increasing use of George Eliot as a touchstone against which other women writers would be compared and found wanting.

By the 1860s, with the phenomenal popularity of the novel, and its dominance by female writers and readers, a division began to emerge between popular and "serious" literature. The more popular a novel, the more appealing to a mass audience, the more suspect the quality of the work.[22] Popular works by women dealing with issues concerning women and often addressed to women were thus dangerously in line for the critical guillotine. W. L. Courtney's *The Feminine Note in Fiction*, written in 1904, epitomizes many of the clichés about Victorian women and their writing – that they are simply imitative, concerned with detail, and overly involved in their works emotionally – coming to the conclusion that "the novel as a work of art" is disappearing because of its dominance by women. He singles out for particular attack what he sees as the tendency of women novelists to be overly didactic and subjective, a criticism still used in recent discussions of Victorian women writers. Here, as elsewhere, we see the strangely self-perpetuating nature of Victorian critical positions on women novelists:

A great creator like Shakespeare or Dickens has a wide impartiality towards all his puppets . . . If a novelist take sides, he or she is lost. Then we get a pamphlet, a didactic exercise, a problem novel – never a work of art. The female author is at once self-conscious and didactic. For reasons which are tolerably clear . . . the beginning of a woman's work is generally the writing of a personal diary.[23]

Over time, we can see that exclusion from the canon was in part the result of the popularity of novels by women in conjunction with their complicated explorations of the woman question.

The novels' popularity with female readers also became problematic. Virginia Woolf's assessment that books about "the feelings of women in a drawing-room"[24] are automatically assumed to be more trivial than books about war is certainly true of the Victorian age and still true today. Terry Lovell argues that throughout history, literary works addressed to women are more likely to be omitted from the canon.[25] Works by women addressed to children, especially those addressed to girls, are thus particularly susceptible to critical neglect. In her chapter for this book, "Phantasies of matriarchy in Victorian children's literature," Alison Chapman argues that its association with women and children continues to lower the status of children's literature; by assuming the disjunction of children's fiction from political issues such as the woman question, contemporary criticism is guilty of reinscribing Victorian gender ideology.

As already noted, another perhaps less visible factor working in the creation of literary reputations in Victorian England was the exaltation of Eliot as the great woman writer and the tendency to use her as a touchstone of artistic excellence, expecting other women novelists to measure up to Eliot's particular strengths and denigrating them when they did not.[26] We see in George Eliot's own essays (such as "Silly Novels by Lady Novelists") as well as in her letters how determined she was to distance herself from other women writers and from the mainstream audience for novels. She reacted bitterly to the comparison of her work with Dinah Mulock Craik's, arguing that hers were a very different kind of novel, not simply read by "novel readers pure and simple."[27] Her novels, often written with an androgynous or even masculine narratorial persona (alongside her masculine pseudonym, of course) who takes authoritatively erudite stances on matters of public concerns, are directed at educated readers, male as well as female.[28] In a letter to Harriet Beecher Stowe in 1869, Eliot makes it clear that her novels are intended primarily for a select few rather than for a popular multitude.[29]

Margaret Oliphant's *Autobiography* throws an interesting light on how women novelists internalized the constant comparisons with Eliot, usually to their own detriment:

George Eliot's life has ... stirred me up to an involuntary confession. How I have been handicapped in life! Should I have done better if I had been kept like her in a mental greenhouse and taken care of? ... I am in very little danger of having my life written, and that is all the better in this point of view – for what could be said of me? George Eliot and George Sand make me half inclined to cry over my poor little unappreciated self... These two bigger women did things which I have never felt the least temptation to do – but how very much more enjoyment they seem to have got out of their life, how much more praise and homage and honour!... I do feel very small, very obscure, beside them, rather a failure all round ... I acknowledge frankly that there is nothing in me – a fat, little, commonplace woman, rather tongue-tied – to impress anyone; and yet there is a sort of whimsical injury in it which makes me sorry for myself.[30]

So despite the real merit and strengths of her novels, Oliphant devalues herself by measuring herself against Eliot as a standard and type of excellence, influenced in part by the assessment of so many critics. Much of her self-abasement specifically relates to her sex – she is a commonplace woman, while Eliot is an extraordinary woman, almost an honorary man by implication. Tricia Lootens argues that nineteenth-century female canonization typically dichotomized women writers, either "casting them as honorary Great Men" or "lauding them as vessels of the unitary, eternal, and ultimately silent sanctity of womanhood."[31] Charlotte Yonge is an example of the latter category, as I argue elsewhere.[32] And Margaret Oliphant ends her autobiography, in which she plaintively describes her decision to focus on supporting her family rather than literary excellence, with an abrupt breaking-off from her narrative and a lapse into silence.

Most pre-feminist studies strongly emphasize that Victorian women novelists do not reach the high canonical standard, as if to justify their own critical project. W.L. Courtney's assessment of woman writers in 1904 set the tone for much of the twentieth century. Amy Cruse, writing of Ouida in 1935, declares that "neither she nor any other of the sensational novelists had the qualities that make the works of the Great Novelists immortal."[33] Vineta Colby takes pains not to make any aesthetic claims for works by Victorian women novelists. Like her Victorian predecessors and later critics, Colby compares Victorian women novelists unfavorably to Eliot:

The trouble with these "singular anomalies" is that they wrote with their brains. George Eliot described a truly cultured woman as one "whose mind had absorbed her knowledge instead of being absorbed by it." Unhappily, the woman novelists who imitated her were absorbed by their knowledge. They displayed it at times gracefully and attractively but more often heavily and clumsily. They used the novels as a medium of instruction; often they exploited it. They were women of intellect, tact, and talent, but they were not artists. That they should have been so widely acclaimed, as most of them were, so honored and influential, is a comment on the power and prestige of the novel itself.[34]

Similarly, Colby makes the following revelatory comment about Mrs. Humphry Ward: "No creative thinker or artist in her own right, she was endowed only with high intelligence, fervent moral conviction, and a warm feminine sympathy for the sufferings . . . of others. The Victorians often confused such talents as these for genius."[35] Thus even critics like Courtney and Colby, who devote entire books to Victorian women novelists, tend to disparage the writers artistically more than the Victorians themselves did.

Until the rise of feminist criticism in the last thirty years, we could attribute the neglect of Victorian women writers to the derogatory associations that Victorians themselves and later critics had with women and writing – particularly if the writing in question was popular, and popular with women readers to boot. But for the most part, while feminist critics have been largely responsible for resurrecting interest in the women in the Victorian period in the last thirty years, they have not considered the works of most noncanonical women novelists in depth. Or when they do consider them in depth, they tend to evaluate the authors according to their degree of feminism or subversiveness, often making derogatory judgments in the process, continuing to use the modernist aesthetic criteria of Courtney and Colby. Elaine Showalter, Patricia Stubbs, Gail Cunningham, Sally Mitchell, and, more recently, Dorothy Mermin come to mind here. While they have all produced distinguished and groundbreaking studies, resurrecting interest in neglected women novelists, they have not really taken the noncanonical women writers very seriously. To be fair, the earliest feminist studies such as those by critics like Showalter, Cunningham, and Mitchell in the 1970s, were written in a historical context where examining forgotten works by Victorian women writers was itself a revolutionary act. It is perhaps unreasonable then to expect, in addition, that these critics should have stepped out of entrenched literary establishment ideas of artistic merit in order to make aesthetic claims for these women writers or to take them seriously as artists. Recent critics, however, like Ann Ardis, are beginning to reevaluate the aesthetic merits of Victorian women writers: in her chapter for this book, "Organizing women: New Woman writers, New Woman readers, and suffrage feminism," Ardis argues that modernism was based on the devaluation of women readers and women's writing and proposes more helpful approaches to the *fin-de-siècle* New Woman writers.

Showalter eloquently describes the impoverishment of the female literary tradition but seems to take for granted that the women novelists she surveys are "minor" and "not great,"[36] dismissing many of them as unimportant: "The feminist writers were not important artists."[37] Equally, Gail Cunningham states that the New Woman novelists "produced nothing of lasting literary merit."[38] Sally Mitchell reacts similarly: "Few of these sensation novels have any claim to literary survival except as a reflection of the decade's interests."[39] Writing of the New Woman

novel, Patricia Stubbs condemns them as overly polemical, being "treat-
ises first, novels second. Many were confused and sentimental, or bald
statements of problems rather than attempts to come to grips with
them."[40]

Popular Victorian women writers are often criticized, then, for being
insufficiently subversive, this judgment being used implicitly as a cri-
terion for their continuing neglect. Stubbs devotes much of *Women and
Fiction. Feminism and the Novel, 1880–1920* to male writers, and dismisses
writers such as Braddon, Broughton, Oliphant, and Ouida as fundamentally conservative, with an "essentially safe, 'establishment' view of
women."[41] Like Stubbs, Mitchell criticizes many novels for having a
limited and conservative scope, focusing on individual relationships
rather than women's role in society.[42] Similarly, arguing that a neglected
Victorian woman author is actually subversive is often used to justify
further consideration and critical reappraisal, as a recent review by
Joseph O'Mealy in *Victorian Studies* of two new books on Oliphant points
out.[43]

In their search for admirable female role models, feminist critics have
found it difficult to engage sympathetically with the apparently conservative characters and agendas of so many novels produced by important
Victorian women writers. When critics do venture out of the narrow
canon, they tend to focus on works like the sensation and New Woman
novels – those, above all, which lend themselves more overtly to feminist
interpretations.

The neglect of most Victorian women writers has created an absurd
situation: we read and study Eliot and the Brontës (and maybe Gaskell)
as if they were the only women writers producing work of literary merit
in the Victorian period; as if their novels were the only interesting and
rewarding works written by women in the Victorian age; as if they wrote
in a critical vacuum, perhaps influenced by their male literary peers but
unaffected by other women writers. While it is true that a relatively
small list of Victorian male writers (such as Dickens, Thackeray, and
Hardy) tend to dominate class reading lists and critical discussions, there
is a far wider range of other male novelists in print and the subject of
critical dialogues: Anthony Trollope, Wilkie Collins, George Gissing,
George Meredith, Benjamin Disraeli, to name just a few. As another
example, almost all the novels written by Wilkie Collins are currently in
print, compared to none by Mrs. Humphry Ward. It is as if, in a
hundred years, future readers might simply read Virginia Woolf and Iris

Murdoch among twentieth-century British women writers, considering other women novelists beneath their notice.

Canons, of course, are dangerous things, liable to blow up as one attempts to tread delicately through the critical war zones. Lootens points out that the embryonic origin of the term "canon" lies in the classical Greek Kanon, meaning, according to Liddell and Scott's *Greek-English Lexicon* "any straight rod or bar."[44] It is exactly this straight and linear characteristic of the canon that makes it sit so uncomfortably with the multivocal qualities of the novel in general, and with the marginalized and multifarious writings of most nineteenth-century women in particular. The inherent and implicit rigidity of what Allan Bloom praises as a "spiritual edifice"[45] is not something I wish to perpetuate. Where I am arguing that currently noncanonical Victorian women novelists should be examined more closely and taken more seriously, I am intending the canon to mean the body of literary works that are in print, written about and discussed, and taught. In effect, I am arguing that the canon should be enlarged, but in some ways I am uncomfortable with the whole concept of a canon that exists, like an exclusive club, to reject candidates seen as less than desirable by a homogenous elite. Rather than argue that the Victorian women novelists discussed in this book should be included in the canon, then, I prefer to make a case that they deserve renewed and sustained attention for their cultural significance and for their aesthetic merits, that their works deserve to be widely available in print and that the writers merit study in university courses alongside Dickens and Eliot.[46]

If we look at literature from the standpoint of cultural studies or from interdisciplinary or sociological perspectives, the value of studying the contributions of neglected Victorian women writers becomes readily apparent. Understanding the whole spectrum of women's literary production is crucial if we want to understand the literary landscape of Victorian Britain, to investigate the female literary tradition, and to comprehend women's history. Additionally, reading canonical works in their literary context enriches our understanding and interpretation, giving us access, for example, to the ways in which Eliot's *Middlemarch*, rather than springing up in glorious and pristine isolation from a writer of genius, is indebted to Harriet Martineau's *Deerbrook* (1839) (a writer for whom Eliot admitted a profound admiration) and Margaret Oliphant's *Miss Marjoribanks* (1866), a novel that was originally attributed to Eliot.[47]

The more complicated question when it comes to studying non-canonical Victorian women authors is the issue of aesthetic value; as critics we are more comfortable with interpretation than evaluation. Elisabeth Jay states correctly that feminist studies have often been criticized for failing to address issues of critical merit in the woman writers they address, perhaps partly in an attempt "to resist the contamination of the male values so firmly imprinted on the traditional tests of literary greatness";[48] ironically, though, Jay herself never quite attempts an overall assessment of Oliphant's literary merit. Although the notion of objective ahistorical and transcultural value has by now largely been exploded, many of us discussing our research on noncanonical Victorian women novelists still face the ubiquitous and overly simplistic question: but are they any good? Often this question can simply be translated as: but are they writing like Eliot or Charlotte Brontë?

Barbara Herrnstein Smith in her useful discussion on the radical contingency of value argues that, rather than being innate or fixed, value is fluid, dependent on the inevitably subjective needs of the individual and the environment. Also, readers will attribute value according to how they classify or label a work: the function of the novels critics choose to foreground depends upon their ideological agenda. It is important, then, to be aware of one's own ideological bias, and of the perils inherent in labeling a piece of work "good" or "not good," "feminist" or "not feminist."

Bearing in mind that the confident directives of taste issued by critics like Matthew Arnold, T. S. Eliot, and F. R. Leavis seem quaint in today's critical climate, there are rewards other than historical and sociological understanding to be gained by reading the writers discussed in this book, as the individual essays powerfully demonstrate. As Alison Chapman's chapter in this book on Victorian children's literature indicates, the works of neglected children's writers such as Maria Molesworth and Jean Ingelow seem as complex, imaginative, and rewarding as those of George MacDonald or Charles Kingsley, authors of better known fantasies. Margaret Oliphant and Charlotte Yonge are as readable, convincing, and as multitextured as Anthony Trollope: Valerie Sanders' exploration of their fictional treatment of matrimony and Monica Cohen's analysis of Oliphant's stylized syntax as an ironic treatment of the woman question both reveal the critical rewards to be gained from a more careful study of these novelists. The vibrant melodramas of Ouida can be immensely absorbing avenues for considering pre-New Woman treatments of women exercising power and sexuality in atypical contexts, as Pamela Gilbert demonstrates in "Ouida and the other New Woman." Mona Caird's *The Daughters of Danaus* and Olive

Schreiner's *The Story of an African Farm* are at least as well crafted, psychologically astute, and emotionally powerful as better-known novels such as George Gissing's *The Odd Women*, as we can see from the wide-ranging contributions of Ann Ardis and Lyn Pykett on the New Woman novelist.

While I am not claiming literary excellence for every Victorian woman novelist, in my own experience and in talking with numerous colleagues and students, the women novelists popularly and critically acclaimed in the Victorian age can prove intensely engaging and re-warding for readers and critics today. It is, however, necessary to be aware of how much Victorian critical mindsets and biases linger, as I hope the preceding examples from twentieth-century criticism demon-strate. It is also important to remember the way in which the canon is self-perpetuating: works with which we are familiar not only remain the ones we associate with literary value, but also become the works that incrementally constitute our definitions and criteria for good art. Hitherto marginalized works are almost inevitably perceived as less valuable: second-rank connotes second-rate. When previously neglect-ed works such as Ouida's *Moths* or Rhoda Broughton's *Not Wisely But Too Well*[49] are reexamined, they are liable to seem exotic, difficult to inte-grate into our existing discussions since they have not been subject to the continuing reshaping for contemporary cultural relevance that Hans Jauss sees as characteristic of canonical works. Then too, many works by Victorian women novelists dealing with the woman question are liable to seem particularly questionable or marginal in relation to our own contemporary "horizons of expectation."[50] Like earlier twentieth-cen-tury critics, we are still uncomfortable with works that seem to have a didactic or polemical element, with novels that seem too subjectively driven by the author's own life and concerns, and we find images of women as conservative angels or anger-driven rebels equally disconcert-ing, in different ways. We must try not to make value judgments based on these responses lest we miss enjoyable texts and oversimplify complex historical and cultural developments.

Alongside the residual ideological limitations of nineteenth-century criticism, I believe that the feminist movement, ironically, has itself complicated the entrance into the canon of most Victorian women novelists, uncomfortable as it is with the treatment of the woman question in so many Victorian novels by women. There is a compelling need to examine these women writers afresh, considering their role in their historical/artistic context as Jane Tompkins urges us to do for American women writers.[51] Above all, we need to recognize what our own ideological agendas are, the extent to which we have inherited unexamined criteria for aesthetic merit, and the ways in which our own woman questions affect our response to Victorian women novelists. In *Sensational Designs*, for example, Tompkins argues that the modernist aesthetic legacy makes readers uncomfortable with the presence of sentimentality or emotion in nineteenth-century American works by women.

In the past few years, Victorian women writers have increasingly attracted critical and popular attention, and this trend seems to be expanding. Novels by Victorian women are regularly being assigned in university courses on Victorian literature and Victorian women, and these women writers have recently been the topic of many lively conference presentations and scholarly discussions. The successful Eighteenth- and Nineteenth-Century British Women Writers Conference is now in its seventh year. Publishers such as Oxford University Press (in their Popular Classics series), Everyman, and Alan Sutton are bringing many noncanonical Victorian women writers back into print. On the World Wide Web, "The Victorian Women Writers Project" based at Indiana University is also making a growing number of works available for readers. At the end of 1996, BBC Radio 4 ran a popular series called "Sensational Women" that included programs on Margaret Oliphant, Rhoda Broughton, Ouida, and Mary Braddon.

A recent *Spectator* review by Claudia Fitzherbert of a new book on Charlotte Yonge acknowledges contemporary interest in forgotten works by Victorian women writers, noting the paradoxically liberating effect of reading even conservative novels by Victorian women: "Whenever I have any doubts about feminism, about where we have got to and where we are going, I return to [Charlotte Yonge's] *The Daisy Chain*, and emerge refreshed and inspired and ready to do battle once more with any fool who dares suggest that the time has come to tinker with the clockwork of the woman's movement."[52]

While the statement above shows how the attitudes to the woman question in novels by Victorian women are still and perhaps inevitably shaping our contemporary responses, we need to reassess the cultural and literary roles and contributions of Victorian women novelists. The complex and engaging body of novels written by Victorian women writers deserves more thorough analysis, particularly in regard to how its reception has been conditioned and complicated by the writers' own complicated positions on the appropriate roles for women in Victorian England.

This book explores a wide range of noncanonical women writers, from Charlotte Yonge to Ouida, from Geraldine Jewsbury to Marie Corelli and E. Nesbit. The chapters mentioned above represent only a few of the broad variety of literary critical approaches and interdisciplinary perspectives covered.

Organized in a loosely chronological fashion, *Victorian Women Writers and The Woman Question* contains four main thematic sections: the three chapters by Valerie Sanders, Anne Humpherys, and Alison Chapman examine, respectively, fictional treatments of marriage in novels by Margaret Oliphant, Charlotte Yonge, and Eliza Lynn Linton, divorce in novels by Mrs. Henry Wood, Lady Charlotte Bury, and Emma Robinson, and phantasies of matriarchy and the maternal in Victorian children's literature. The following chapters by Alexis Easley and Monica Cohen analyze the rhetorical devices through which Harriet Martineau and Margaret Oliphant articulate their ambivalence to the woman questions. The third section contains a cluster of chapters which investigate literary treatments of women and work from mid- to late-century, focusing particularly on portraits of women writers and painters. These chapters start with June Sturrock's contextualisation of Charlotte Yonge within debates over literary women in the 1850s, continue with Lyn Pykett's discussion of women's writing of the 1890s, and conclude with Dennis Denisoff's discussion of the works of Geraldine Jewsbury, Dinah Mulock Craik, and Mary Elizabeth Braddon. The fourth and final section contains chapters by Pamela Gilbert, Ann Ardis, Beth Sutton-Ramspeck, Amelia Rutledge, and Annette Federico, exploring New Woman novelists as well as their predecessors and their successors, tracing the connections between them. The novelists covered in this last section include Ouida, Mrs. Humphry Ward, and Marie Corelli, as well as an extremely wide range of New Woman novelists.

Moving from fictional treatments of marriage and divorce to maternity and woman's work, from textuality to sexuality and political involvements, and spanning the time-period from early Victorian to the Victorian legacy in Edwardian England, this study responds to and problematizes the woman question in previously neglected Victorian fiction by women. This book attempts to delineate the range of sophisticated, historically grounded, theoretically informed and broadly interdisciplinary reconsiderations of the full spectrum of Victorian women novelists that we have lacked until now and need so urgently. Ultimately, the aim of *Victorian Women Writers and the Woman Questions* is to expand

the limited landscape of Victorian novels by women, focusing renewed
and serious attention on the women writers forgotten or neglected by
literary history, and in the process also expanding and radically
reevaluating our reading of "the Victorian."

NOTES

1 Elaine Showalter, *A Literature of Their Own: British Women Novelists from Brontë to Lessing* (Princeton, NJ: Princeton University Press, 1977), p. 7.
2 See, for example: Nancy Fix Anderson, *Woman Against Women in Victorian England. A Life of Eliza Lynn Linton* (Bloomington and Indianapolis: Indiana University Press, 1987); Ann Ardis, *New Women, New Novels* (New Brunswick, NJ: Rutgers University Press, 1990), Elisabeth Jay, *Mrs. Oliphant: A Fiction to Herself. A Literary Life* (Oxford: Clarendon Press, 1995); Dorothy Mermin, *Godiva's Ride: Women of Letters in England, 1830–1880* (Bloomington: Indiana University Press, 1993); Lyn Pykett, *The "Improper" Feminine: The Women's Sensation Novel and the New Woman Writing* (London and New York: Routledge, 1992); Valerie Sanders, *Eve's Renegades: Victorian Anti-Feminist Women Novelists* (London: Macmillan, 1996); John Sutherland, *Mrs. Humphry Ward* (Oxford: Clarendon Press, 1990).
3 Harriet Martineau, *Autobiography* (London: Smith, Elder, 1877), p. 402. Philippa Levine's *Feminist Lives in Victorian England. Private Roles and Public Commitment* (Oxford: Basil Blackwell, 1990) and Candida Ann Lacey's edited book, *Barbara Leigh Smith Bodichon and the Langham Place Group* (New York and London: Routledge, 1987) both contain valuable background on the women's movement in Victorian England. For more detail on sexual politics and "feminism," see Susan Kingsley Kent's *Sex and Suffrage in Britain, 1860–1914* (Princeton, NJ: Princeton University Press, 1987) and Lucy Bland's *Banishing the Beast: English Feminism and Sexual Morality, 1885–1914* (London: Penguin, 1995).
4 Charlotte Yonge, *The Clever Woman of The Family*, 1865 (London: Virago, 1985), p. 3.
5 *Ibid.*, p. 365.
6 *Ibid.*, p. 367.
7 Mary Elizabeth Braddon, *Lady Audley's Secret*, 1862 (Oxford: Oxford University Press, 1987); Mrs. Henry Wood, *East Lynne*, 1861 (London: J. M. Dent, 1984).
8 Along with New Woman novelists, sensation novelists have attracted the bulk of the relatively small amount of critical attention paid to noncanonical Victorian women novelists. See Ann Cvetkovich, *Mixed Feelings: Feminism, Mass Culture, and Victorian Sensationalism* (New Brunswick and London: Rutgers, 1993); Winifred Hughes, *The Maniac In The Cellar: Sensation Novels of the 1860s* (Princeton, NJ: Princeton University Press, 1980); Sally Mitchell, *The Fallen Angel. Chastity, Class and Women's Reading, 1835–1890* (Bowling Green,

OH: Bowling Green University Popular Press, 1981); Lyn Pykett, *The "Improper" Feminine*, Natalie Schroeder, "Feminine Sensationalism. Eroticism, and Self-Assertion: M. E. Braddon and Ouida," *Tulsa Studies in Women's Literature* 7. 1 (Spring 1983), 87–104; R. C. Terry, *Victorian Popular Fiction* (London: Macmillan, 1983).

9 Eliza Lynn Linton, *The Rebel of the Family*, 3 vols. (London: Chatto and Windus, 1880).

10 *Ibid.*, vol. I, p. 73.

11 *Ibid.*, vol. I, p. 9.

12 For more discussion of Linton's life and works, see Herbert Van Thal, *Eliza Lynn Linton. The Girl of The Period* (London: George Allen & Unwin, 1979), Anderson, *Woman Against Women*, and Sanders, *Eve's Renegades*.

13 Sarah Grand, *Ideala* (London: Richard Bentley & Son, 1889), p. 228.

14 *Ibid.*, p. 240.

15 *Ibid.*, p. 296.

16 Kate Flint's *The Woman Reader. 1837–1914* (Oxford: Clarendon Press, 1993) is a fascinating investigation into the position(s) of the Victorian woman reader.

17 See, for example, Ellen Miller Casey, "'Edging Women Out?': Reviews of Women Novelists in the *Athenaeum*, 1860–1900," *Victorian Studies* 39. 2 (Winter 1996), 151–71; Elaine Showalter, *A Literature of Their Own*; Gaye Tuchman, *Edging Women Out: Victorian Novelists, Publishers, and Social Change* (New Haven, CT: Yale University Press, 1989); and Nicola Diane Thompson, *Reviewing Sex: Gender and the Reception of Victorian Novels* (London and Basingstoke: Macmillan, and New York: University Press, 1996).

18 Mitchell, *The Fallen Angel*, p. 140.

19 Felix Alan Walbank (ed.), *Queens of the Circulating Library. Selections from Victorian Lady Novelists, 1850–1900* (London: Evans Brothers, 1950), p. 196.

20 *Ibid.*, p. 298.

21 Tricia Lootens, *Lost Saints. Silence, Gender, and Victorian Literary Canonization* (Charlottesville and London: University Press of Virginia, 1996), p. 13.

22 My chapter on Anthony Trollope in *Reviewing Sex* discusses at length the emerging distinctions between popular and "serious" literature in literary criticism from the 1860s.

23 W. L. Courtney, *The Feminine Note in Fiction* (London: Chapman and Hall, 1904), p. xiii.

24 Virginia Woolf, *A Room of One's Own* (San Diego, New York, London: Harcourt Brace Jovanovich, 1984), p. 77.

25 Terry Lovell, *Consuming Fictions* (London: Verso, 1987).

26 Elizabeth Langland's *Nobody's Angels. Middle-Class Women and Domestic Ideology in Victorian Culture* (Ithaca and London: Cornell University Press, 1995) contains a fascinating discussion of Oliphant and Eliot in relation to each other which assesses their strength and differences, rather than using Eliot as the model against which Oliphant will be judged.

27 Gordon S. Haight (ed), *The George Eliot Letters*, 9 vols. (New Haven, CT: Yale

University Press, 1954–74), vol. III, p. 302.

28 Susan Sniader Lanser's *Fictions of Authority. Women Writers and Narrative Voice* (Ithaca: Cornell University Press, 1992) contains useful and relevant discussion of issues of narratorial voice for female authors. See especially her discussion of male narrators and pseudonyms (pp. 17–19).

29 Eliot's letter to Harriet Beecher Stowe reads as follows: "I am beginning to see with new clearness, that if a book which has any sort of exquisiteness happens also to be a popular widely circulated book, its power over the social mind, for any good, is after all due to its reception by a few appreciative natures, and is the slow result of radiation from that narrow circle. I mean, you can affect a few souls, and that each of these in turn may affect a few more, but that no exquisite book tells properly and directly on a multitude however largely it may be spread by type and paper" (*Letters*, vol. V, p. 30).

30 *The Autobiography and Letters of Mrs. M. O. W. Oliphant*, ed. Mrs. Harry Coghill (London: William Blackwood, 1899), pp. 5–8.

31 Lootens, *Lost Saints*, p. 10.

32 Nicola Thompson, "The Angel in the Circulating Library: Charlotte Yonge's *The Heir of Redclyffe*," in *Reviewing Sex*, pp. 87–107.

33 Amy Cruse, *The Victorians and Their Books* (London: George Allen & Unwin, 1935), p. 329.

34 Vineta Colby, *The Singular Anomaly. Women Novelists of the Nineteenth Century* (New York: New York University Press, 1970), p. 11.

35 *Ibid.*, p. 113.

36 Showalter, *A Literature of Their Own*, p. 7.

37 *Ibid.*, p. 31.

38 Gail Cunningham, *The New Woman and The Victorian Novel* (London: Macmillan, 1978), p. 19.

39 Mitchell, *The Fallen Angel*, p. 90.

40 Patricia Stubbs, *Women and Fiction. Feminism and the Novel, 1888–1920* (London: Methuen, 1981), p. 118.

41 *Ibid.*, p. 39.

42 Mitchell, *The Fallen Angel*, p. 142.

43 In his review of D.J. Trela's *Margaret Oliphant: Critical Essays On A Gentle Subversive* (Selinsgrove: Susquehanna University Press, 1995) and Margarete Rubik's *The Novels of Mrs. Oliphant: A Subversive View of Traditional Themes* (New York: Peter Lang, 1994), O' Mealy states that "[T]he starting point for this Oliphant revival, indeed the main selling point, shared by the Margarete Rubik and D. J. Trela books is the notion of 'subversion.' Margaret Oliphant, long thought a hopelessly stuffy and conventional Victorian, is actually a rebel." *Victorian Studies* 39.2 (Winter 1996), 249–51.

44 Lootens, *Lost Saints*, p. 5.

45 Allan Bloom, *The Closing of The American Mind* (New York: Simon & Schuster, 1987), p. 53.

46 Recent influential discussions of canons and canonicity include Barbara

Herrnstein Smith's *Contingencies of Value. Alternative Perspectives for Critical Theory* (Cambridge, MA: Harvard University Press, 1988) and John Guillory's *Cultural Capital. The Problem of Literary Canon Formation*, (Chicago: Chicago University Press, 1993).

47 Harriet Martineau, *Deerbrook*, 1839 (Garden City: Dial Press, 1984); Margaret Oliphant, *Miss Marjoribanks*, 1866 (London: Virago, 1988).

48 Elisabeth Jay, *Mrs. Oliphant: "A Fiction to Herself,"* p. 289.

49 Louise de la Ramée (Ouida), *Moths*, 3 vols. (London: Chatto and Windus, 1880); Rhoda Broughton, *Not Wisely But Too Well*, 1867 (London: Alan Sutton, 1993).

50 Hans Robert Jauss, "Literary History," in H. Adams and L. Searle (eds.), *Critical Theory Since 1965* (Tallahassee: University Press of Florida, 1986) p. 166.

51 Jane Tompkins, *Sensational Designs: The Cultural Work of American Fiction 1790–1860* (Oxford and New York: Oxford University Press, 1985).

52 Claudia Fitzherbert, "Review of *Charlotte Yonge* by Alethea Hayter," *The Spectator* (December 14–21, 1996), 63–5.

WORKS CITED

Anderson, Nancy Fix, *Woman Against Women in Victorian England. A Life of Eliza Lynn Linton*, Bloomington and Indianapolis: Indiana University Press, 1987.

Ardis, Ann, *New Women, New Novels*, New Brunswick, NJ: Rutgers University Press, 1990.

Armstrong, Nancy, *Desire and Domestic Fiction: A Political History of The Novel*, New York: Oxford University Press, 1987.

Bakhtin, M. M., *The Dialogic Imagination*, Austin: University of Texas Press, 1981.

Bland, Lucy, *Banishing the Beast: English Feminism and Sexual Morality, 1885–1914*, London: Penguin, 1995.

Bloom, Allan, *The Closing of The American Mind*, New York: Simon & Schuster, 1987.

Braddon, Mary Elizabeth, *Lady Audley's Secret*, 1862, Oxford: Oxford University Press, 1987.

Broughton, Rhoda, *Not Wisely But Too Well*, 1867, London: Alan Sutton, 1993.

Caird, Mona, *The Daughters of Danaus*, London: Bliss, Sands, and Foster, 1894.

Colby, Vineta, *The Singular Anomaly. Women Novelists of the Nineteenth Century*, New York: New York University Press, 1970.

Courtney, W. L., *The Feminine Note in Fiction*, London: Chapman and Hall, 1904.

Cruse, Amy, *The Victorians And Their Books*, London: George Allen & Unwin, 1935.

Cunningham, Gail, *The New Woman and The Victorian Novel*, London: Macmillan, 1978.

Cvetkovich, Ann, *Mixed Feelings: Feminism, Mass Culture, and Victorian Sensationalism*, New Brunswick and London: Rutgers, 1993.

Fitzherbert, Claudia, "Review of *Charlotte Yonge*, by Alethea Hayter," *The Spectator*, December 14–21, 1996, 63–65.

Flint, Kate, *The Woman Reader. 1837–1914*, Oxford: Clarendon Press, 1993.

Gissing, George, *The Odd Women*, 3 vols., London: Lawrence and Bullin, 1893.

Grand, Sarah, *Ideala*, London: Richard Bentley & Son, 1889.

Guillory, John, *Cultural Capital. The Problem of Literary Canon Formation*, Chicago: University of Chicago Press, 1993.

Haight, Gordon S. (ed.), *The George Eliot Letters*, 9 vols., New Haven: Yale University Press, 1954–74.

Herrnstein Smith, Barbara, *Contingencies of Value. Alternative Perspectives for Critical Theory*, Cambridge, MA: Harvard University Press, 1988.

Hughes, Winifred, *The Maniac in the Cellar: Sensation Novels of the 1860s*, Princeton, NJ: Princeton University Press, 1980.

Jauss, Hans Robert, "Literary History," in H. Adams and L. Searle (eds.), *Critical Theory Since 1965*, Tallahassee: University Press of Florida, 1986, pp. 349–66.

Jay, Elisabeth, *Mrs. Oliphant: A Fiction to Herself. A Literary Life*, Oxford: Clarendon Press, 1995.

Kingsley Kent, Susan, *Sex and Suffrage in Britain, 1860–1914*, Princeton, NJ: Princeton University Press, 1987.

Lacey, Candida Ann, (ed.), *Barbara Leigh Smith Bodichon and the Langham Place Group*, New York and London: Routledge, 1987.

Langland, Elizabeth, *Nobody's Angels: Middle-Class Women and Domestic Ideology in Victorian Culture*, Ithaca and London: Cornell University Press, 1995.

Levine, Philippa, *Feminist Lives in Victorian England. Private Roles and Public Commitment*, Oxford: Blackwell, 1990.

Linton, Eliza Lynn, *The Rebel of the Family*, 3 vols., London: Chatto and Windus, 1880.

Lootens, Tricia, *Lost Saints. Silence, Gender, and Victorian Literary Canonization*, Charlottesville and London: University Press of Virginia, 1996.

Lovell, Terry, *Consuming Fictions*, London: Verso, 1987.

Martineau, Harriet, *Autobiography*, London: Smith, Elder, 1877.
  Deerbrook, 1839, Garden City: Dial Press, 1984.

Mermin, Dorothy, *Godiva's Ride. Women of Letters in England, 1830–1880*, Bloomington: Indiana University Press, 1993.

Miller Casey, Ellen, "'Edging Women Out?': Reviews of Women Novelists in the *Athenaeum*, 1860–1900," *Victorian Studies* 39.2 (Winter 1996), 151–71.

Mitchell, Sally, *The Fallen Angel. Chastity, Class and Women's Reading, 1835–1880*, Bowling Green, OH: Bowling Green University Popular Press, 1981.

Oliphant, Margaret, *Miss Marjoribanks*, 1866, London: Virago, 1988.
  The Autobiography and Letters of Mrs. M. O. W. Oliphant, ed. Mrs. Harry Coghill, London: William Blackwood, 1899.

O'Mealy, Joseph, Review of *The Novels of Mrs. Oliphant: A Subversive View of Traditional Themes*, by Margarete Rubik, and *Margaret Oliphant: Critical Essays On A Gentle Subversive*, ed. D. J. Trela, *Victorian Studies* 39.2 (Winter 1996), 249–51.

Pinney, Thomas, (ed.), *Essays Of George Eliot*, New York: Columbia University Press, 1963.
Poovey, Mary, *Uneven Developments: The Ideological Work of Gender in Mid-Victorian England*, Chicago: University of Chicago Press, 1988.
Pykett, Lyn, *The "Improper" Feminine: The Women's Sensation Novel and the New Woman Writing*, London and New York: Routledge, 1992.
Ramée, de la, Louise (Ouida), *Moths*, 1880.
Sanders, Valerie, *Eve's Renegades: Victorian Anti-Feminist Women Novelists*, London: Macmillan, 1996.
Schreiner, Olive, *The Story Of An African Farm*, 2 vols., London: Chapman and Hall, 1883.
Schroeder, Natalie, "Feminine Sensationalism, Eroticism, and Self-Assertion: M. E. Braddon and Ouida," *Tulsa Studies in Women's Literature* 7.1 (Spring 1983), 87–104.
Showalter, Elaine, *A Literature of Their Own: British Women Novelists from Brontë to Lessing*, Princeton, NJ: Princeton University Press, 1977.
Sniader Lanser, Susan, *Fictions of Authority. Women Writers and Narrative Voice*, Ithaca: Cornell University Press, 1992.
Stubbs, Patricia, *Women and Fiction. Feminism and the Novel, 1888–1920*, London: Methuen, 1981.
Sutherland, John, *Mrs. Humphry Ward*, Oxford: Clarendon Press, 1990.
Terry, R. C., *Victorian Popular Fiction*, London: Macmillan, 1983.
Thompson, Nicola Diane, *Reviewing Sex: Gender and the Reception of Victorian Novels*, London: Macmillan; New York: New York University Press, 1996.
Tompkins, Jane, *Sensational Designs: The Cultural Work of American Fiction 1790–1860*, Oxford and New York: Oxford University Press, 1985.
Tuchman, Gaye, *Edging Women Out: Victorian Novelists, Publishers, and Social Change*, New Haven: Yale University Press, 1989.
Van Thal, Herbert, *Eliza Lynn Linton. The Girl of the Period*, London: George Allen & Unwin, 1979.
Walbank, Felix Alan (ed.), *Queens of the Circulating Library. Selections from Victorian Lady Novelists, 1850–1900*, London: Evans Brothers, 1950.
Wood, Henry Mrs., *East Lynne*, 1861, London: J. M. Dent, 1984.
Woolf, Virginia, *A Room Of One's Own*, San Diego, New York, London: Harcourt Brace Jovanovich, 1984.
Yonge, Charlotte, *The Clever Woman of The Family*, 1865, London: Virago, 1985.

Marriage and the antifeminist woman novelist

Valerie Sanders

> All the world believed that she did really love her black-haired,
> florid, big-fisted Plutus, who was not a gentleman for all his acres;
> and that he in turn loved his faded, elderly, ultra-refined wife; and
> the belief counted as a medal of gold and a chain of silver in their
> honour.[1]

This cynical comment from Eliza Lynn Linton's novel *Patricia Kemball*
describes the marriage of Jabez Hamley, a self-made businessman and
bully in the Bounderby mould, with the ladylike Rosina Kemball,
twenty years his senior. In many respects it represents the low water-
mark reached by marriage in the English middle-class novel three
quarters of the way through the century, when images of early Dick-
ensian dimpling girl-brides and rosy-cheeked children were looking
outmoded, even to Dickens himself. Of course the unequal marriage –
whether in terms of age or status – had long been the staple material of
comedy; but in the later Victorian novel, it becomes a new source of
tragic social concern, as, for instance, in the marriage of Dorothea and
Casaubon in *Middlemarch*. Moreover, it was not just the unequal marriage that novelists explored, but the failed marriage of all kinds. It was
as if the Matrimonial Causes Act of 1857, which recognized a more
widespread need for divorce, gave novelists fresh license to query the
state their writing traditionally celebrated as the desirable norm.

The novelists one might have expected to correct the picture are the
antifeminists: novelists such as Charlotte M. Yonge, Eliza Lynn Linton,
Mary (Mrs. Humphry) Ward, and Margaret Oliphant, who agreed that
women essentially belonged at home – ideally as wives, but failing that,
as dutiful single daughters or sisters. Their novels concentrate on the
Victorian household as the site of adventure, the testing ground of moral
probity and individual resilience. Although they explore other options
for women, especially higher education and work outside the home,

these novelists usually decide, like their literary predecessors, that death or marriage is the only realistic possibility for their heroines; yet the marriages they portray involve half-hearted endings, bizarre alliances, and an underlying atmosphere of sexual distaste. Now largely excluded from the literary canon, mainly because of their unfashionable commitment to women's domestic role, they appear, on close reading, considerably more ambivalent than has been fully recognized. This chapter will explore the gaps between their official support for marriage, and their private reservations about it, focusing on their rhetorical deconstruction of the Victorian middle-class ideology of marriage. Their novels become a troubled site of struggle, a place where the meaning of marriage is repeatedly contested, in the Bakhtinian sense, and its instability as an institution heightened by debate and example. Moreover, their image of marriage becomes progressively more caricatured at the husband's expense, revealing a surprisingly strong undercurrent of contempt for men. The implications of this for a wider understanding of Victorian private life will be considered at the end of the discussion.

If marriage was the norm in Victorian middle-class England, it was a highly uneasy norm, constantly under attack from lawyers, reformers, moralists, and feminists. The Victorians talked constantly about wedlock: in their letters, diaries, biographies, and novels. *Poole's Index to Periodical Literature* for 1887–92, under "Marriage," charts their mounting anxiety about its difficulties: "Disparity of Age in," "Unhappiness in; are Women to Blame?," "Why Men do not Marry," "Failures in, Some." In 1888, 27,000 letters flooded into the *Daily Telegraph* in response to Mona Caird's essay on "Marriage" in the *Westminster Review*, and when Harry Quilter published a selection under the heading *Is Marriage a Failure?* many of his correspondents clearly thought it was, and welcomed the chance to say so. Even Elizabeth Rachel Chapman, a pro-marriage theorist, conceded that: "the once sacred and once theoretically indissoluble life-tie between husband and wife has become, in short, an open question."[2]

Joan Perkin argues that most couples accepted the *status quo*: "The majority of women preferred not to know they were living in subjection, did not care about lack of political rights, believed change was unlikely and would involve considerable risk if it came, or just did not have the stomach for the fight"[3] – a view very close to Oliphant's. Several notorious cases in public life would have made them aware of the extremes of marital unhappiness: Caroline and George Norton, whose public battles led to the Infant Custody Act of 1839 and married women's property reform in the 1850s; John Stuart Mill, who met the married Harriet Taylor in 1830 and was unable to marry her himself until 1851 (her husband having died in 1849); Charles Dickens, who publicly announced his separation from his wife, Catherine, in 1858, after the births of ten children; and Marian Evans, who "eloped" with the married George Henry Lewes in 1854: the year the Ruskins' disastrous marriage was annulled on grounds of non-consummation. George Eliot subsequently married John Cross, who was twenty-one years her junior; while a twenty-seven-year age gap separated Mark Pattison, Rector of Lincoln College, Oxford, from his wife Emilia Frances Strong. Pat Jalland cites several cases of elderly men marrying young girls: a situation that "could arouse great abhorrence."[4] Novels by antifeminist women seem to have reflected this more uneasy image of marriage prevalent by the second half of the century, and writers were especially intrigued by queasy age-differences.

Margaret Oliphant, Charlotte Yonge and Eliza Lynn Linton all reached their maturity as novelists at a time when marriage was coming under serious critical scrutiny. None had any personal reason for feeling positive about it. Oliphant, who had married her cousin Frank in 1852 at the age of twenty-four, was widowed in 1859: none of her six children outlived her, though two difficult sons, Cyril and "Cecco", survived till their thirties. Eliza Lynn married William James Linton (twice widowed, with several children) in 1858, but they soon became incompatible, separating in 1864. Charlotte Yonge never married at all, and like the others, records in her autobiography a strong sense of her parents' temperamental differences. Linton and Yonge both had dominant fathers and weak mothers (Linton's died when she was a baby), while Oliphant had a highly competent and loving mother but a shadowy father. Her brother also made an inadequate husband, and landed on her, with his motherless children, in 1870. All three novelists are reticent about their personal lives in any direct, confessional sense, but must have been aware that as a spinster, a widow, and a separated woman, as childless wife or bereaved mother, each had conspicuously failed to live up to the ideal of a true woman's life as the middle-class culture of their age defined it.

In their nonfictional writing on marriage, the antifeminist women novelists had to confront the fact of sweeping changes in public opinion between the 1850s and 1890s. It was impossible for them to remain entirely untouched by the storm: instead, they made grudging concessions, in favor of easier divorce laws, or in recognition of bad husbands.

But they also eschewed logical argument and based their diagnosis of the health of Victorian marriage on an impressionistic response to their own disappointed idealism, while trying to believe in the possibility of happy marriage for fictional versions of themselves: a confused standpoint that multiplies the ideological nuances of their writing, and widens the gap between formal statements of their views and their fictional illustration.

CHARLOTTE M. YONGE

Yonge wrote only of her childhood in her unfinished autobiography, but commented at greater length on singleness and marriage in *Womankind* (1876), a review of middle-class Christian women's roles. Conceding women's inferiority to men, *Womankind* focuses on woman as the helpmeet, which Yonge considered the highest and only real purpose in a woman's life. Her assumption again is that most normal women will marry: yet occasional ambiguities in the text expose Yonge's more worldly-wise consciousness that the ideal state can go awry. She divides wives into four kinds: "the cowed woman, the dead-weight, the *maîtresse femme*, and the helpmeet,"[5] a list like Linton's collection of female caricatures in *The Girl of the Period* and elsewhere. Discussing the "oppression" of women, she argues that the unmarried suffer only from not having the vote: "It is the wife who is the injured creature" (*Womankind*, p. 235).

Yonge's attitude to marriage in her novels remains equivocal. Big supportive families are the backbone of her society, but within them are complex emotional allegiances and disagreements, guilty secrets and wasting diseases. Exhausted mothers die after giving birth to eleven or twelve children, as happens in *The Pillars of the House* (1873). When *The Daisy Chain* (1856) begins with Dr. May, notorious for his "headlong driving,"[6] accidentally killing his wife in a carriage accident, six weeks after the birth of her eleventh child, Yonge symbolically implies that marriage is reckless of women's lives, especially as the accident also cripples their eldest daughter, Margaret, herself on the brink of engagement to an heroic but debilitated sailor, Alan Ernescliffe. As it is, their relationship never progresses beyond bedside chivalry, and much of Margaret's life, as Yonge summarizes it, has been wasted in the fruitless emotions of an imitation-marriage, a mock life-cycle of female devotion: "The twenty-five years' life, the seven years' captivity on her couch, the anxious headship of the motherless household, the hopeless betrothal, the long suspense, the efforts for resignation, the widowed affections, the slow decay, the tardy, painful death agony – all was over" (*The Daisy Chain*, p. 575).

Her sister Flora, almost as ill by the end of the novel, marries George Rivers, who is her intellectual inferior; loses her first baby to neglect and opium addiction, and has little to rejoice over even when her second is born. Without blaming the institution of marriage as such, Yonge certainly censures Flora's worldliness in choosing the type of husband she does and pushing him into an unsuitable political career (a plan condoned by the more cynical Oliphant in her novels). The eldest brother, Richard, a clergyman, tells Flora she must bear with her life, "'unless some leading comes for an escape'" (p. 591), the very suggestion of "escape" being surprising for Yonge; yet the only truly happy marriage in the novel is that between Norman May and Meta Rivers – who promptly leave the family and Victorian society to become missionaries in New Zealand.

Left behind by everyone is Yonge's most popular heroine, Ethel May, who at the beginning of the novel has an authentic fifteen-year-old's curiosity about romance and lovers: "'How did lovers look?' was a speculation which had, more than once, occupied Ethel" (pp. 269–70). Flora's engagement dismays her because she believes "'there ought to be superiority on the man's side'" (p. 351), but her own fledgling romance with Norman Ogilvie founders on her loyalty to her father: "Widowed as he was, she knew that he would sorely miss her, and that for years to come she should be necessary at home" (p. 386). Critics have long recognized that Yonge places good daughterhood above the claims of conventional wifehood, even though there are times when Ethel feels bored at home, undervalued, and frustrated; yet aspects of this episode remain unsettling. Norman Ogilvie soon marries a wealthy neighbor in accordance with his parents' wishes, while Ethel's father has his other children to care about, "and she had begun to understand that the unmarried woman must not seek undivided return of affection ... but must be ready to cease in turn to be first with any" (p. 593). There is a futility about Ethel's sacrifice, made in a moment of teenage devotion to her father, a sense that she deserves better; and yet Ethel also seems too original to marry, too intellectual to subordinate her strong personality to a husband's. Her singleness is probably accepted by most readers with a mixture of regret and relief, though the choice seems very stark and oddly irreversible for such a young girl. It was as if Yonge wanted to protect her favorite from being diminished by a sexual relationship.

Marriage itself, meanwhile, can either strengthen or warp weak natures: possibilities further explored in *The Clever Woman of the Family* (1865). Rachel Curtis, though intellectual, is in many ways the complete opposite of Ethel. Scornful of marriage, rather than curious about it, but with little to do at home, she is frustrated by the prolonged state of childishness imposed by her singleness, and at the age of twenty-five has reached a crisis in her life. She feels it is time to declare herself a spinster, telling her sister Grace: "'From this moment we are established as the maiden sisters of Avonmouth, husband and wife to one another, as maiden pairs always are.'"[7] This might have been an opportunity for Yonge to investigate the emotional alternatives for single women as Rachel plays at married couples with her sister: an option that recurs when her widowed cousin Fanny returns home from the colonies with seven children, and "Rachel's heart throbbed with Britomart's devotion to her Amoret" (*The Clever Woman*, p. 8). But, like Jane Austen in *Emma*, Yonge declines to substitute female friendship for marriage as a long-term choice. As with Austen, same-sex devotion seems to be seen as an immature state, a preparation for the firmer guidance that only men can provide, even though Fanny Temple's marriage is one of Yonge's most grotesque. At sixteen she married her father's friend, General Sir Stephen Temple, aged sixty: a marriage duplicated by Bessie Keith with Lord Keith, who proposes first to Fanny. All the Curtis sisters know of Fanny after her marriage was that "she had much ill-health and numerous children, and was tended like an infant by her bustling mother and doting husband" (p. 5), the wife becoming a generational amalgam of parent and child: grown-up enough to have children of her own, but still an infantilized pet to her husband and mother.

Throughout the novel, Yonge reinforces the sense of a society in which the mismatching of old and young is not uncommon. Fanny's odd family of countless small boys seems to confirm the sexual unnaturalness of her union, as does Bessie Keith's acquisition, by marriage, of seven grandchildren – her husband's elder daughter being only three years older than Bessie herself. Lord Keith's two daughters were themselves married in odd circumstances, as his brother, Colin Keith, explains: "'Isabel he married when she was almost a child to this Comyn Menteith, very young too at the time... It is all rack and ruin and extravagance, a set of ill-regulated children, and Isabel smiling and looking pretty in the midst of them'" (p. 152); while Mary, the younger daughter, chose her own husband, but now lives on limited means in Trinidad. The Keith marriage, seen as even more grotesque than

Fanny's with Sir Stephen Temple, ends as most unsuitable marriages do in Yonge's novels – in the deaths of both parties. Of the two marriages finally left to stand, one is between a "thirty-three years' old bride upon crutches" (Ermine Williams) (p. 355), and a prematurely aged soldier (Colin Keith), though unlike Margaret May and Alan Ernescliffe, they do at least survive to enjoy their happiness and have an adopted child (Bessie's orphaned son). The other is between Rachel Curtis and Alick Keith, which now works only because Rachel has been chastened into giving up her egotistical ambitions.

Few girls in Yonge's novels have an entirely easy passage from irresponsibility into the cares of marriage and motherhood, and even Rachel is often crossed by a husband who is ironic and sarcastic with her. Yonge's marriages, founded as they frequently are on a shaky basis of invalidism, and disparity of age or intellect, generally cause more problems than they solve. This is especially true of a later novel, *The Three Brides* (1876), which stresses the incongruity of three brothers' marriages. Arriving home on the same day, the new brides are not at all what their husbands' family expect. One sickly South African bride arrives without her husband, who is still abroad; the albino clergyman son has married a bouncy extrovert from a military background; and the eldest, Raymond, brings home a cousin obsessed with the superiority of her own branch of the family.

Nicola Thompson has argued that Yonge has largely been neglected by critics because her "ideas and depiction of gender roles seem so impossible to translate as covert rebellion."[8] In fact, her novels query the assumption that wifehood is the natural destiny of women, while remaining perplexed about the alternatives. *The Daisy Chain* and *The Clever Woman* explore both the emotional emptiness of the single woman's life and the feverish disorder of the wife's. Neither is entirely satisfactory, and the truly happy marriage, Yonge indicates, is rare; yet by embedding her distorted love stories in sprawling family sagas she was able to make subversive suggestions without antagonizing generations of devoted readers. Like Oliphant in her Carlingford Chronicles, Yonge emphasizes the trivia of daily life and its frustrations as the context for marital disillusionment and anxiety. She turns marriage into one of many domestic troubles, often self-inflicted, and chosen by the weaker members of the family, requiring an extensive exercise in self-discipline for its survival.

MARGARET OLIPHANT

Although Oliphant admired her mother as a great household manager, her own marriage was destabilized by the bad relationship between her husband and her mother. When Frank Oliphant first proposed to her, her instinctive answer was "an alarmed negative, the idea having never entered my mind. But in six months or so things changed. It is not a matter into which I can enter here."[9] Making full allowance for autobiographical reticence, this is nevertheless a pointedly tight-lipped refusal to tell the story of her own courtship, and particularly odd in a novelist whose main theme was marriage. Such references as she does make allude more often to underlying disagreements than to shared happiness. Her brother was "discontented and wounded" (*Autobiography*, p. 36) by the change in his family's living arrangements; while Oliphant commented on her early married life: "I, for my part, was torn in two. I have gone through many sorrows since, but I don't know that any period of my life has ever contained more intolerable moments than those first years that should have been so happy" (p. 37).

When they reached Rome, where Frank died (having deceived his wife as to how ill he was), the Oliphants came to know Robert and Geraldine Macpherson, another couple struggling with a resident mother-in-law. "There used to be a fierce row often in the house, from which he would stride forth plucking his red beard and sending forth fire and flame" (p. 75). Men in Oliphant's life constantly had to be humored. The real support came from women, such as her "big Jane," who helped with the children, Geraldine Macpherson, Jane Carlyle, and two Oliphant nieces, Madge and Denny. Even so, Oliphant often sounds grudging about other women: her real passion was for her "babies" and later her two grown-up sons, for whom she mourns desperately in the uncut version of her *Autobiography*. A disbeliever in second marriages, Oliphant spent her long widowhood clinging to the dwindling remains of her family and trying to live a normal woman's life. In the event, it eluded her, as it did Yonge and Linton.

In their periodical writing, Oliphant and Linton tackled the big issues of the day: votes for women, the divorce laws, higher education, inequality, and motherhood, conceding that some women were undoubtedly unlucky in their experiences, but refusing to see this as a reason for drastic change. "I admit for my part the superiority of sex," Oliphant said in 1880. She was certain that men's greater physical strength would "keep women in subjection as long as the race endures," and that as a consequence, women cherished a "sense of injustice."[10] Oliphant's opinions in her later articles are often difficult to pin down. Aware of all that was being said on both sides of the debate, she sounds bewildered and frustrated, coy and ironic. Though in this article she discusses the suffrage, what really concerns her is men's ingratitude to women for all their hard work, declaring the "sentiment of men towards women ... thoroughly ungenerous from beginning to end, from the highest to the lowest" ("The Grievances of Women," p. 710). Oliphant's personal feelings seem to have been less directly engaged by the public debates than by her personal circumstances; yet doubting whether many women were really suffering as much as the sensationalists made out, she was against legislating for a minority. Ultimately, she felt the complexities of private life were beyond the reach of lawyers because the "bond of marriage is too intimate, and the parties are left too completely at each other's mercy, to make any external code absolutely supreme between them."[11]

Oliphant's late novel *Kirsteen* (1890) begins, like *The Clever Woman of the Family*, with the marriage of a young girl to a man old enough to be her grandfather – but pursues the story far more adventurously. Refusing to marry an elderly suitor her father has chosen for her, and whose generosity would help her family enjoy a better life, Kirsteen leaves Glendochart to marry her sister Mary, and runs away to London, establishing herself successfully as a mantua-maker, because she is too honorable to break her pledge to Ronald Drummond, her younger lover serving in India. Kirsteen never marries, nor does she die; and therefore breaks the mold of the Victorian heroine who generally embraces one or other of the standard fates. Oliphant had long been tempted to reward her heroines with an independent working life rather than with marriage, but had usually succumbed to critical expectations. At the end of *The Curate in Charge* (1876), she stages an open debate about the convenient marriage-plot, complaining that her heroine's resolve to work and bring up her half-brothers ought to "come to some great result in itself." It would have been more challenging than to have her marry, which is "simply a contemptible expedient."[12] Oliphant goes further than Yonge in deflecting pity from her unmarried heroines, and making their decisions seem worthwhile; yet she too had difficulty in rejecting the marriage-plot outright, or adopting it uncritically. Elizabeth Langland has recently shown how women in Oliphant's novels "use men to consolidate their own and middle-class control."[13] Marriage becomes acceptable to Oliphant if it gives her "unpleasant" heroines a vicarious career and strengthens their role as middle-class managers.

Elisabeth Jay has discussed Oliphant's later novels which deal with the subject of marriage breakdown and the entirely different mental worlds occupied by husband and wife. The Carlingford novels of her middle period, on the other hand, focus on improbable courtships and unequal marriages, where all the superiority is on the woman's side, especially in *Miss Marjoribanks* (1866) and *Phoebe Junior* (1876), two novels that are exceptionally cynical about marriage. The context for courtship in an Oliphant novel is often the mother's negative experience of marriage, as with Kirsteen's mother: "Her husband was an arbitrary and high-tempered man, whose will was absolute in the family, who took counsel with no one, and who, after the few complaisances of a grim honeymoon, let his wife drop into the harmless position of a nonentity, which indeed was that which was best fitted for her."[14] Similar positions are occupied by the invalidish Mrs. Marjoribanks and Mr. Copperhead's wife in *Phoebe Junior*, Oliphant's task being to save the high-spirited daughters in each of these novels from going the way of their mothers. The only solution appears to be to give them feeble-minded husbands, such as Tom Marjoribanks and Clarence Copperhead: though in each case, the heroine could have married someone with more intellectual appeal.

Lucilla Marjoribanks reads like a satire on Yonge's Ethel May. She too commits herself to her widowed father (also a doctor), accepting that she "must sacrifice her own feelings, and make a cheerful home for papa";[15] but there the resemblance ends. Where Ethel was thin and scholarly, Lucilla is plump and practical, an egotistical manager, whose apparent devotion to her father is really a cover for an ambitious social campaign in Carlingford. Frequently described as a "genius," Lucilla outgrows household management and goes in for politics by proxy; in the meantime risking her dwindling chances of marriage with a compatible man. Oliphant is at her most interesting where she frankly discusses Lucilla's personal crisis of confidence in her single life. Like Yonge's Rachel Curtis, she has reached the "term of young ladyhood" (*Miss Marjoribanks*, p. 394), but has nothing more satisfying to put in its place, and when her father dies, she has fewer options than her servant Thomas, who thinks of going into the public house business. Subtly dissecting Lucilla's motives, Oliphant recognizes that while she wants to contribute something to society, she also wants a life of her own. Marriage with her cousin Tom will at least give her a grander project: the reform of Marchbank village. In a painfully comic scene with her old friend Mrs. Chiley, however, Lucilla's choice of husband is mercilessly

mocked."[Mrs. Chiley] said herself afterwards that she felt as if somebody had discharged a pistol into her breast" (p. 491), an incongruously
tasteless image in this context of small town life; while in Grange Lane
itself "there was first a dead pause of incredulity and amazement, and
then such a commotion as could be compared to nothing except a
sudden squall at sea" (p. 494). As both Oliphant and Lucilla do their best
to persuade doubters that this is the best marriage for her, Oliphant
concludes that if nothing else, Lucilla gets to keep her own surname, and
symbolically her own identity. Oliphant sidesteps passion altogether,
and offers no hints of future babies.

Her later heroine, Phoebe Junior, makes a similar kind of marriage,
that will give her something practical to do in the public sphere; and
another May family, the children of a widowed clergyman, seem to
satirize Yonge's pious Mays. Ethel's impatience with the younger
children is here blown into Ursula's utter exasperation with her family;
while the generation of young adults in the novel generally has far more
common sense than the older people who are meant to guide them.
With several young men to choose from, including Ursula's personable
brother Reginald, the forthright Phoebe Junior throws herself away on
Clarence Copperhead, a comic buffoon who is even worse than Flora
May's George Rivers. As she eats breakfast with her lover and grandfather, Phoebe wonders whether all men are such braggarts, and
Oliphant comments: "Phoebe had more brains than both of her inter-
locuters put together, and half-a-dozen more added on."[16] Even
Oliphant's most vibrant heroines are selfish and calculating – especially
in planning their emotional lives. On the very brink of her marriage
proposal from Clarence, Phoebe can snatch a pleasanter evening with
Reginald, which Oliphant admits was "very wrong," but not unnatural:
"She was anxious that Clarence should come back to her, and ask her to
be his wife; and yet she was pleased to be rid of Clarence, and to give her
whole attention and sympathy to Reginald, trying her best to please
him" (*Phoebe Junior*, p. 268). Oliphant's style has a bluntness and brutality that leave no romantic illusions unshattered. Her heroines reform
marriage from within, rejecting the life of childbearing and submission
that their mothers suffered, and subtly adjusting the balance of power,
so that the estate management or parliamentary speech-writing fall to
their lot, while their husbands provide the public facade. Images of
romantic love are few in Oliphant's novels, and even those that exist,
such as Kirsteen's sister Anne's devotion to her handsome doctor
husband and children, tend to be undermined by suggestions of self-

interest, or else come to nothing, like Kirsteen's romance with Ronald.

Oliphant should be viewed as a key figure in the de-romanticizing of marriage in preparation for Ibsen and the New Woman of the 1880s and 1890s. Her blunt cynicism still has the power to shock, as she demonstrates how women were prepared to weigh up all the pros and cons of a marriage-proposal, and act to further their own ambitions, rather than in response to any emotional impulse. Sexual needs are scarcely acknowledged: partly from prudery, but also because Oliphant genuinely seems to have felt that other issues were more important. Because her own views on the woman question were uncertain, because she distrusted theory in general, and theories of group behaviour in particular, she developed her own idiosyncratic response to the debates about women's independence. Her novels place young women in positions where they have to make active decisions about their future, in order to avoid lives of low-status drudgery, without the spiritual comfort Yonge provides for her put-upon heroines, such as Ethel May. When they choose marriage, Oliphant repeatedly implies that they choose a tawdry conventionality, for which she, as author, has to apologize.

ELIZA LYNN LINTON

Eliza Linton, the most virulently antifeminist of the three novelists discussed here, was also the most outspoken against marriage, which she saw both as "slavery" and a "lottery."[17] Simultaneously she believed that all sweet good girls needed the support of a strong man in marriage, and that marriage could often be deeply frustrating to both parties, largely because of the woman's impatience with domesticity. Her own most satisfactory relationships in life were with an older man she could treat as a father-substitute (Walter Savage Landor), or with younger women of the next generation (Beatrice Harradan and Beatrice Sichel), who were ideal daughter-substitutes. She also had step-children, but most of her relationships were short-lived, broken up by death or marriage. She clung to the idealized picture of the happy young wife and mother as the true destiny of her sex – perhaps all the more tenaciously as her own experience proved how difficult it was to attain. "The Love, the Home, the Motherhood, the Matronship – all, all have gone – died – and will never wake up to life again!" she mourned when her marriage collapsed, "and yet I long for love and I pine for a home."[18] It was as if she needed to believe in it the more her own knowledge of society made her cynical and bitter: and by the 1890s, she was viewing society as having gone wildly out of control. When she wrote on "The Philosophy of Marriage" for Harry Quilter's book (*Is Marriage a Failure?*), she blamed not just the institution of marriage itself, but the conditions of the English home that fostered mutual boredom between husband and wife. Believing, in any case, that few men were naturally monogamous, Linton warned: "And we must always remember that, if a man finds it an agony to see the same woman at breakfast for three hundred and sixty-five days in the year, the woman does not find the same man a Proteus of joy and romance; and the chances are that she is just as much bored by him as he is by her."[19] Linton found herself in a difficult position. As the author of the notorious *The Girl of the Period* (1868), which deplored the passing of the sweet-natured feminine woman in favor of the over-educated, swearing, coarse-minded modern hoyden, she was bound to see home and marriage as the natural destiny of the ideal girl. Motherhood she doggedly viewed as the summit of women's happiness, and completely incompatible with a working life. Beginning her career as a radical who even wrote a defense of Mary Wollstonecraft, Linton was, like Oliphant, emotional and inconsistent in her stance on women's rights, attacking the sickly sentimentality surrounding women as the "sacred sex," while actively contributing to this image herself. Her ideal world contained noble virile men and devoted feminine women, on the ancient Greek model. Higher education, work outside the home, the vote and divorce were, as in Oliphant's case, issues less emotionally compelling than the omnipresence of bad behavior: the slide into surliness and cynicism, cruelty and competition, which she saw as desexing women and making them impatient with the quiet life of home and motherhood. By 1891 she was deploring:

The married woman who is content with marriage, maternity, and domestic life alone is as rare a being as the black swan of the past. It all depends on her temperament where she seeks her distractions – whether in art, politics, philanthropy, money-making, or love. In any case, marriage is of the nature of an episode rather than the completed drama of her life; and even as an episode it is one of which she wearies sooner than man.[20]

Usually seen as a virulent reactionary, Linton at least recognized that the divorce laws were too inflexible, and that human nature (always, to her, "a sadly rickety kind of thing"[21]) required more sensitive legislative machinery to handle its emotional vagaries.

The world depicted in her novels is of parents planning mercenary marriages for their daughters, and daughters fighting snobbish attitudes (or succumbing to them) about middle-class women going out to work;

while the standard wicked husband is old, cold, fastidious, and exacting: for example, St. John Aylott in *Sowing the Wind* (1867), and Launcelot Brabazon in *The One Too Many* (1894). Aylott even attempts baby-murder, and beats his wife, Isola, who exclaims: "'Marriage! was this marriage! did wifehood mean degradation, slavery, submission to insult, the loss of self-respect?'"[22] Jabez Hamley, in *Patricia Kemball*, hopes his old wife will die, leaving him free to marry the cousin's child he has raised as a daughter.

The claims of marriage, work, and feminism are further debated in *The Rebel of the Family* (1880), through the contrasting experiences of the Winstanley sisters. While Thomasina, the worldly eldest, is content to buttress the family's finances by a marriage of convenience to the middle-aged Mr. Brocklebank, and the youngest, Eva, tries to elope, Perdita, the "Rebel" of the title, entertains old-fashioned romantic ideas of wifehood, in preference to the liberated, lesbian lifestyle of Bell Blount, a woman's rights activist. "'Oh, but being married to a good man and having children of your own is better than all this,' said Perdita, with strange passion. 'After all, work is only a substitute.'"[23] This goes to the heart of Linton's philosophy and blurs the impression of Perdita's rebellion: no longer the firebrand daughter wishing to over-turn society, Perdita merely wants a job until she finds someone agree-able to marry. When this turns out to be a humble chemist, Leslie Crawford, with a mad wife in the Rochester style, but a knack of being there when Perdita feels suicidal, the critics were understandably con-fused. Was Linton sanctioning this marriage or satirizing it? The *Satur-day Review* was particularly unsure about Leslie Crawford, wondering whether "there is not a considerable touch of sarcasm in the author's eloquent approval of her heroine's marriage with a chemist and drug-gist, whom she exalts into a hero because he has pulled her back from the brink of the pond in Kensington."[24]

Worse confusion arises in *The One Too Many*, where Linton recognizes only two kinds of femininity: the abject and the ignorant, in Moira West, and the bohemian and coarse, in the group of four Girton girls, led by Effie Chegwin. At the beginning of the novel Moira is forced to marry the middle-aged and fastidious Launcelot Brabazon, for the unconvinc-ing reason that Mrs. West finds her the "one too many" at home (she has only one other daughter, so this seems a poor excuse). Avoiding any direct portrayal of their sexual incompatibility, Linton focuses on their intellectual differences: Brabazon becoming the dictatorial teacher, "jailer" and "tyrant," while Moira dwindles into a feather-headed dunce, the image of perfect femininity, graceful, weak, passive, and limp. Linton protested that she never intended her to be perfect, but the novel's confused crosscurrents arise from the absence of positive examples either of womanhood or marriage, examples also frequently missing from her other novels. Inevitably, the reader warms to Effie Chegwin and her parents, who are liberal-minded, relaxed, and cheerful. "'I would send my mother to blazes before I would sell myself to a man I did not love,'" Effie declares.[25] On the other hand, even Effie's parents freeze at the thought of her marrying a common policeman, a prospect that also outrages her three Girton "pals." Linton herself has mixed feelings about it, suggesting that Effie's willingness to sacrifice herself for the man she loves at least shows genuine womanly devotion (vol. III, p. 242); but the thrust of the novel is completely in conflict with its professed dedication to "the Sweet Girls Still Left Among Us who have no part in the new revolt but are content to be dutiful, innocent, and sheltered."

It is clearly unwise to generalize about Victorian antifeminist women novelists on the basis of only a few novels. On the other hand, those selected for discussion were some of the most widely read, and, Linton's apart, the most accessible today, besides having a considerable amount in common with one another. They all explore the histories of women who find it difficult to marry, as much because of psychological resistance as lack of opportunity. In each case, the novelist pushes to the limit her reservations about marriage; she tries to find alternatives, and is equally uneasy about them. The caricaturing of men, which began with Flora's husband, George, in *The Daisy Chain*, intensifies with Oliphant's Clarence Copperhead, and Linton's Launcelot Brabazon. Husbands such as Tom Marjoribanks and Alick Keith, who escape caricature, are often emasculated, while the women (except for Moira) are emotionally complex, intelligent, and unfulfilled. Overshadowed in literary history by the sensation novel of the 1860s and the outspoken New Woman novel of the 1890s, such as Grant Allen's *The Woman Who Did* (1895), the antifeminist woman's novel has undeservedly slipped from view and its skeptical critique of marriage been underestimated.

In fact, these novels expose the full extent of the conservatives' self-doubt over the marriage question. Purporting to uphold the ideals of romantic courtship and marriage, they launch their heroines into a world of selfish maneuvering, where to be innocent is to be unhappy, and to be married a practical compromise. The cleverest women, such as Oliphant's, survive, but the traditional happy ending is widely questioned, and the novels are at their most interesting where they deliberately distort it. They go much further than their better-known predecessors, Charlotte Brontë and George Eliot, who usually supply their heroines with second opportunities for contentment, in that they question whether marriage *is* a credible, even desirable, romantic solution. Mediated in bold language, a rhetoric of shock and disgust, the marriages described in these novels reflect a society in love with social advancement to the exclusion of women's emotional and intellectual fulfillment. If antifeminist women were having doubts about the certainty of domestic happiness, the "gender crisis" of the 1880s onwards assumes even greater proportions than cultural historians have recognized. It was eventually left to Mrs. Humphry Ward, the youngest of the antifeminist women novelists, to restore some tremulous physical consciousness to the fictional portrayal of men and women in love, and to suggest that a marriage between equals could enrich the lives of both.

NOTES

1 Eliza Lynn Linton, *Patricia Kemball* (London: Chatto and Windus, 1875), p. 180.
2 Elizabeth Rachel Chapman, *Marriage Questions in Modern Fiction, and Other Essays on Kindred Subjects* (London and New York: The Bodley Head, 1897), p. 10.
3 Joan Perkin, *Women and Marriage in Nineteenth Century England* (London: Routledge, 1989), p. 257.
4 Pat Jalland, *Women, Marriage and Politics 1860–1914* (Oxford: Clarendon Press, 1986), p. 82.
5 Charlotte Yonge, *Womankind* (London: Mozley and Smith, 1876), p. 179.
6 Charlotte Yonge, *The Daisy Chain, or Aspirations: A Family Chronicle* (London: Macmillan, 1856), p. 34.
7 Charlotte Yonge, *The Clever Woman of the Family* (1865; repr. London: Virago, 1985), p. 1.
8 Nicola Diane Thompson, *Reviewing Sex: Gender and the Reception of Victorian Novels* (London: Macmillan; New York: New York University Press, 1996), p. 107.
9 *The Autobiography of Margaret Oliphant*, ed. Elisabeth Jay (Oxford: Oxford University Press, 1990), p. 33.
10 Margaret Oliphant, "The Grievances of Women," *Fraser's Magazine* 101 (May 1880), 698.
11 Margaret Oliphant, "Mill on the Subjection of Women," *Edinburgh Review* 130 (October 1869), 581.
12 Margaret Oliphant, *The Curate in Charge* (1876; repr. Gloucester: Alan Sutton, 1985), p. 193.

13 Elizabeth Langland, *Nobody's Angels: Middle-Class Women and Domestic Ideology in Victorian Culture* (Ithaca and London: Cornell University Press, 1995), p. 180.
14 Margaret Oliphant, *Kirsteen* (1890; repr. London: Everyman, 1984), p. 2.
15 Margaret Oliphant, *Miss Marjoribanks* (1866; repr. London: Virago, 1988), p. 26.
16 Margaret Oliphant, *Phoebe Junior* (1876; repr. London: Virago, 1989), p. 316.
17 Eliza Lynn Linton, "The Modern Revolt," *Macmillan's Magazine* 23 (December 1870), 147; "Our Civilization," *Cornhill Magazine* 27 (June 1873), 675.
18 G. S. Layard, *Mrs. Lynn Linton: Her Life, Letters and Opinions* (London: Methuen, 1901), p. 107.
19 Eliza Lynn Linton, "The Philosophy of Marriage," in Harry Quilter (ed.), *Is Marriage a Failure?* (London: Swan Sonnenschein, 1888), p. 198.
20 Quoted by Joan Perkin in *Women and Marriage*, p. 289.
21 Eliza Lynn Linton, "The Judicial Shock to Marriage," *Nineteenth Century* 29 (May 1891), 696.
22 Eliza Lynn Linton, *Sowing the Wind*, 3 vols. (London: Tinsley Brothers, 1867), vol. III, p. 254.
23 Eliza Lynn Linton, *The Rebel of the Family*, 3 vols. (London: Chatto and Windus, 1880), vol. I, p. 286.
24 *The Saturday Review*, November 20, 1880, p. 650.
25 Eliza Lynn Linton, *The One Too Many*, 3 vols. (London: Chatto and Windus, 1894), vol. I, p. 216.

WORKS CITED

Caird, Mona, "Marriage," *Westminster Review* 130 (August 1888), 186–201.

Chapman, E. R., *Marriage Questions in Modern Fiction, and Other Essays on Kindred Subjects*, London and New York: The Bodley Head, 1897.

Heilbrun, C. J., *Hamlet's Mother and Other Women*, New York: Columbia University Press, 1990.

Jalland, Pat, *Women, Marriage and Politics 1860–1914*, Oxford: Clarendon Press, 1986.

Jay, Elisabeth, *Mrs Oliphant: A Fiction to Herself. A Literary Life*, Oxford: Clarendon Press, 1995.

Langland, Elisabeth, *Nobody's Angels: Middle-Class Women and Domestic Ideology in Victorian Culture*, Ithaca and London: Cornell University Press, 1995.

Layard, G. S., *Mrs. Lynn Linton: Her Life, Letters and Opinions*, London: Methuen, 1901.

Linton, Eliza Lynn, "The Judicial Shock to Marriage," *Nineteenth Century* 29 (May 1891), 691–700.

  "The Marriage Tie: Its Sanctity and Abuse," *New Review* 6 (February 1892), 218–28.

  "The Modern Revolt," *Macmillan's Magazine* 23 (December 1870), 142–49.

  The One Too Many, 3 vols., London: Chatto and Windus, 1894.

"Our Civilization," *Cornhill Magazine* 27 (June 1873), 671–78.

Patricia Kemball, London: Chatto and Windus, 1875.

The Rebel of the Family, 3 vols., London: Chatto and Windus, 1880.

Sowing the Wind, 3 vols., London: Tinsley Brothers, 1867.

Oliphant, Margaret, *The Curate in Charge*, 1876, repr. Gloucester: Alan Sutton, 1985.

"The Grievances of Women," *Fraser's Magazine* 101 (May 1880), 698–710.

Kirsteen, 1890, repr. London: Everyman, 1984.

"Mill on the Subjection of Women," *Edinburgh Review* 130 (October 1869), 572–602.

Miss Marjoribanks, 1866, repr. London: Virago, 1988.

Phoebe Junior, 1876, repr. London: Virago, 1989.

Autobiography, ed. Elisabeth Jay, Oxford: Oxford University Press, 1990.

Perkin, Joan, *Women and Marriage in Nineteenth Century England*, London: Routledge, 1989.

Quilter, Harry (ed.), *Is Marriage a Failure?* London: Swan Sonnenschein, 1888.

Rose, P., *Parallel Lives: Five Victorian Marriages*, London: Penguin, 1984.

Thompson, Nicola Diane, *Reviewing Sex: Gender and the Reception of Victorian Novels*, London: Macmillan; New York: New York University Press, 1996.

Yonge, Charlotte, *The Clever Woman of the Family*, 1865, repr. London: Virago, 1985.

The Daisy Chain, or Aspirations: A Family Chronicle, 1856, repr. London: Virago, 1982.

The Three Brides, London: Macmillan, 1876.

Womankind, London: Mozley and Smith, 1876.

Breaking apart: the early Victorian divorce novel

Anne Humpherys

In 1881 Emile Zola complained that legalized divorce would be the ruin of literature because it would make marital misery solvable and thus rob the novelist of his subject matter.[1] But despite Zola's anxieties, when expanded access to divorce came to France and England, literature was not ruined, but instead new subjects and new structures developed to integrate marital breakdown and remarriage into the plot. In fact, the introduction of divorce into the conventional marriage plot resulted in a disruption of form that made the novel more multi-voiced, more diffuse, more open-ended – divorce, in other words, is a factor in the development of the modernist and postmodernist experiments in narrative form.

Naturally, since divorce was practically impossible before the mid-nineteenth century, only a handful of novels talked about it in the first half of the century. But the debates about divorce reform in the decade leading up to the passage of the Matrimonial Causes Act of 1857 (known popularly as the Divorce Reform Act) were coupled with a small flurry of narratives which were at least partially about divorce, the most well known though not necessarily the most interesting being *Hard Times* (1854) by Charles Dickens.

After the passage of the Matrimonial Causes Act in 1857, there was a slow but steady increase in the number of novels that featured divorce – as an action thought about, or sometimes attempted, or less frequently, achieved. Not until the 1880s, however, did divorced characters figure in significant ways in the novel. But many of the themes and narrative methods of these later divorce novels[2] are adumbrated in the early fictional attempts to examine through the lens of divorce issues raised by unhappy marriages and the inequality of women under the law.

In the following chapter, I survey these thematic innovations and narrative methods in the divorce novel from the late 1830s to the early 1860s, and then examine in detail three novels whose power and interest is at least partly due to the introduction of divorce into the plot.

Two legal facts are essential to this discussion. First, when a woman married, she literally ceased to be a person under the law of coverture, which stated that the wife's interests were represented by her husband. The justification for this drastic disenfranchisement was that if the wife had rights separate from her husband the harmony of marriage would be destroyed. The consequences were that if the marriage went bad, a wife had no legal recourse.

The second fact is that before the 1857 Matrimonial Causes Act, divorce was available but only as a prerogative of the very wealthy, mainly men, its justification being to prevent "spurious offspring" from inheriting big estates. The only legal ground or cause for divorce thus was adultery. Women could also sue for divorce, but in their case the adultery had to be "aggravated" by incest or bigamy. Only four women had successfully petitioned Parliament for a full divorce before 1857, only three of them between 1827 and 1857 as compared to 140 full divorces granted to men during the same period.

Three separate legal actions, including a private bill in the House of Lords, were necessary. There was a somewhat more easily achieved judicial separation "from bed and board," but women in that position had no legal status – no right to their own earnings nor to access to their children. Nor could either party remarry.

A Royal Commission of Divorce was set up in 1850 and issued a three-volume report in 1853 in which it proposed no change in the law concerning separation and divorce, but rather a major reconstruction of the courts involved in divorce actions. A bill to that end was introduced in 1854 but failed; it was introduced again in 1857 and passed. This Matrimonial Causes Act was quite conservative, not touching the double standard or traditional patriarchal structures, but it did increase the availability of both legal separation and full divorce for the middle classes and for women, and increasing numbers of both groups took advantage of it after 1857.[3] There were a couple of important new provisions in the 1857 Act – one, the protection of judicially separated women's property, and two, the addition of cruelty and desertion for two years to the aggravated causes for divorce for women. (The double standard in divorce was not abolished until 1923, and grounds other than adultery were admitted only after 1937.)

The debates about divorce reform, which actually extended over several decades, and the expectations raised by the passing of the 1857 Act established a context in which women's concerns about their disadvantaged position in marriage could be narrated. The pattern in which this concern is represented is consistent enough to be a trope: a brutal and/or egregiously adulterous husband is repeatedly excused, forgiven, and often nursed by the heroic wife until finally he or she dies as in *The Tenant of Wildfell Hall* by Anne Brontë (1848), or in a few cases she runs away (*Stuart of Dunleith* by Caroline Norton, 1851), or in even fewer cases, the husband reforms, as in *Thrice His* by Louisa Jane Campbell (1866), though the wife in that novel dies anyway. For the purposes of discussion here, I will call this narrative pattern the "Caroline Norton plot" after the real-life woman who was forever linked in the public mind with the agitation for reform of women's legal status and whose own life contained many of the elements of the fictional trope.[4]

But not all of the early divorce novels had long-suffering wives as their protagonists: a minority had the "Jane Eyre plot," one in which the *husband* has been tricked into a bad marriage or his wife turns bad quickly, and then he falls in love with a good woman who should be his wife. These novels are sometimes narrated from the heroine's point of view, as in *Jane Eyre*, and sometimes from the husband's, as in Ouida's first novel, *Held in Bondage* (1863).

Most of the fifteen early divorce novels (from 1837–69) that I have identified fall into one of these two plot patterns, though the three more interesting ones discussed below modify the tropes. Among the novels that do fit the two tropes, there are differences, of course, but for all, the narrative issue is the same: first, if, and then how to extricate the heroine or hero from the mistaken marriage, and second, whether to allow her or him to make a second more fulfilling one. All of the early divorce novels share an uncertainty about second marriages because of the confusion about whether marriage is a sacrament (and therefore indissoluble) or a civil contract which can be legally canceled.[5]

Another narrative problem in these novels is how to achieve the separation from an undesirable spouse without the heroine, whether she be the abused wife or the second love, losing the reader's sympathy. That is, the problem is to maintain her heroine status as innocent and capable of unlimited self-sacrifice and still reward her with love and happiness. This problem provides the total narrative drive of *The Tenant of Wildfell Hall*.

There are at least four types of resolution to this narrative problem in these early novels. In the most common one, the unsatisfactory partner dies, as in *Jane Eyre*, *David Copperfield*, *Middlemarch*, or most astonishingly, *Paul Ferroll* (1855) by Caroline Clive, in which the hero murders his wife in the first lines of the novel, spends the rest of the novel married to his beloved second wife, and finishes by going to America with their daughter and escaping all punishment.

Two, the abused partner, usually the wife, dies after years of mistreatment in extended scenes of pathos, as in Caroline Norton's *Stuart of Dunleith* or in one of the double plots in *Cheveley* (1839) by Bulwer Lytton's estranged wife Rosina. Three, there is a separation or divorce, either discussed as in *Hard Times* (1854), or begun as in *Stuart of Dunleith* or *Thrice His*, or actually achieved as in Thackeray's *The Newcomes* (1858) or Trollope's *Phineas Finn* (1869). The results of the divorce or even judicial separation, however, are always disastrous for the woman.

The fourth resolution is bigamy either attempted or achieved, as in *Jane Eyre*, or the anonymous *Clara Harrington* (1852), or John Harwood's *Lord Lynn's Wife* (1864), a type of plot that increased after the enactment of the 1857 bill. In fact, I think (others have said the same thing) that the first literary response to divorce law reform was a rush of novels not about divorce but about bigamy because, though divorce (including judicial separation) might seem tantalizingly available as a resolution to an unsatisfactory marriage after the new law, this possibility was strongly countered by the deep shame and severe social ostracism that was attached to divorced women. Thus, the expectations that a bad marriage could (and should) be ended so that a new and better marriage might be achieved which were raised by the new Divorce Reform Act were frequently represented in popular fiction by the bigamy plot, most often, as in *Jane Eyre*, when the abused partner is the husband. In the bigamy plot, the second marriage could be examined but its illegality enabled the author to avoid the marriage as a sacrament or civil contract issue.

Most of the divorce novels before the 1857 Act were of the Caroline Norton type, that is their intent was to represent the terrible position of married women who had depraved or unscrupulous husbands. But although the sufferings of the heroines in these novels made clear the injustice of the legal inequality in marriage, redress seemed impossible. Because of the wife's total dependence on her husband, even judicial separation could not be attempted without his consent and financial support, and in any case if separated, the woman had no right to keep or even see her children. This legal situation coupled with the shame attached to either separation or full divorce meant there was little that a heroine who was to keep the reader's sympathy could do. She either had to stay with the abusive husband, which defeated the purpose of the exposé by reaffirming the cultural expectation that the role of women is to serve and endure, or become a version of a fallen woman by leaving him, whether to return to her parents (*Hard Times*), to elope with another man (*The Newcomes* and Mrs. Henry Wood's *East Lynne*), or to seek a legal separation or full divorce, such as is attempted in Emma Robinson's *Mauleverer's Divorce*.

This contradiction between the intent to expose legal injustice and the denial of any remedy is introduced in one of the many subplots in Thackeray's *The Newcomes*, where Barnes Newcome's violent abuse of his wife, who was forced by her ambitious family to marry him, is unbearable for the reader as well as for her. But her escape with the man whom she wanted to marry and who has continued to love and care for her, followed by her subsequent divorce and remarriage, does not save her narratively, for the minute she leaves her husband's house, she is condemned not only by society, but more importantly by the narrator and behind him the author, neither of whom, however, can offer a single suggestion as to what else she could have done. Even Caroline Norton, who did separate from her abominable husband and who led the battle for the right of a separated woman to keep her children and her earnings, in her vaguely autobiographical novel, *Stuart of Dunleith*, allows her abused heroine to run away, even to begin legal proceedings for a divorce, but in the end can think of no better resolution for that heroine except for her to die without redress, comfort, or satisfaction in what is one of the most painful deathbed scenes I know of in nineteenth-century fiction.

In many novels whose whole point is to call for redress for women's inequality under the marriage law, this contradiction can destabilize the narrative and open fissures through which new types of narrative structures and closures are tried, not always successfully. For example, there can be an elongated exposition – that is the presentation of the heroine's sufferings (as in *The Tenant of Wildfell Hall*, where the long and repetitive detailing of Helen Huntingdon's unhappy marriage takes up over half the novel) at the expense of narrative development and climax. This narrative pattern, by constantly delaying the climax, that is some action presumably on the part of the wife, and the resulting closure, develops a plot with a different rhythm, one not based on the Aristotelian exposition, climax, and denouement. Rather such a plot develops through incremental repetition and leads to either a new beginning, a new narrative (as in *The Tenant*, when Helen's return to nurse her dying husband begins the story anew), or to a collapse of the climax and closure into a final few pages (as in an interesting novel by John Lang, *The Ex-Wife* [1859]).

Another narrative structure that attempts to deal with this contradiction is the split plot, where one wife fulfills the long-suffering and passive "feminine" role while another wife tries out, usually with bad results, other alternatives, including elopement, separation, and divorce. *Mauleverer's Divorce* is the best example of this split, though *Hard Times* is a variant of it in that Stephen Blackpool acts out the Jane Eyre plot while Louisa acts out the Caroline Norton plot.[6]

The variations in the tropes result in interesting narrative experiments, and I want to look more closely at three novels which call up but then undercut the tropes partly because they refuse the motivation implied in both the Caroline Norton and the Jane Eyre plots – that is, the presence of a violent, abusive or otherwise totally unacceptable partner. With one exception, the undesired partners in these three novels, though flawed, have many good qualities. Therefore abuse is not the only motive for the divorce. This complication of motive doubles the narrative, not plot and subplot, but plot and counterplot, two plots that comment on and in two cases undermine each other.

The first of these novels was written long before the 1857 Act: *The Divorced* by Lady Charlotte Bury[7] in which the divorce has taken place before the narrative begins. The second, *Mauleverer's Divorce* by Emma Robinson[8] (1858), is set before the Act but written during the debates. In it two divorces are attempted, that by a women failing, that by a man succeeding. The third is the immensely popular *East Lynne* by Mrs. Henry Wood (1861), written in the years immediately following the Matrimonial Causes Act and seemingly accepting of divorce which allows a second marriage.

Lady Bury's 1837 silver fork novel *The Divorced* is probably the product of the publicity surrounding the divorce of Lord Ellenborough in 1830, which, notorious in its collusion (where the husband and wife agree beforehand to the evidence that will result in a divorce), led to intense debates about divorce reform. Conventional in almost all ways, the novel features stereotypical characters: the protagonists are aristocrats, and minor characters include the faithful maid, the frustrated spinster, the overly indulgent mother, the self-sacrificing daughter. Chance and coincidence determine the plot, which details the blighting of the hopes and eventually the lives of the children of the second marriage, and the coarsening of the noble lover and second husband through the social ostracizing of his wife. Though the theme is the destructive effects on all parties in a divorce, the wife is most severely punished. She loses both her children to death, her husband to suicide, her fortune, her status, and eventually her own life.

But several elements in this novel, which was reissued unchanged in the year just after the 1857 Act was passed, subvert some of its conventionality. The first is its "donée", as Henry James would say. *The Divorced* is, ironically, given its very early date, the only nineteenth-century divorce novel I have identified which is solely concerned with the second marriage, thus making it the only novel that is clearly neither a "Caroline Norton" nor a "Jane Eyre" story. This is singular enough, since the way in which society expressed its disapproval of divorce was to act as though the wife had died, and in fact Lady Howard, the wife in *The Divorced*, has a son by her first husband who thinks she is dead. In all other early divorce novels, when the wife leaves her husband she essentially drops out of the story, even as she disappears from people's conversation. By writing a novel that focused on the second marriage *after* the divorce, Lady Bury was breaking both a social and a narrative taboo.

Perhaps she could do so because the convention of the silver fork novel promised revelations about the private lives of the aristocratic world, and divorces were the prerogative of the rich landed gentry. One of the characters says about the divorced Lady Howard "nowadays these things are quite common"[9] – and this in 1837! Lady Bury also wanted to criticize the double standard by which society ostracizes the female divorcée but not the male seducer.

But Lady Bury makes an even more surprising break with narrative and social convention: the text is actually sympathetic towards the wife even as it is determined to punish her. Though Lady Howard suffers for her "crime," her unswerving love for Lord Howard, her tenderness for their children, her meekness and forgiveness in the face of her second husband's blaming her for their situation, her reluctance to assert her feelings or rights, give her many of the traits of a conventional heroine and command the reader's sympathy. Lord Howard's slow loss of love for her seems more the result of his weak character than the divorce, and in any case his decline is depicted with such sophisticated psychological insight that it creates even more sympathy for his wife.

Moreover, though making the point that the second marriage can never be happy or successful, and that any resulting children will inevitably suffer for the sins of the parents (in this case they are denied the lovers they desire and then die), the novel also takes an unusual turn which inserts a competing narrative into the conventional moralistic one. Lady Bury's novel is unique among the early divorce novels, and as far as I know, all nineteenth-century divorce novels, because the motivation for elopement, divorce, and remarriage is not a brutal or inadequate spouse (Lady Howard's first husband is a good if stiff man), but rather a passionate love for another, one who is equally noble and good.

The counter story of Lord and Lady Howard's love emerges slowly and in fragments through details given in conversation between the two of them as well as exchanges among other characters. As we piece it together, their love story sets up resonances with one of the West's great myths – that of doomed, star-crossed romantic love – the love of Tristan and Isolde, Paolo and Francesca, Romeo and Juliet. The intermittent eruption into the surface story of this powerful myth disrupts meaning by making it hard to know how to judge the characters' actions. The text certainly details the devastating effect of their social ostrasizing on their love, but it also suggests that this love, with the support and comfort they have given each other for over twenty years of their banishment and isolation, and their commitment to each other, yet just might have been worth all the costs of divorce. More than once Lady Howard says she has no regrets, and the novel opens with an epigraph from Byron: "I've lost all for love but I regret nothing."

I do not want to claim too much for Lady Bury's novel. But Emma Robinson's *Mauleverer's Divorce* is another matter. This fascinating novel has many concerns: Welsh nationalism, inheritance laws, parliamentary debates, Puseyitism. But as the title and subtitle – "a story of a woman's wrongs" – suggest, its central concern is women's inequality in marriage and under the law. Thus this would appear to be a novel of the "Caroline Norton" type. However, Robinson does not limit her story to an exposition of these wrongs nor does she resolve them by the death of one or more of the parties, as Lady Bury, Caroline Norton, Anne Brontë, and others do. Rather she introduces divorce as a remedy.

Though the novel was written during the final stages of debate on the 1857 Matrimonial Causes Act and published just after it was passed, the novel is set in the 1840s and so the two divorce actions in the novel are initiated under the old law. Much of the social criticism is directed against two elements of the old divorce law that were reformed by the new: the conservatism toward women in the Ecclesiastical Courts which controlled divorce actions prior to the new law, and the inability of separated married women to protect their earnings from the depredations of their husbands. From this point of view *Mauleverer's Divorce* is part of the divorce reform debates. But what destabilizes the conventional narrative is the conflicting attitudes toward divorce.

The marriage triangles in this novel are constructed of both the

"Caroline Norton" and the "Jane Eyre" plots, that is one marriage has an abused wife (Sophia) with a drunken, violent, adulterous, and spendthrift husband (Luxmoor), and the other a spoiled but not vicious husband (Scarlatt Suett, a kind of Rochester figure) who is married to the narrator Hugh/Helana but in love with Sophia. Part of the instability in this novel results from this doubling, for the novel is narrated in the first-person by Hugh/Helana, the wife in the "Jane Eyre" plot whose husband is in love with the abused wife in the "Caroline Norton" plot. Because the story is narrated by the Bertha figure in the Jane Eyre plot, whom as we know now can be either the abused or the unsuitable wife depending on the point of view, the novel manages to present all varieties of argument about divorce in sorting out the rights and wrongs of the situation. Clearly divorce is a good thing for abused wives, but there is that problem of second marriages. As the Bible says, "Whoever putteth away a wife, and marrieth another, committeth adultery; and whosoever marrieth her that is put away from her husband, committeth adultery."[10]

In *Mauleverer's Divorce* the statement that marriage is indissoluble is expressed by the narrator and focus, Hugh/Helana, who seems at the beginning to fulfill all the expectations of a conventional heroine. She is innocent and pure, maternal, obedient, and in the beginning endlessly forgiving and tolerant of her irritable husband. The subtitle, "a story of a woman's wrongs," refers to her. Thus her negative view of divorce might seem the message we are meant to take away. But her argument is subverted by an equally strong assertion in the text that Sophia as an abused wife – and the abuses are egregious: drunkenness, adultery, bastardy, beatings, stealing, fraud – should be able to get a divorce. Further, as Sophia says, and even Hugh/Helana agrees, the denial of that remedy causes tragedy for all four of the protagonists as well as the innocent Vivien ApHowel who loves and tries to save Hugh/Helana. "Might Sophia have been not only an unharmful but useful and salutary member of society," Hugh/Helana muses, "but for the reprobate vileness of that man's conduct towards her? Had there even been a possible release for her from his pestilent association, might she have righted herself by the force of her own strong mind, and the balancing influence of early good impressions?"[11]

One of the narrative consequences of this tension is that we increasingly experience the first-person narrator Hugh/Helana as unreliable. This shifts the interest off the other characters and onto her – what are *her* motivations? what role does *she* play in her own tragedy? As the novel develops in its jerk and start way – there are at least three different climaxes which lead to new expositions, new rising actions, and new climaxes – the focus of the novel becomes not the machinations of the "villain" Scarlatt or the "villainess" Sophia (who both are described by the narrator in these conventional terms), but rather the tortured, paranoid consciousness of the narrator Hugh/Helana.

Justifying her refusal to treat her faithless husband gently, as Sophia and Vivien – one her enemy and the other her faithful supporter – urge, Hugh/Helana pettishly declares "Where I was not *all*, I determined to be *nothing*."[12] After blackening Sophia's character and betraying her whereabouts to her brutal husband from whom she has been hiding, Hugh/Helana says, "I own I did not sufficiently discriminate mere suspicions, the accusations of enemies, from certainties."[13]

Moreover this destabilizing of the narrator's reliability results in a subversion of closure. On the surface the rewards and punishments are conventional: the abusive husband Luxmoor dies of the DTs and Sophia, the second wife of Hugh/Helana's divorced husband, dies in premature childbirth. Vivien, Hugh/Helana's rejected would-be lover and savior, who allowed himself to be manipulated by Scarlatt and Sophia, also dies. But Scarlatt, Hugh/Helana's adulterous husband, goes unpunished and in fact gets the money, the title, the estate, and the children, while Hugh/Helana, the putative heroine, is stripped of wealth, her children, and divorced from her husband, who has been able to manufacture a charge of adultery with Vivien against her and get a divorce. Hugh/Helana's remedy is to retire to the island of Madeira to write this book to defend her innocence since she was not able to do so at her divorce trial. (One of the major injustices in both the old and the new divorce laws, one which Caroline Norton was active in exposing, was that respondents, usually women, could not testify in their own defense in court nor could their barristers cross-examine witnesses. This was not changed until 1869.) "I seem to have turned a gaze at once microscopic and all-embracing on my past career," Hugh/Helana says at the beginning of the novel. "At last I comprehend it in its entirety!"[14]

But through the three volumes that make up her defense, she consistently undermines her own story, especially as it is framed in binary melodramatic terms – she as victim and Sophia as villainess. As quoted before, Hugh/Helana admits that Sophia would have thrived without her brutal husband. In fact, Hugh/Helana has been an enemy to Sophia as much as Sophia to her: she is directly responsible for Sophia being denied her divorce since Hugh/Helana revealed to the court a letter that suggested Sophia condoned[15] her husband's behavior by accepting him back after he had beaten and robbed her.

Also, by spitefully betraying Sophia's whereabouts to her husband, Hugh/Helana also robs Sophia of her means to a livelihood. (Luxmoor takes, as he is legally entitled to, all the money she makes.) Hugh/Helana recounts Sophia's efforts to befriend and help her, in particular to help her breach the rift with her husband. Sophia becomes the loved caretaker of Hugh/Helana's children, whom the latter had abandoned to pursue her fleeing husband: "And yet in the absorption of my agony, these very children themselves – I scarcely embraced them! – certainly shed no tears over them – when I parted from them that day, leaving them only in the charge of a few scared domestics, whom I imagined still faithful to me."[16]

But most important, the supposed villainess Sophia is given the last words in the novel to justify herself. Hugh/Helana, the controller of the narrative, at the end of her own effort at self-vindication, quotes Sophia's last letter of explanation in full and *does not respond to it.* Thus, the novel ends with Sophia's voice and Sophia's story. Beaten, robbed, and forced to support her husband's bastard children, unable to get a divorce, and further subjected to the jealousy, humiliations, and outright maliciousness of Hugh/Helana's actions towards her, Sophia ends the novel with a narration of *her* wrongs not those of the narrator and supposed heroine Hugh/Helana's, thus destabilizing the reference of the subtitle, "a story of a woman's wrongs."

"Cruel and remorseless laws [of marriage and divorce] have done this for me – for you – for all whom the misfortune of my position have involved," Sophia writes. "Will they never be changed? Will no hero of civilization arise – no statesman, worthy of the name – who despising the interested and superstitious clamour certain to howl and hiss around him in the effort – will no one restore to woman some portion of the rights due to the human form she bears?"[17] The destabilizing effect of this shift to Sophia's story at closure is further reinforced because her final words echo the author Emma Robinson's first words, her dedication of her novel to Lord Palmerston, the Prime Minister who kept Parliament in session through a hot and humid August in 1857 until it passed the Matrimonial Causes Act: "despising the clamours of interested and bigoted factions, he first of all English statesmen has commenced the generous justice of restoring the sexes to a legal equality."

The impact of this closure is unsettling for the reader, at least for this reader.[18] Narrative expectations have led us to rely on Hugh/Helana's first-person report, though we may have suspected her of overreactions and not a little paranoia. But at the end, we are asked to identify with Sophia, whom Hugh/Helana has called a liar, a manipulator, a fraud, and her deadly enemy. Finally, then, we question the very possibility of narrative certainty in this text; though the closure and in particular its reference to the dedication invite us to read back to make meaning of the narrative, we cannot do so, for this closure leaves open all questions: not just what happens to Hugh/Helana and Scarlatt and their children, but more importantly, whose version of what happened is right – the narrator's or Sophia's? Closure, then, is undermined as neatly as in any *roman nouveau* or postmodernist text one could name.

The introduction of divorce into these two novels of inappropriate and unhappy marriages results in mixed responses to marriage as an institution and divorce as a remedy. The contradictory positions about the priority of romantic love to marriage in *The Divorced* and the questioning of the permanence of the marriage bond in *Mauleverer's Divorce*, plus the reluctance in both novels to assign full responsibility for the miserable outcomes to only one person, destabilize narrative authority and narrative closure.

Mrs. Henry Wood's vastly popular *East Lynne*, published four years after the passage of the Matrimonial Causes Act, seems more assured in its use of divorce as a plot event. Though the introduction of divorce still results in a double plot, it is linear rather than simultaneous in its development. First the novel tells its version of the Jane Eyre story of a man who makes a mistaken marriage while the right woman waits. Divorce enables the closure of this plot. At the same time the divorce generates another narrative, one the novel really wants to tell – the more emotionally powerful story of the Fatal Return, a mythic story in which a marriage partner is thought dead, the remaining partner remarries, and then the first partner secretly returns. In this case the first wife reenters the family as a governess for her own children.

The divorce of Lady Isobel Carlyle by her husband Archibald Carlyle after she elopes with Francis Levison is presented as an inevitable action, taking only five months from her elopement to the final judgment. She is anxious for the divorce so her lover can marry her before their child is born. In the event he does not, telling her it would be a disgrace for his family, he having inherited a title, if he married a divorced woman. This is the most bitter aspect of her punishment for leaving her marriage to date, but worse is to come, for no matter how understandable her

actions or repentance, she is to be punished by witnessing the happiness
of her supplanter and the death of her oldest child.

   East Lynne is conventional in its attitude toward divorce: the erring
wife and the seducer are punished. Further, it is a Jane Eyre narrative in
its social criticism of the idealized "angel in the house." The good
second wife Barbara Hare is sensible and active. The inadequate first
wife, on the other hand, is an idealized angel like the protagonist of *Lady
Audley's Secret*, published by Elizabeth Braddon in the next year. Lady
Isobel is beautiful, with black curls, delicate, "wondrously gifted by
nature, not only in mind and person, but in heart ... generous and
benevolent"[19] but also helpless, clinging, dependent, and weak. Carlyle
falls in love with her for these traits, even as does Sir Michael Audley
with Lucy Graham.

   These very traits, however, make the women unsatisfactory wives.
However, in *East Lynne*, Wood complicates the issue of culpability by
making it clear that Carlyle shares responsibility for the catastrophe,
thus modifying the Jane Eyre trope and showing the impact of changing
notions of masculine behavior in marriage that were being worked out
in part by the Divorce Court judgments.[20] To him his wife is a beautiful
possession; he never tries to understand her. He leaves her alone to be
bullied by his unpleasant sister (whom he banishes from the house for his
second wife). He does not even think about the problems presented by
her having no money and no companions. Lady Isobel is blamed for not
confiding in her husband about either her misery over Miss Carlyle's
tyranny or her jealousy of Barbara Hare. But equally, Carlyle's failure to
confide in his wife about why he spends so much time with Barbara and
at late hours (they confer about her brother's situation) brings about
Isobel's fall. Carlyle goes about his business, never sharing his life with
his wife, oblivious to her pleas to stay with her, to ask Levison to leave.
The villain Francis Levison finds it easy, thus, to convince her that her
husband doesn't care for her and is carrying on an affair with Barbara.
Lady Isobel's very "angelic" qualities – passivity, weakness, and dependence – make her an easy target for his seduction. Unlike the
situation in *The Divorced*, where true love and passion motivated the
elopement and complicated the moral position of the novel, here conventional female weakness and male villainy are responsible for the
flight of Lady Isobel.

   Archibald Carlyle's failures as a husband the first time round (he
learns and is an ideal husband the second time) complicate the reader's
response to her flight. As in *Mauleverer's Divorce*, it is uncertain whether

Lady Isobel is the abused or the unsatisfactory wife. But even though the stern narrator admits that such a marriage may be a disaster, she denies any redress to the wife: "Whatever trials may be the lot of your married life, though they may magnify themselves to your crushed spirit as beyond the endurance of woman to bear, *resolve* to bear them ... bear unto death, rather than forfeit your fair name and your good conscience."[21]

After Lady Isobel runs away with Levison and is divorced, she needs to die in order to enable her ex-husband to marry the right woman. Barbara Hare doesn't think Lady Isobel being alive is an impediment to remarriage, but Carlyle does, and he quotes the same Biblical phrase used in *Mauleverer's Divorce*: "Whosoever putteth away his wife, and marrieth another, committeth adultery."

Everyone thinks Lady Isobel does die in a train wreck, and with that reported death the Jane Eyre plot can be fulfilled with the marriage of two people meant for each other. Except *East Lynne* does not end with the happy ending of Barbara's "Reader, I married him." In fact, the divorce and falsely reported death which enable the marriage of Carlyle and Barbara is the beginning of the powerful story of the Fatal Return of a woman who is thought dead coming back unknown (because disfigured) as a governess to her own children. In this story, Lady Isobel becomes the heroine rather than the villainess. She suffers all and for all and thus ironically fulfills the idealized angel in the house trope perfectly.

The emotional power of *East Lynne* and the reason it was so enormously successful as a novel and as a play both in Britain and the United States during the rest of the century lies in the voyeuristic experience of watching[22] the tortured feelings of rage, jealousy, love, guilt, desire, and frustration that are the product of the extended encounters between the unrecognized and powerless woman and her children and her lost husband. Though the narrator insists that Lady Isobel's emotional torture is just punishment for her elopement, as readers we experience sympathy with her as she nurtures her children while Barbara neglects them. Isobel has no right to accept and reciprocate their love, nor more practically to insist on medical treatment for the ailing William. This is particularly excruciating as he dies slowly of consumption. Her death follows his shortly, a necessary event to introduce further emotional intensity in a recognition and forgiveness scene and to bring the Fatal Return story to closure. The Fatal Return story over, the Jane Eyre story comes to its final closure with Carlyle and Barbara happy and content, he pledging his troth in words reminiscent of Jane and Rochester: "My wife, my darling, now and forever."[23]

Novels like *Mauleverer's Divorce* and *East Lynne* were part of the long process of naturalizing divorce in the nineteenth century.[24] But while divorce was slowly naturalized, the uncertainty about the moral status of second marriages remained. While the bigamy and Fatal Return plots first enabled novelists to examine second (and always better) marriages without having to take on that problem, gradually novels began to look at divorce and second marriages directly even as the early novel by Lady Bury had done. When they did so, as in *Keynotes* by George Egerton (1893) and *Jude the Obscure* by Thomas Hardy (1895), they abandoned the early Caroline Norton and Jane Eyre plots and substituted fragmentary and circling plot structures that point to modernist experimental forms for the novel.

NOTES

Research for this essay was made possible by several PSC-CUNY Research Awards. An early version was delivered in 1996 at the Eighteenth- and Nineteenth- Century Women Writers Conference.

1 Emile Zola, "Le divorce et la littérature," *Le figaro* (February 14, 1881), p. 8.
2 I use the term "divorce novel" somewhat loosely here: in some of these early novels separation or full divorce is considered but in others more desperate and in several cases illegal types of "divorce" substitute for the legal remedy: running away, bigamy, murder. Defined in this way, the field of early divorce novels includes some dozen, including *Jane Eyre* (1847) and *The Tenant of Wildfell Hall* (1848).
3 Gail Savage, "'Intended Only For the Husband': Gender, Class, and the Provision for Divorce in England, 1858–1868," in Kristin Ottesen Garrigan (ed.), *Victorian Scandals: Representations of Gender and Class* (Athens: University of Ohio Press, 1990), pp. 11–12.
4 See Mary Poovey, "Covered but Not Bound: Caroline Norton and the 1857 Matrimonial Causes Act," in *Uneven Developments: The Ideological Work of Gender in Mid-Victorian England* (Chicago: University of Chicago Press, 1988), pp. 51–88.
5 Much of the general public discussion and debate in the half century after 1857 was organized around this question, which was first introduced in 1836 when the government accepted the legality of civil marriages.
6 See my article on this subject, "Louisa Gradgrind's Secret: Marriage and Divorce in *Hard Times*," *Dickens Studies Annual* 25 (1996), 177–96.
7 Lady Bury (Charlotte Susan Maria, née Campbell, 1775–1861). "She was born the youngest daughter of the Duke of Argyll. At 21, she married Colonel John Campbell, who died in 1809, leaving her with nine children. For nine

years, she was lady in waiting to Queen Caroline and later (1838) published an indiscreet diary of her experiences in the royal household. In 1818, she married Edward Bury (d. 1832), Rector of Lichfield, and bore him two more children. She wrote lively silver fork novels, which did well for her and Colburn, her publisher . . . These include *The Exclusives* (1830); *The Disinherited and the Ensnared* (1834); *The Devoted* (1836); *The Divorced* (1837); *Family Records* (1841); *The Manoeuvering Mother* (1842); *The Lady of Fashion* (1856)." John Sutherland, *The Stanford Companion to the Victorian Novel* (Stanford, CA: Stanford University Press, 1990), p. 95.

8 "Emma Robinson (1814–90) was born in London, the daughter of an Oxford Street bookseller. Few details of her life are known. Her father (d. 1856) apparently disapproved of her writing (her novels were accordingly published anonymously) and publicized them *as not* by her. His behavior was regarded as eccentric in literary circles. She never married, and went mad in later life. Robinson's novels largely comprise florid Ainsworthian historical romances and include: *Whitehall* (1845), set in the Court of Charles I; *Caesar Borgia* (1846), a work considered immoral by the standards of the day; *The Maid of Orleans* (1849); *Owen Tudor* (1849). Out of the run of Robinson's normal style is *The Gold Worshippers* (1851), 'a future historical novel.' In the late 1850s, Robinson turned to more domestic themes with: *Mauleverer's Divorce, A Story of Woman's Wrongs* (1858); *Which Wins, Love or Money?* (1862). Robinson wrote plays, received a small Civil List pension in 1862, stopped publishing around 1868 and died in the London County Lunatic Asylum in Norwood." Sutherland, *Stanford Companion*, p. 541.

9 Lady Charlotte Bury, *The Divorced*, 2 vols. (London: Henry Colburn, 1837), vol. II, p. 94.

10 Both this quotation and the one Carlyle uses in *East Lynne* (on page 55) are versions of Matthew 5:32: "Everyone who divorces his wife, except on the grounds of inchastity, makes her an adulteress; and whoever marries a divorced woman commits adultery."

11 Emma Robinson, *Mauleverer's Divorce: A Story of a Woman's Wrongs*, 3 vols. (London: Charles J. Skeet, 1858), vol II, p. 152.

12 *Ibid.*, vol. III, p. 100.

13 *Ibid.*, vol. III, p. 179.

14 *Ibid.*, vol. I, p. 16.

15 Condonation is "the pardon of a marital offence by the other spouse, and the subsequent resumption of cohabitation and sexual relations." Laurence Stone, *The Road to Divorce* (Oxford: Oxford University Press, 1990), p. 206. Condonation, under both the old and the new law, was sufficient to deny a divorce. In fact, proved condonation forced the court to deny the petition for divorce, a legal situation that the Divorce Court judges in the early days frequently complained about.

16 Robinson, *Mauleverer's Divorce*, vol. III, p. 265.

17 *Ibid.*, vol. III, p. 379.

18 It is notoriously difficult to determine how any particular text was received

by contemporaries. I have found no notices or reviews of *Mauleverer's Divorce*.

19 Mrs. Henry Wood, *East Lynne* (1861; London: J. M. Dent, 1984), p. 9.

20 See A. James Hammerton, *Cruelty and Companionship: Conflict in Nineteenth-Century Married Life* (London: Routledge, 1992) for a discussion of changing attitudes toward masculinity and marriage.

21 Wood, *East Lynne*, p. 289.

22 See my article in which I first identified the Fatal Return trope, "*Enoch Arden*, the Fatal Return, and the Silence of Annie," *Victorian Poetry* 30 (1992), where I discuss at length the most well-known version of this voyeurist pleasure in Tennyson's *Enoch Arden*: Enoch looking through the window at Annie his wife, his two children, her new husband John, and their new baby, pp. 334–35.

23 Wood, *East Lynne*, p. 639.

24 The most important event in the naturalizing of divorce was the establishing of a Divorce Court in London which, coupled with daily press reports of the Divorce Court actions, created a sense (inaccurate) of the prevalence of divorce. In my chapter "Coming Apart: The Divorce Court and the Press," in Laurel Brake and David Finkelstein (eds.), *Defining Centres: Nineteenth-Century Media and the Construction of Identities* (London and New York: Macmillan, 1999), I discuss the role of the press reports of the Divorce Court proceedings in the construction of new attitudes toward divorce. See also Hammerton, *Cruelty and Companionship*, chapter 4.

WORKS CITED

Braddon, Mary Elizabeth, *Lady Audley's Secret*, 1862, Oxford: Oxford University Press, 1987.

Brontë, Anne, *The Tenant of Wildfell Hall*, 1848, Oxford: OxfordUniversity Press, 1993.

Brontë, Charlotte, *Jane Eyre*, 1847, London: Penguin, 1996.

Bury, Lady Charlotte, *The Divorced*, 2 vols., London: Henry Colburn, 1837.

Dickens, Charles, *Hard Times*, 1854, London: Penguin, 1969.

Clive, Caroline, *Paul Ferroll*, London: Saunders and Otley, 1855.

Hammerton, A. James, *Cruelty and Companionship: Conflict in Nineteenth-Century Married Life*, London and New York: Routledge, 1992.

Humpherys, Anne, "*Enoch Arden*, the Fatal Return, and the Silence of Annie," *Victorian Poetry* 30 (1992), 331–42.

"Louisa Gradgrind's Secret: Marriage and Divorce in *Hard Times*," *Dickens Studies Annual* 25 (1996), 177–96.

Norton, Caroline, *Stuart of Dunleith*, 3 vols., London: Colburn, 1851.

Poovey, Mary, "Covered but Not Bound: Caroline Norton and the 1857 Matrimonial Causes Act," in *Uneven Developments: the Ideological Work of Gender in Mid-Victorian England*, Chicago: University of Chicago Press, 1988.

Robinson, Emma, *Mauleverer's Divorce: A Story of a Woman's Wrongs*, 3 vols., London: Charles J. Skeet, 1858.

Savage, Gail. "'Intended Only for the Husband'": Gender, Class, and the Provision for Divorce in England, 1858–1868," in Kristin Ottesen Garrigan (ed.), *Victorian Scandals: Representations of Gender and Class*. Athens: University of Ohio Press, 1992.

Stone, Laurence, *The Road to Divorce*, Oxford: Oxford University Press, 1990.

Thackeray, W. M. *The Newcomes*, 1855, Oxford: Oxford University Press, 1990.

Wood, Mrs. Henry, *East Lynne*, 1861, London: J. M. Dent, 1984.

CHAPTER 4

Phantasies of matriarchy in Victorian children's literature

Alison Chapman

> Yet women have a mission! aye, even a political mission of im-
> mense importance! which they will best fulfil by moving in the
> sphere assigned them by Providence; not comet-like, wandering in
> irregular orbits, dazzling indeed by their brilliancy, but terrifying
> by their eccentric movements and doubtful utility.[1]

This chapter addresses the maternal in noncanonical children's literature by women as a trope that exposes the blind spot of the dominant
Victorian gender ideology. Far from entrenching the feminine within
the domestic and private, phantasies of the maternal expose motherhood as the vehicle for a transgressive agency which crosses that artificial divide, the separate spheres of activity.[2] Although children's literature is specifically addressed to children and to mothers who read aloud
to them, the literature is inherently interwoven with the nineteenth-
century debate about the political valency of motherhood and its pervasive influence upon children. This chapter explores a group of noncanonical children's writers – Maria Louisa Molesworth, Julia Horatia
Ewing, Frances Browne, and Jean Ingelow – in terms of the representation of the maternal. In particular, I am interested in the tensions
produced by the attempted containment of middle-class women within
the domestic sphere, which is contingent upon the assertion of female
influence upon children and upon patriarchs in the public sphere.

The children's literature written by these authors does not explicitly
address the woman question, nor were the authors in any way actively
involved in women's enfranchisement. As a result of her religious
convictions, Ingelow firmly rejects supporting the women's movement.[3]
Although Molesworth's separation from her husband in 1879 results in a
more progressive attitude to the sphere of women's activities, her fiction,
like Ewing's, has been taken to be complicit with the conservative
containment of female activities within the home, which has un-

doubtedly contributed to their noncanonical status.[4] But, in different ways, the children's fiction of these authors offers phantasies of matriarchy which constitute a rhetorical and thematic challenge to the containment and disenfranchisement of mothers.

Studies of Victorian children's literature generally assume that it is entirely distinct from other fiction of the period. Of course, children's literature was marketed and consumed as an entirely separate genre, but critical approaches which repeat its isolation ironically tend also to repeat a trope of containment which this fiction puts into question.[5] In other words, despite new studies which expose the subversiveness of much Victorian children's fiction, by insisting on the separateness of that genre, such studies reinscribe the Victorian ideology of the separate spheres of gendered activity. Such an ideology of separation marginalizes children's fiction securely within the domestic space of the home, a space that is demarcated as the other side of the binary from public and political discourse. This chapter, positioned in a collection that considers noncanonical novels for adults, seeks to expose and to challenge the containment of children's literature in Victorian and contemporary academic critique, by arguing that this very trope of containment is precariously both the ground and vanishing point of gender (and also genre) ideology.

The mid-century saw a rapid blossoming of fiction for children which is coterminous with two ideological shifts crucial to the formation of the woman question: the domestication of fantasy and the ascendancy of the concept of the "Angel in the House." The new literary market satisfied the urgent need for children's moral education that arose with the increasing emphasis upon domestic maternal influence. The change in the attitude to the relationship between child and mother produced, in particular, an increase in the numbers of works of didactic and Evangelical fiction that incorporate the new mode of domesticated fantasy, justified as a vehicle for moral education.[6]

This mode of fantasy is itself produced by the shift in the ideology of the home. The subversive and radical implications of the fantastic were caught up in the new commercialized representations of private space, symbolized by the Great Exhibition of 1851 which offered for the gaze of the consumers a plethora of fetishised domesticated objects.[7] As Barbara Garlick argues, the new emphasis on the domestic sphere serves to make fantasy familiar and commercial. Fairy paintings and fairy tales are produced to satisfy middle-class tastes and, crucially, are not only domesticated but placed specifically in the nursery. And, as part of the process of familiarization, the feminine is represented and contained as passive otherness.[8] In this way, fantasy becomes one of the discourses that serves to maintain the ideology of the separate spheres.

Alongside the new mode of tamed and commodified fantasy, the new ideology of the home produced that most insidious, elusive, and pervasive of creatures: the "Angel in the House," institutionalized by Coventry Patmore's poem of the same name, published 1854–62. This ideal of the domesticated, confined, ethereal, and asexual wife and mother attempts to position woman's influence safely within the home. Two other contesting ideologies, the "Angel out of the House" and the "Female Saviour," attempt to position women's influence elsewhere: the former in philanthropic works, without challenging patriarchal authority; the latter in a radical vision of female leadership as the corrective to masculinist society. Crucially, however, distinctions between this ideological trinity are often impossible to disentangle; in this way, women's influence seeps out of bounds and unsettles the definitions of femininity upon which each side involved in the woman question base their assumptions.[9]

I want to illustrate what happens when one of the most notable proponents of the Angel in the House fails, despite herself, to contain the maternal within the domestic sphere. As representative literature of the Angel of the House thesis, Elizabeth Helsinger, Robin Sheets, and William Veeder's survey *The Woman Question* turns to Sarah Lewis' *Woman's Mission* (1839), which articulates woman's powerful domestic influence as wife and mother; but the influence is effectively a double bind that leaves women always both influential and restrained: "Admitting no inferiority except in terms of physical strength, Lewis describes women as morally superior to men, and she invests their duties with social, political, and religious significance... The terms Lewis helped define – 'mission', 'sphere', and 'influence' – were invoked throughout the period to awaken women's aspirations *and* to curtail their activities" (p. 5)[10] The double bind becomes a familiar icon of the feminine, serving both to empower (and eroticize) the feminine at the same time as it contains and controls. Judith Lowder Newton, in her discussion of the development of the ideology of the separate spheres, points out that, in effect, valorizing women's position within the home ends up emphatically separating power and influence. While, in women's advice manuals and in contemporary journals, power is ascribed to men, woman's influence is secret, unobtrusive, and unobserved.[11] As Sarah Lewis comments, "power is principally exerted in the shape of authority, and is limited in its sphere of action. Influence has its source in human sympathies, and is as *boundless* in its operation" (p. 13; my italics). In her analysis of women's fiction from *Evelina* to *The Mill on the Floss*, Newton discerns women's writing as: "both the locus of compensating fantasies and the site of protest, actions expressive of the authors' powers" ("Power and the Ideology," p. 771). These novels, Newton argues, assert female power not as influence, but as ability and agency.

Turning back to *Woman's Mission*, I wish to argue that it is a paradigmatic text that, far from limiting the influence of wives and mothers to the domestic sphere, ends up, despite itself, suggesting that female aspirations cannot be so easily contained. This is a form of agency that acts, in contradistinction to Newton's notion of power, *from within* the discourse of "boundless influence." By valorizing female power as a moral agent for the regeneration of the political sphere, Lewis exposes the slippery boundaries between private and public, the domestic and the workplace. Central to the argument of *Woman's Mission* is the formative influence that mothers have on their sons:

Principles have their chief source in influences; early influences, above all; and early influences have more power in forming character than institutions or mental cultivation; it is therefore to the arbiters of these that we must look for the regenerating principle. We must seek, then, some fundamental principle, some spirit indefatigable, delighting in its task, and which may pervade the whole of society. Such a principle we find in family affection, – especially in maternal affection. Have we, then, been too bold, in asserting that women may be the prime agents of God in the regeneration of mankind? (pp. 19–20)

The rhetorical question discloses a radical subtext: maternal agency overcomes the "impediments" of the separation of the spheres: "Maternal love [is] the only purely unselfish feeling that exists on this earth; the only affection which (as far as it appears,) flows from the loving to the beloved object in one continual stream, uninterrupted by those impediments which check every other. Disease, deformity, ingratitude – nothing can check the flow of maternal love" (p. 128). Lewis excuses the pervasiveness of the influence as divinely sanctioned by God, but the influence is nevertheless fluid and unrestrained. Sarah Lewis' Angel in the House is a mother who precipitates the institution *and* subversion of the boundaries of social and psychic space and, inevitably, the security of gender identity.

But this combination of institution and subversion is also characteris-

tic of the genre of children's fiction by women. The relationship between fantasy, Angels, and influence produces a concern that the
growth of children's literature is out of control, and that this has
negative implications for maternal influence. Mrs. Molesworth, perhaps
one of the most prolific writers for children (she published over one
hundred novels), warns about this dangerous new surfeit of children's
books. While admitting that she might be charged with the same
complaint, Molesworth laments the new market for children's books
which tempt children to treat books as replaceable commodities. She
compares this attitude to her own childhood memories of the books
passed down by her mother and grandmother – for, in previous generations, the scarcity of children's books made each valuable and well
known. She tells of the exchange of each treasured book (whose cover
and texture she can vividly recall) among family members, so that they
were known intimately and lovingly: "we – for I was one of a party of
brothers and sisters at home – and our companions all read the same
stories, and talked them over together much more exhaustively than it is
possible now, when 'publications for the young' are issued by hundreds
and more yearly."[12] The implication is that the contemporary production of children's books makes them less familiar and carelessly read and
treated: thus, paradoxically, the proliferation of fiction defamiliarizes
children to the literature and to its moral message. This is the flipside of
commodification: although the domestication of fantasy fails to contain
the feminine, as illustrated by Lewis, the generic implications are that
children's literature loses its association with the feminine in its commerce with the marketplace. Thus, the ideology that fails to fix maternal
influence within the home may also loosen the correspondence of the
feminine with the genre of children's literature.

Molesworth's concern that commodification sullies children's literature may be read as conservative and elitist. But her remedy is to assert
maternal influence in a way that allows for its transgressive potential
despite a masculine marketplace. In contrast to this masculinization of
the literary marketplace, which positions books as replaceable commodities, Molesworth emphasizes the memory of the books of her mother
and grandmother as an alternative literary heritage. This is offered with
the acceptance of her own proliferous output which necessarily means
that she has a position in the masculine sphere of labored activity. But by
suggesting the greater value of the maternal books, Molesworth sets up a
"female genealogy" *alongside* the marketplace. This is Luce Irigaray's
term for an alternative female symbolic which can bring about new

relations between the sexes and bring the maternal to a new signification: "it is ... necessary, if we are not to be accomplices in the murder of
the mother, for us to assert that there is a genealogy of women. There is
a genealogy of women within our family: on our mothers' side we have
mothers, grandmothers, and great-grandmothers... Let us try to situate
ourselves within this female genealogy so as to conquer and keep our
identity."[13]

Molesworth's lament for the new devaluation is rendered more acute
with her insistence upon the "influence of fiction upon children's minds
and character" ("Story-Reading and Story-Writing," p. 772). But this
beneficial feminine moral and educative influence, which influences the
public sphere by proxy,[14] is contingent upon the mother's absence:
precisely the symbolic murder of the mother that Irigaray laments.
Sarah Lewis insists that the maternal influence must be coterminous
with the renunciation of self, for only in the act of self-sacrifice can
women attain the purity of motive that enables their moral influence to
pervade the public sphere. In other words, only by erasing her own
subjectivity can the mother ensure the stability of the separate spheres.
But in this very act of vanishing, maternal influence is located in the
fluid and unstable interface *between* the separate spheres, at the interval
or boundary itself, that Lewis is also trying to maintain. Further, in
order to justify women's remove from direct political influence, and
arguing for the necessity of women's containment in the domestic
sphere, *Woman's Mission* rhetorically collapses the distinction between
feminine and masculine norms, while trying to securely domesticate and
contain the maternal:

[the mother] is, so to speak, the guardian angel of man's political integrity...
This is the true secret of woman's political influence, the true object of her
political enlightenment. Governments will never be perfect till all distinction
between private and public virtue, private and public honour, be done away!
Who so fit an agent for the operation of this change as an enlightened, unselfish
woman? (p. 66)

Denied direct participation in politics and government, the maternal
agency nevertheless might ultimately dissolve the demarcation between
public and private but only with the erasure of maternal subjectivity.

In fact, along with the domestication of fantasy from the mid-nineteenth century there is a proliferation of phantasies of domestication,
and phantasies of matriarchy, established at the expense of the mother's
presence. The transgressive influence of the Angel in the House is, in

these terms, only possible by virtue of a symbolic matricide which refigures the mother's absence in terms of political and legal existence as the grounds upon which a new symbolic economy can be established. Irigaray argues that Western culture is founded on the death of the mother and that this must be resisted if a new symbolic economy is to come about. But, in these Victorian stories for children, the repression of the mother allows her figurative return in other female guises as the first step to signifying from within androcentrism what Irigaray terms "the bodily encounter with the mother."[15]

For Molesworth, Ewing, Browne, and Ingelow, the mother's absence induces a proliferation of maternal substitutes in the guise of aunts, grandmothers, or the motherly behavior of a child to his or her sibling. Molesworth's *The Boys and I* (1882), for example, is narrated by fourteen-year-old Audrey, who gives an account of an episode when she was nine when her parents went abroad and left her with two younger brothers, Tom and Racey. Audrey has always thought of herself as a second mother to the boys: "I never minded a bit, however much mother petted the boys – I felt as if I was like her in that – we were like two mothers to them I sometimes pleased myself by fancying."[16] The children are sent to live with Uncle Geoff in London and his unfamiliarity with children makes their lives miserable. Audrey is determined to assume maternal responsibilities for her brothers in the face of a hostile patriarchal household: she informs the boys, "I want you to count me first – like as if I was instead of mother, you know. That's what mother wants" (p. 77). Uncle Geoff notes with amusement Audrey's maternal role: "so you're to be the boys' little mother – eh, Audrey? . . . It's a great responsibility, isn't it? You'll have a good deal to do to teach *me* my duty too, won't you?" (p. 71).

The children's plan to run away to their nurse (who has left them suddenly because her mother is dying) is foiled by a combination of the vagaries of the postal system and the intervention of "Miss Goldy-hair," whom the children had met when she came to view their family home when it was up for sale and named her because of her golden hair (p. 35). The children lose their way while illicitly trying to post a letter to their nurse, informing her of their plans for escape, and mistake Miss Goldy-hair's house for Uncle Geoff's. Miss Goldy-hair is the superlative Angel in the House: recently motherless herself, she devotes all her time to the care of orphans in a home established by philanthropic ladies. The children immediately equate Miss Goldy-hair with their absent mother: she kisses them and lays out the tea tray like mother (pp. 181–82). In fact,

Miss Goldy-hair puts an end to Audrey's uncomfortable rebellion against her uncle and his housekeeper, Mrs. Partridge, and Audrey's concurrent reiteration of her maternal role, by teaching Audrey to see that her uncle merely misunderstands children.

For Audrey and Tom, however, Miss Goldy-hair is not only a mother substitute, but she is invested with a psychic phantasy of the maternal. The morning after their encounter with Miss Goldy-hair, Audrey and Tom assess her appearance as an angel, or fairy, in the house:

> here I must really put down what I said, whether it vexes someone or not –
> "Tom, do you know, I think her face is just exactly like an angel's when you look at it quite close."
> "Or a fairy's," said Tom.
> "No," I said, "an angel's. Fairies are more merry looking than she is. She has such a kind, sorry look – that's why I think her face is like an angel's." (p. 198)

But, most significantly, the phantasy of the maternal associated with Miss Goldy-hair interrupts the narrative and threatens Audrey's careful control of events. Audrey's mother insists that she must write her tale in strict chronological order and without revision or deletion:

> Afterwards, I will tell you what put it in my head to write [the narrative] down. If I told you now you wouldn't understand – at least not without my telling you things all out of their places – ends at the beginning, and middles at the end; and mother says it's an awfully bad habit to do things that way. It makes her quite vexed to see any one read the end of a book before they have really got to it... And I can't score through anything, and just leave it as it came into my head to write it all down. (pp. 7–8)

Despite mother's injunction that everything must keep to its chronological place, the maternal substitute, Miss Goldy-hair, repeatedly interrupts the narrative out of her place and at the expense of their biological mother's presence. For example, in a discussion of her problems with her uncle's housekeeper, Mrs. Partridge, Audrey comments: "I can see all how it was quite plainly now – now that I have so often talked it over with mother and with aunt – (but I am forgetting, I mustn't tell you that yet)" (p. 145). A few pages later, Audrey laments her inability to keep her narrative "straight": "you see I want to make up my story as like a proper one as I can, in case aun– oh, there I am again, like a goose, going to spoil it all!" (p. 150).

What interrupts the narrative out of its chronological sequence is the fact of Miss Goldy-hair's marriage to Uncle Geoff, when the children are sent off to visit their nurse. But Audrey cannot keep Miss Goldy-hair in her proper chronological or ideological position. As the domestic and philanthropic angel, the narrative tries and fails to contain her in her own superlative domestic sphere, her proper ideological position. But the narrative's insistent punctuation of the transformation of Miss Goldy-hair into a motherly aunt constantly returns to the fact of maternal substitution and the absence of the mother. Miss Goldy-hair's position as the Angel in the House *par excellence* is displaced into a patriarchal space as a female genealogy which transforms Uncle Geoff's seemingly horrific household into a nurturing home at the explicit cost of the presence of the children's biological mother. And, in the final paragraphs, when the parents have returned, Audrey is anxious to reassure us that: "you have *no idea* how fond mother and auntie are of each other" (p. 264); and indeed we don't, for mother is curiously voiceless and displaced from the happy ending of her own maternal return.

A similar narrative disruption occurs with genealogies of maternal figures in other novels, but most typically involving grandmothers. Mrs. Molesworth articulates what was seen as the special affinity between grandmothers and granddaughters in "Story-Reading and Story-Writing." Molesworth argues that children should be protected from what they will learn with adulthood: an awareness of "the sadder facts of our complex human nature." But, with old age, Molesworth argues that there is a return to the perception of childhood: "as the 'eventide' approaches, with a wonderful return to the faithful child-nature, we come to believe again in the 'light' as the reality."[17] Frances Browne's fairy story, *Granny's Wonderful Chair* (1857), positions the grandmother as the agent for Snowflower's entry into an initially hostile public and patriarchal sphere, King Winwealth's court. Through the storytelling powers of her grandmother's chair, Snowflower impresses the King, who grants her a higher courtly status in gratitude for each story the chair narrates. When it is discovered that the teller is in fact the King's brother, trapped by a curse in the cushion of the chair, Snowflower is made the King's heiress. Through her grandmother's agency, and in her absence, Snowflower transgresses her gender and class identity and establishes a female genealogy alongside the patriarchal court.[18] Molesworth's *"Grandmother, Dear": A Book for Boys and Girls* (1878) similarly anticipates the return of the children in grandmother's care to their decidedly patriarchal home. The children, whose mother is dead, visit their grandmother in France with their aunt. They invest their grandmother with fantastic/phantastic qualities. Sylvia comments: "she would almost do for a fairy godmother, if only she had a stick with a golden knob."[19] Their grandmother has an ethereal beauty and wisdom that the children are in awe of, and "the look in her eyes had a tenderness and depth which can only come from a life of unselfishness, of joy and much sorrow too – a life whose lessons have been well and dutifully learnt, and of which none has been more thoroughly taken home than that of gentle judgement of, and much patience with, others" (p. 7). Grandmother, explicitly, takes the place of the children's mother but in a way that repeatedly exposes the mother's absence. The care of her daughter's children recalls for the grandmother the absence of her daughter:

grandmother watched [the grandchildren] from the window, and thought how pretty they looked, and the thought carried her back to a time – not so very long ago did it seem to her now – when their mother had been just as bright and happy as they – the mother who had never lived to see them as babies . . . It was a blessing, a very great blessing and pleasure to have what she had so often longed for, the care of her little daughters to herself. (p. 157)

The story that grandmother tells from her own childhood, at the request of the children, insists upon the affinity between grandmothers and grandchildren at the cost of the absence of the mother. She tells how she came to be close to her grandmother: "to the last she was able to sympathise in all my girlish joys, and sorrows, and difficulties" (p. 146). Molly comments: "Like you, grandmother, dear . . . She must have been just like you" (p. 146). By the end of the novel, the children's stay with grandmother has conditioned them within an emphatically maternal symbolic for a return to England, to a new family home with their father. The phantasy of matriarchy continues to be proleptically imagined in this new patriarchal sphere.

By contrast, Julia Horatia Ewing's *Mrs. Overtheway's Remembrances* emphasizes explicitly the sense of loss in the affinity between grandmother figures and little girls.[20] Molesworth criticizes the children's fiction of Ewing, who was her rival in the literary marketplace, for excessive morbidity: "children should not be saddened before their time, while yet, on the other hand, they should not be deceived" ("Story-Reading and Story-Writing," p. 774). Ewing's fiction does address more explicitly than Molesworth's a profound loss within childhood itself, a loss generated by the absence of the mother which grandmother figures try to cover over. Ida is orphaned and stays with an unsympathetic uncle. She watches the elderly lady across the street –

Mrs. Overtheway – regularly going to church, and imagines she has the happiness that Ida lacks: "she believed her friend to be old, immeasurably old, indefinitely old: and had a secret faith that she had never been otherwise. She felt sure that … she helped herself at meals, and went to bed according to her own pleasure and convenience; was – perhaps on these grounds – utterly happy, and had always been so" (p. 4). Ida falls ill as a result of gathering flowers for Mrs. Overtheway, and Mrs. Overtheway comes to visit and tells Ida stories about her past. Her last "remembrance," Kerguelen's Land, is actually the story of Ida's father who has returned after being shipwrecked and who has written asking the neighbor to break the unexpected news of his return gently. Through Mrs. Overtheway's friendship, Ida recovers her domestic position in her father's house, much like the children in "*Grandmother, Dear*" are prepared for their return to their father. Ida's return carries the psychic influence of Mrs. Overtheway, whose stories she narrates to her father. The implication is that the continuing psychic influence of the maternal figure upon Ida mediates between Ida and her father. Jean Ingelow's "Grandmother's Shoe" (1865; reprinted in *Studies for Stories*) suggests a similar influence of a grandmother figure upon a child temporarily lodging with a Quaker family. The grandmother appears cold and stern, but a moment of empathy with the child enables her to negotiate the rather harsh religious expectations of the household and be reconciled to the father of the house, while reminding us of the awesome power of grandmother's influence – even, in one instance, denoting the presence of God.[21]

The children's story of the period which suggests most forcefully the potential of mobile and uncontainable maternal influence to mediate between the spheres is another of Ingelow's Evangelical narratives, "The Cumberers" (1868). Here, a female community is described that combines the qualities of the public and private sphere and that suggests the fluidity between them. The narrator, Miss T., due to ill health, has been left by her parents as the paying guest of a family who live by the sea. The family is made up entirely of the Misses Perkins, daughters of a deceased clergyman. The story begins with a lengthy description of each sister and the household role of each and the lesson which Miss T's stay there has taught her: "the place each is fitted to fill in this world" (*Studies for Stories*, p. 2). It transpires that each has a position in the household economy which juxtaposes the necessary commerce of capitalism with a feminine economy of the gift, or of charity – all, except the "cumberer," Amelia. Each sister's roles and duties are outlined, with a comment on the effect to the household management if they were to die. The eldest sister, Robina,

kept the house; and half its comfort, and nearly all of its superfluities, certainly arose from this circumstance. Assuredly she was not intellectual, but her love of order, economy, and regularity made her a very useful person. And I saw that if she were to die, her sisters, independently of their affection for her, would miss her sorely from their household. (p. 3)

The narrator stresses the importance and utility of Miss Perkins in her household: "she might perhaps have been called a twaddler in society, but in her own sphere she was useful and beloved" (p. 5); and, moreover, she charitably helps the neighborhood's poor. The next eldest sister, Anne, takes sole care of the garden; Robina explains: "we could not afford to keep a man: it would not pay us, but all that Anne can raise is pure gain; for we save seeds, and exchange cuttings with our neighbours... Now I say that providence fits us beautifully for our separate spheres: for Anne is able to sit indoors very little" (p. 6). Along with the repetition of the gift economy, Robina stresses the loss that Anne's death would be to the household: "I don't know what we should do without her, I am sure; for I don't know anything more melancholy than living in a garden full of weeds" (p. 7). The next sister, Sarah, is similarly indispensable. Her function is the sewing for the house, as well as some work for poor neighbors: "'it would be a sad thing for us, and for a good many beside, if anything were to happen to Sarah'" (p. 9).

Each sister has her proper sphere and function; but the place of each in the economy of the self-sufficient household redistributes the distinction between public and private, domestic and workplace, for each is seen in different ways to be involved in commerce and in charitable work. This economy is meant to illustrate the moral duty of getting by on a limited income, but it ends up subverting the ideological construction of the private sphere as alien to the workplace. The Perkins' transgressive economy incorporates feminine accomplishments into the masculine attributes of the public sphere. But this mediation between the spheres is based on the value of each sister, which is described in terms of the *absence* of each in the economy, her loss to others if she died. Once again, the radical value of the maternal figures is established in terms of absence – in this case, death of the sisters. But the narrator then turns to Miss Amelia, the sister who has the misfortune to act as a "cumberer": "my doubts were (among others) what the mission of Miss Amelia Perkins could possibly be in this world, and my speculations were (among others) as to who would be the worse off if she were taken from it, and who would be the better" (p. 9). Amelia "never did anything," "there were no duties that she habitually performed; there was no place that she occupied" (pp. 9–10). As the typically "redundant" female, Amelia threatens to overbalance the economy of the household precisely by having no function. Her status as a cumberer is illustrated, furthermore, by her typically feminine ways, her entrenchment within the domestic sphere: she spends her time on feminine accomplishments to the detriment of household tasks. Through not having a role at all, through functioning outside of the household economy, Amelia illustrates the danger of refusing to cross over the boundaries of the separate spheres. Although the story is overtly didactic, and designed to teach young girls the value of their domestic duties, it also conveys how those duties cannot be contained in the domestic and private space assigned to them, but have commerce with the public sphere in a way that transforms both. All the Misses Perkins, except Amelia, are types of the Angel in the House whose functions mediate between and reorganize the separate spheres, rather than merely entrench the values of domesticity. Amelia's reward is to marry badly, to spend an inheritance unwisely, and to give up her two eldest children to her sisters while she goes abroad "to practise such economy as should enable [her] to return to [her] native country" (p. 92). Amelia's profligate lifestyle costs her more than her children and her home – it illustrates the dangers of existing wholly within a constricting feminine sphere.

Finally, and in some senses as an allegory of the process I have been analysing, I turn to Jean Ingelow's *Mopsa the Fairy* (1869), which dramatizes the domestic matriarch's transgressive influence which seeps its way into both the psyche and the public political sphere. The novel narrates the journey through fairyland of Jack, the little boy who vanishes down a tree trunk, and who is given charge of a growing fairy, Mopsa. The first section of the novel gives Jack a maternal function as he protects and nurtures Mopsa. But Mopsa grows up alarmingly quickly to become the queen of Fairyland, and so displaces Jack as the novel's protagonist. This is a problematic utopia of feminine power; as Nina Auerbach and U. C. Knoepflmacher point out, Mopsa must expel Jack in order to reign.[22] Enfranchisement is commensurate with loss and renunciation. Jack feels the loss acutely: "he longed to stay in that great place with Queen Mopsa – his own little Mopsa, whom he had carried in his pocket, and taken care of, and loved" (p. 310).

But, although Mopsa's matriarchy is established at the expense of her childhood friend, and childhood itself, it does not also cost a renunciation of the maternal subject. Indeed, Jack's banishment as the original maternal figure precipitates a multiplication of maternal figures; a rhetorical move seen in other children's fiction. Jack acknowledges, however, the necessity of estrangement from his charge: "Mopsa did not need him, she had so many people to take care of her now" (p. 310). Further, the narrative not only suggests fluidity in Mopsa's reign between the separate spheres – but, significantly, it is a fluidity that is continued upon Jack's return to his home, which repeats the phantasy/fantasy of matriarchy he experienced in Fairyland. Jack is returned to what is emphatically "his father's house" (p. 313). To Jack, this home is "not in the least like anything that he had seen in Fairyland, and he began to forget the boy-king, and the applewoman, and even his little Mopsa, more and more" (p. 314). Jack sits on his father's knee and "thought . . . what a great thing a man was; he had never seen anything so large in Fairyland, nor so important; so, on the whole he was glad he had come back, and felt very comfortable" (p. 314). But, as Auerbach and Knoepflmacher argue (*Forbidden Journeys*, pp. 211–12), the mother's relation to the son and the father reinscribes Mopsa's matriarchy on a psychic level, as she reads aloud the ballad of the lost shepherdess:

> Over the hills her voice is heard,
>   She sings when the light doth wane:
> "My longing heart is full of love.
>   When shall my loss be gain?
> My shepherd lord, I see him not,
>   But he will come again."
>
> (pp. 315–16)

The iteration of this ballad by the mother casts maternal presence as contingent upon the anticipation of a return of matriarchy to Jack's real world. The mother subverts the containment and domestication of the maternal and keeps in play the memory of matriarchy, of female political enfranchisement that fractures the boundaries of the domestic sphere. The result is an assertion of maternal subjectivity and presence coterminous with a subversive transgression and redistribution of the binary public/private. The irony of the novel's abrupt closure – "That's all" (p. 316) – reminds us of the lack of causality and rationality in Mopsa's kingdom – "That that is, is" (p. 296), a fairy maxim – and translates the ending into the reminder of the shimmering possibilities of matriarchy from within a redistribution of gender ideology.

Intriguingly, the transgressive and mediatory power of the maternal figure is represented by John Millais' illustrations to the novel (figures 4.1 and 4.2). When Mopsa becomes the Queen of the Fairies her depiction radically alters. Suddenly she acquires a heavy bosom (particularly for a ten-year-old), dark hair (previously depicted blond), and her profile resembles the image of Queen Victoria as Mopsa comforts Jack on his departure from Fairyland. This resemblance interrupts the fantasy/ phantasy with a reminder of a political context to the novel, the nineteenth-century matriarch, which suggests that the interface between fantasy and politics is more unstable than the reassuringly abrupt end might indicate. The maternal Angel in the House, whose position of influence is located in the interstice between the spheres, gives way in *Mopsa the Fairy* to a matriarch whose power is established at the expense of childhood, but which nevertheless also figures the maternal as a fully present subject who subverts the ideology of the separate spheres from within. Millais' illustration points to the endlessly subversive psychic influence of mothers upon little boys and patriarchal fathers. In contrast to Lewis' horror in the epigraph at her vision of mothers "wandering in irregular orbits" out of their domestic sphere with "doubtful utility," the subversive influence in Ingelow's novel is a mediating link to the fantasy world which gestures to Mopsa's matriarchy as already a political reality.

The Angel in the House, in fact, might be the mediatrix *par excellence.* The Angel in the House not only dramatizes the instability of borders but also intimates a new social structure in which what patriarchy splits – private and public, feminine and masculine, domestic and political – might be healed. In her manifesto for a new relationship between the sexes, Luce Irigaray posits the angel as the messenger or mediator that is located in the position of the "excluded middle" between such terms as masculine and feminine, woman and divine. Irigaray suggests that the angel rhetorically moves between categories and allows for their symbolic redistribution, for "*angels* would circulate as mediators of that which has not yet happened, of what is still going to happen, of what is on the horizon."[23]

Reading Irigaray's mediating angel alongside the Victorian Angel in the House exposes the possibilities of the Victorian female mediatrix as a negotiator between not only the separate spheres, but between the collapse of women into the maternal and the political subject position that conventionally belongs to the masculine identity. From the place of the angel, the influence of mothers exceeds its domestic boundaries, just

4.1　*The Apple Woman*, by John Millais, 1869.

4.2   *The Queen's Farewell*, by John Millais, 1869.

as Victorian children's fiction exceeds its designation as a domestic, private, and feminine genre. And, as the "guardian angel" of the moral education of children (in particular, but not exclusively, of the little boy), the subversive power of the maternal initiates a redistribution of symbolic structures that had denied the maternal direct political agency.[24] The children's fiction of Ingelow, Browne, Molesworth, and Ewing thus both exposes the slipperiness of the attempted containment of maternal influence *and* dramatizes its transgression; for, like Jack's mother, the fiction is written to be read aloud to children, with profound subliminal implications. Like *Mopsa*'s combination of maternal and political agency, Victorian women's fiction for children constitutes a radical critique and a subversive reorganization of gender and genre boundaries.

NOTES

1 (Sarah Lewis), *Woman's Mission*, 2nd edn. (London: John W. Parker, 1839), pp. 46–47.

2 Throughout the essay, "phantasy" is meant as a psychoanalytical term which denotes a psychic drama; "fantasy" is a literary or aesthetic term which refers to a genre.

3 The *Times'* obituary states that Ingelow "resolutely shrank from the Woman's Movement" (July 21, 1897).

4 See Roger Lancelyn Green, *Mrs. Molesworth* (London: The Bodley Head, 1961) and Marghanita Laski, *Mrs. Ewing, Mrs. Molesworth, Mrs. Hodgson Burnett* (London: Arthur Barker, 1950).

5 Compare Maria Louisa Molesworth, "On the Art of Writing Fiction for Children," *Atalanta* 6 (May 1893), 583–86.

6 See J. S. Bratton, *The Impact of Victorian Children's Fiction* (London and Totowa, NJ: Croom Helm/Barnes and Noble, 1981), and David Grylls, *Guardians and Angels: Parents and Children in Nineteenth-Century Literature* (London and Boston: Faber, 1978).

7 For a useful account of the Great Exhibition, see Thomas Richards, *The Commodity Culture of Victorian England: Advertising and Spectacle, 1851–1914* (Stanford, CA: Stanford University Press, 1990).

8 Barbara Garlick, "Christina Rossetti and the Gender Politics of Fantasy," in Kath Filmer (ed.), *The Victorian Fantasists: Essays on Culture, Society and Belief in the Mythopoeic Fiction of the Victorian Age* (London: Macmillan, 1991), pp. 133–52 (p. 133).

9 Elizabeth K. Helsinger, Robin Lauterbach Sheets, and William Veeder (eds.), *The Woman Question: Society in Britain and America, 1837–1883*, 3 vols. (Chicago: Chicago University Press, 1989 [1983]), vol. I, p. xv.

10 Sarah Lewis notes that: "it *is* an apparent inconsistency to recommend at

the same time expansion of views and contraction of operation"; but, she argues, this is faulty reasoning which ignores that it is natural for women to be confined to the domestic sphere and to renounce themselves (*Woman's Mission*, pp. 48–49).

11 Judith Lowder Newton, "Power and the Ideology of 'Women's Sphere,'" reprinted in Robyn R. Warhol and Diane Price Herndl (eds.), *Feminisms: An Anthology of Literary Theory and Criticism* (New Brunswick, NJ: Rutgers University Press, 1993), pp. 765–80.

12 Maria Louisa Molesworth, "Story-Reading and Story-Writing," *Chamber's Journal* (November 5, 1898), 772–75 (p. 772).

13 Luce Irigaray, "The Bodily Encounter With the Mother," in *The Irigaray Reader*, ed. Margaret Whitford (Oxford: Blackwell, 1991), pp. 34–46 (p. 44). Irigaray is never explicit about defining the genealogy; but it is not to be taken as simply a separate woman's (literary) tradition, for it must have active commerce with paternal genealogies.

14 See also Maria Louisa Molesworth, "The Best Books for Children," *Pall Mall Gazette* (October 29, 1887), 5, which articulates the convention that mothers make the best readers of stories to children.

15 "The Bodily Encounter," pp. 42–43. Compare Lewis: "the character of the mother may often be said to influence the fate of the son long after she has ceased to exist. Her image, engraven on his heart in life, or speaking from the tomb in death, will still interpose itself between him and objects unworthy of his choice" (*Woman's Mission*, pp. 35–36).

16 Maria Louisa Molesworth, *The Boys and I: A Child's Story for Children* (London: Chambers [1882]), p. 19.

17 Molesworth, "Story-Reading and Story-Writing," p. 774.

18 Frances Browne's fairy story, *Granny's Wonderful Chair* (New York: Macmillan [1857] 1939).

19 Maria Louisa Molesworth, *"Grandmother, Dear": A Book for Boys and Girls* (London: Macmillan, 1878), p. 3.

20 See Julia Horatia Ewing, *Mrs. Overtheway's Remembrances and Other Stories* (London: Dent [1869]).

21 Reprinted in Jean Ingelow, *Studies for Stories from Girls' Lives*, 5th edn. (London: Strahan, 1868).

22 Nina Auerbach and U. C. Knoepflmacher (eds.), *Forbidden Journeys: Fairy Tales and Fantasies by Victorian Women Writers* (Chicago: University of Chicago Press, 1992), pp. 209–10.

23 Luce Irigaray, *An Ethics of Sexual Difference* (London: Athlone Press, 1993 [1984]), p. 15.

24 See Helsinger, Sheets, Veeder, *The Woman Question*, vol. II, chapters 1 and 2.

WORKS CITED

Auerbach, Nina, and U.C. Knoepflmacher (eds.), *Forbidden Journeys: Fairy Tales and Fantasies by Victorian Women Writers*, Chicago: University of Chicago Press, 1992.

Bratton, J. S., *The Impact of Victorian Children's Fiction*, London and Totowa, NJ: Croom Helm/Barnes and Noble, 1981.

Browne, Frances, *Granny's Wonderful Chair*, New York: Macmillan (1857), 1939.

Ewing, Julia Horatia, *Mrs. Overtheway's Remembrances and Other Stories*, London: Dent, 1869.

Garlick, Barbara, "Christina Rossetti and the Gender Politics of Fantasy," in Kath Filmer (ed.), *The Victorian Fantasists: Essays on Culture, Society and Belief in the Mythopoeic Fiction of the Victorian Age*, London: Macmillan, 1991, pp. 133–52.

Green, Roger Lancelyn, *Mrs. Molesworth*, London: The Bodley Head, 1961.

Grylls, David, *Guardians and Angels: Parents and Children in Nineteenth-Century Literature*, London and Boston: Faber, 1978.

Helsinger, Elizabeth K., Robin Lauterbach Sheets, and William Veeder (eds.), *The Woman Question: Society in Britain and America, 1837–1883*, 3 vols., Chicago: Chicago University Press, 1989 (1983).

Ingelow, Jean, *Studies for Stories from Girls' Lives*, 5th edn., London: Strahan, 1868.

Irigaray, Luce, *An Ethics of Sexual Difference*, London: Athlone Press, 1993 (1984).

The Irigaray Reader, ed. Margaret Whitford, Oxford: Blackwell, 1991.

Laski, Marghanita, *Mrs. Ewing, Mrs. Molesworth, Mrs. Hodgson Burnett*, London: Arthur Barker, 1950.

(Lewis, Sarah), *Woman's Mission*, 2nd edn., London: John W. Parker, 1839.

Molesworth, Maria Louisa, "The Best Books for Children," *Pall Mall Gazette* (October 29, 1887), 5.

The Boys and I: A Child's Story for Children, London: Chambers, 1882.

"Grandmother, Dear": A Book for Boys and Girls, London: Macmillan, 1878.

"On the Art of Writing Fiction for Children," *Atalanta* 6 (May 1893), 583–86.

"Story-Reading and Story-Writing," *Chamber's Journal* (November 5, 1898), 772–75.

Newton, Judith Lowder, "Power and the Ideology of 'Women's Sphere,'" reprinted in Robyn R. Warhol and Diane Price Herndl (eds.), *Feminisms: An Anthology of Literary Theory and Criticism*, New Brunswick, NJ: Rutgers University Press, 1993, pp. 765–80.

Richards, Thomas, *The Commodity Culture of Victorian England: Advertising and Spectacle, 1851–1914*, Stanford, CA: Stanford University Press, 1990.

The Times, obituary of Jean Ingelow (July 21, 1897).

CHAPTER 5

Gendered observations: Harriet Martineau and the woman question

Alexis Easley

The career of Harriet Martineau is difficult to place in a feminist narrative of literary history. Although Martineau was a life-long advocate of women's rights,[1] she disapproved of feminists who drew attention to their personal lives in their work.[2] In her *Autobiography*, Martineau criticizes the feminist who "[violates] all good taste by her obtrusiveness in society . . . oppressing every body about her by her epicurean selfishness every day, while raising in print an eloquent cry on behalf of the oppressed."[3] Such selfish feminist activities, Martineau claimed, had the effect of drawing attention to the identity of the writer instead of furthering actions and ideas that would enable women to overcome confining social roles. For this reason, Martineau carefully avoided direct association with the feminist movement, preferring to campaign for women's rights as a behind-the-scenes journalist and power broker.

Because Martineau was less "visible" in pursuing her feminist agenda than activists such as Josephine Butler and Emily Davies, her work has received little attention in recent histories of Victorian feminism.[4] The purpose of this chapter is not to "rescue" Martineau from this obscurity but to interrogate the notion of obscurity itself in the history of nineteenth-century feminism. Focusing on Martineau's early career in the 1820s and 1830s, I argue that she actively sought anonymity and objectivity in her work as a means of distancing her gender and identity from her writing. This enabled her to express a more "objective" perspective on women's issues and to communicate her ideas to a mixed-gender audience. Through various forms of low-profile activism, Martineau defined feminism as an activity, rather than as a public identity, which would enable women to criticize oppressive social conditions without having to assume roles as "public women."

In the first part of this chapter, I demonstrate how Martineau used the anonymity of periodical writing to give the impression of objectivity in her early essays on the woman question. I then point out the ways she maintained this personal distance in her early sociological works, *Society in America* (1837) and *How to Observe Morals and Manners* (1838). In the third part of this chapter, I examine how Martineau was able to translate this distanced narrative perspective on women's issues into domestic fiction, specifically her first novel, *Deerbrook* (1839). In all of these works, Martineau defines feminism in contradictory terms – as a private, yet politicized, activity that enables women to exert influence on key social issues while still avoiding the public gaze. Further, she demonstrates how women can use subversive forms of social observation and indirect activism as a means of exerting influence on matters of social and political concern to women. I conclude by reflecting on the legacy of Martineau's early contributions to the woman question in terms of her later career and the ongoing development of feminist thought.

In 1829, Martineau marked the beginning of her literary career[5] by recording a series of private resolutions in her journal. She writes, "After long and mature deliberation, I have determined that my chief subordinate object in life shall henceforth be the cultivation of my intellectual powers, with a view to the instruction of others by my writings."[6] In order to accomplish this goal, she vowed "to consider [her] own interests as little as possible, and to write with a view to the good of others; therefore to entertain no distaste to the humblest literary task that affords a prospect of usefulness."[7] In this way, Martineau defined herself as a conduit through which "useful" knowledge would be imparted to society at large, rather than as a creator of original ideas.

When defining herself as an author and social reformer, Martineau had few positive models of women writers who had succeeded in this task. The work of Mary Wollstonecraft would seem to have provided Martineau with a model of female activism; however, though Martineau agreed with many of Wollstonecraft's views on the woman question, she was repelled by her scandalous public persona.[8] For Martineau, the controversy over Wollstonecraft's personal life detracted from the "usefulness" of her reformatory project. What was needed was a depersonalized voice that could speak more dispassionately and objectively about the social inequities faced by women. In addition to distancing herself from Wollstonecraft's style of feminist activism, Martineau was also wary of being identified as a literary bluestocking.[9] As Sylvia Meyers points out, while in the eighteenth century the term "bluestocking" was used to refer to a specific circle of writers, by the early nineteenth century it was used more broadly – and often pejoratively – to refer to any woman with literary ambitions.[10] In the popular press of the early nineteenth century, bluestocking writers were often viewed as intellectual exhibitionists who publicly displayed their knowledge and achievements in upper-class salons and *conversazioni*.

Although during various periods of her career Martineau was cast into the bluestocking mold by critics, she always attempted to distance herself from what she saw as a negative cultural stereotype. In her *Autobiography*, she tells how at age eighteen she made a practice of conducting her studies surreptitiously, lest she be accused of "blue-stockingism which could be reported abroad."[11] Throughout her career, Martineau continued to define her intellectualism and activism against the materialism and display of upper-class salons, where sex and identity were used as a means of self-promotion. One of the most important factors that enabled Martineau to engage in this private form of public activism was the convention of anonymity in early and mid-Victorian periodicals. Since the narrative voice of many reform-minded periodicals was assumed to be masculine, Martineau often used a masculine voice when writing her essays. This enabled her to speak out on controversial issues – especially the woman question – with the appearance of objectivity since as a "man" she could not be accused of writing on behalf of the female sex or in reference to her own personal difficulties.

Martineau wrote her first anonymous essays on women's issues for the *Monthly Repository*, a Unitarian periodical edited by Robert Aspland. Because Martineau strove to complicate the gender of her narrative voice in these early essays, she often expressed conflicting viewpoints on the role of women in society. For example, in her essay, "On Female Education," published in 1822, Martineau placates conservative readers by claiming that a woman's primary role is to serve as "domestic companion" to her husband.[12] But interspersed with this essentializing discourse on women's "nature" is a persuasive defense of women's right to equal education. She argues that in most educational settings, the female child "is probably confined to low pursuits, her aspirings after knowledge are subdued, she is taught to believe that solid information is unbecoming her sex, almost her whole time is expended on light accomplishments, and thus before she is sensible of her powers, they are checked in their growth."[13] In this way, Martineau expresses progressive views on women's education without seeming to commit herself – and readers – to an extremist stance. If these viewpoints had been attached to a feminine signature, most likely they would have been dismissed as bluestocking diatribe. By posing as a bourgeois male journalist, Martineau was careful to steer clear of any such identification. She writes, "I do not desire that many females should seek for fame as authors" and goes on to outline a course of reading that includes study of "living languages."[14] Such statements are of course ironic – and perhaps hypocritical – considering that Martineau is herself an author who signs her article with a Latin pseudonym, Discipulus. But such a stance was unavoidable for women who participated in public discourse during the 1820s – a time when there were few positive cultural stereotypes of the "public woman."

However, the narrative voice of Martineau's periodical essays was far from being strictly a defensive maneuver; in fact, throughout her career, she actively constructed a narrative persona that was detached from her gender as a way of creating the appearance of "objectivity" in her many discourses on the woman question. Of course, as Linda Peterson and Deirdre David have suggested, Martineau's appropriation of masculine discourse also to some extent reflects her internalization of patriarchal ideology.[15] By employing the discourses of the public sphere, she reinforced the very system that necessitated her masculine disguise. However, by insisting that women be "heard but not seen" in political debates, Martineau also attempted to secure the right of women to participate in public discourse.

Martineau constructed a contradictory role for the woman activist that was neither strictly public nor private. Writing in the privacy of her own home, she could make a living and participate in public debates while still avoiding the accusation of egotism and personal bias. At the same time, by participating in public debates as a journalist, she could influence the direction of society as a whole. Likewise, while she might employ "masculine" rhetoric in her reviews and essays, she might also broaden the audience for discussion of women's issues. For Martineau, the feminist message was more important than its messenger, whose personal bias, gender, and vanity could interfere in the process of communicating vital moral and political lessons. As we will see, this was a point of view she encouraged readers to adopt as well, so that they, too, could learn to engage in "objective," yet gender-sensitive, forms of cultural criticism.

Once Martineau began publishing books under her own name in 1832, she had more difficulty maintaining the objectivity she desired for expressing her viewpoints on the woman question. After the publication of *Illustrations of Political Economy* (1832–34), a serialized collection of didactic stories based on the principles of political economy, Martineau was catapulted into literary stardom. Suddenly she was no longer the obscure journalist who campaigned for women's rights under the guise of anonymity; she was the newly crowned feminine genius, whose growing literary reputation was called upon to be of service to a variety of radical causes. While Martineau in many ways enjoyed the fame associated with her literary success during the 1830s, she was still somewhat uneasy about her new public role. As a literary celebrity, she found it increasingly difficult to speak out on women's issues from a depersonalized point of view.

One way Martineau regained this perspective was to travel abroad, where she could write about radical issues – including the woman question – without being exposed to excessive and damaging forms of public attention. In 1834 she traveled to America, where she remained for two years, collecting data and impressions for her major sociological study, *Society in America* (1837). In writing this study, Martineau claimed to "compare the existing state of society in America with the principles on which it is professedly founded; thus testing Institutions, Morals, and Manners by an indisputable, instead of an arbitrary standard."[16] With this goal in mind, Martineau conducted a minute examination of American society from a variety of domestic, social, and political standpoints, including a sharp critical analysis of the disenfranchisement of women and slaves.[17] By claiming to address women's issues in the context of a foreign political and domestic culture, Martineau was able to give the impression that she was speaking on behalf of the citizens of another country, rather than in her own personal or national interest. Of course in reality Martineau intended her cultural critique to extend far beyond America's national boundaries. In a letter to William J. Fox, she writes that the purpose of *Society in America* was in part to promote the "revision in [parliament] of all laws regarding Woman; to set a watch on all legal proceedings [which] relate to women; & to expose her whole state."[18]

Martineau provided readers with the tools to understand and question conventional gender roles by defining feminism as an activity aimed at "seeing" and "writing" other cultures from a gender-sensitive point of view. In order to examine the specific feminist activities Martineau was advocating in *Society in America*, it is useful to examine its companion text, *How to Observe Morals and Manners* (1838), which spells out her techniques of cultural criticism. This how-to book was intended to train tourists to develop their "powers of observation," which would enable them to come to a broader, more scientific, understanding of the morals and manners of other cultures.[19] This claim to scientific objectivity was counterbalanced by the explicitly politicized point of view that Martineau hoped to train her readers to adopt. As Richard Stein points out, Martineau was attempting to produce a form of "subjective objectivity," which incorporated the individuality of the observer, producing "not so much a neutral record of impersonal facts as a passionate search for truths essential to individual and social improvement."[20]

Martineau's proposals for analyzing social institutions from a gendered point of view are especially innovative. "The degree of the degradation of woman," she writes, "is as good a test as the moralist can adopt for ascertaining the state of domestic morals in any country."[21] She goes on to list various benchmarks against which societies must be judged in order to determine their level of social "progress":

Where he [the observer] finds that girls are committed to convents for education, and have no alternative in life but marriage, in which their will has no share ... [he may presume that] domestic employments of the highest kind are undesired and unknown. He may conclude that ... for one more generation at least, there will be little or no [social] improvement. But where he finds a variety of occupations open to women ... he may conclude that here resides the highest domestic employment which has yet been attained, and the strongest hope of a further advance.[22]

Here Martineau associates the development of society with the occupational and vocational status of women. Of course by presenting Anglo-Protestant culture as the "strongest hope" for overall human advancement, she also expresses a colonialist perspective. In an earlier passage, Martineau compares the "slavery" of the "Indian squaw" to that of the women of "France, England, and the United States ... [who are] less than half-educated, precluded from earning a subsistence ... and prohibited from giving or withholding their assent to laws which they are yet bound by penalties to obey."[23] In this way, Martineau privileges a colonialist perspective while at the same time pointing to the cross-cultural nature of gender oppression.

In addition to analyzing the overall social status of women, Martineau encourages travelers to focus their analysis on the institution of marriage within foreign cultures. She laments that "by no arrangements yet attempted have purity of morals, constancy of affection, and domestic peace been secured."[24] Problems with marriage as an institution are attributable to the social construction of gender roles. On one hand, males are brought up to prize a "shallow" sense of honor and a sense of "feudal ambition" in their relationships with women.[25] Women, for their part, are "educated to consider marriage the one object in life, and therefore to be extremely impatient to secure it."[26]

When discussing problems associated with marriage as an institution from a cross-cultural perspective, Martineau goes beyond the boundaries of her original project of giving "travelers" the tools to observe and understand foreign cultures; here, and elsewhere, the observant gaze is turned inward on British culture itself as a means of judging its collective "health" against a series of feminist benchmarks. By providing readers with the tools to analyze other cultures – and their own – from a gender-sensitive perspective, Martineau provided a new form of feminist activity that could be employed on an international journey or a walk down the streets of London. In this way, she fostered a feminist consciousness among middle-class readers, encouraging them to view gender roles as categories generated by a given set of institutional arrangements, rather than as "natural," God-given identities. When viewed as dynamic and socially constructed, gender roles become a temporary "problem" that must be overcome in order to facilitate overall social progress.

By focusing her critique on other cultures, specifically on America, Martineau attempted to address gender issues with an indirect approach that enabled her to maintain a claim to "objectivity." She also attempted to maintain this distanced perspective by employing a "scientific" approach to writing that examined "facts" and "institutions" instead of individual cases. Once Martineau made the decision to train her critical eye more directly on English culture, she found it more difficult to gain this same sense of personal distance from the feminist issues she was committed to advocating. How was she to write about the institutional oppression of women in England without falling into the trap of "epicurean selfishness" that she so disliked in public discourse on the woman question? Her answer – at least temporarily – was to turn to domestic fiction.

Martineau claimed that her decision to write *Deerbrook* (1839), her first novel, was premised on her desire to escape the "constraint of the effort to be always correct, and to bear without solicitude the questioning of my correctness."[27] While in the past the claim to "scientific" observation had provided her with the authority to be an advocate for radical causes, including the woman question, it also had subjected her to criticism by those who questioned her ability to produce reliable data.[28] Afraid of "losing nerve" in her reformatory project, she turned to fiction as a way of more freely expressing her moral viewpoints: "my heart and mind were deeply stirred on one or two moral subjects on which I wanted the relief of speech, or which could be as well expressed in fiction as in any other way, – and perhaps with more freedom and earnestness than under any other form."[29] It is difficult to know what these "two moral subjects" might have been, but it is likely that women's issues – particularly problems associated with marriage as an institution and the lack of vocational opportunities for intellectual women – were still on her mind as she began her first novel. Martineau no doubt felt that such issues could be addressed "with more freedom" in a domestic novel since as a form of "feminine" writing it was held to a lower critical standard than more "serious" forms of nonfiction, such as political tracts and sociological studies. For this reason, it provided her with more license to analyze the social roles of women in contemporary British culture.[30] After all, her earlier contributions to the debate over the woman question had been either in the form of anonymously published periodical essays or in the form of sociological analyses of distant societies; thus, in order to analyze women's issues in contemporary British culture without being branded as an exhibitionist bluestocking, she needed to address them from behind the veil of fictionality.

Written contemporaneously with *How to Observe Morals and Manners*, *Deerbrook* demonstrates how gender-sensitive forms of observation can lead to deeper understanding of the material and moral conditions that impede women's social progress and consequently the advancement of society as a whole. However, because the domestic novel by convention was focused on the fate of individuals, rather than more broadly on the progress of social institutions, Martineau needed to employ narrative tools that would enable her to analyze the general social issues that the specific instances in her novel were intended to illustrate. More specifically, Martineau needed to find a way to work within the conventions of the "marriage-plot" associated with domestic fiction[31] while at the same time criticizing marriage as an institution in need of reform.

On the surface, *Deerbrook* seems to be a love story in the manner of Jane Austen, where intricate and often humorous social relations are used to examine moral issues associated with domestic relations. The novel's marriage-plot has troubled feminist critics over the years because it seems to reinforce conventional gender relations and class hierarchies. As Valerie Sanders points out, *Deerbrook* is "unsatisfying because of its refusal to follow through the implications of its many statements about love, self-repression, marriage, and women's career prospects: statements which are often made in impassioned, isolated speeches to other women."[32] Likewise, Deirdre David views the novel as evidence of Martineau's retreat into a more conservative political position that "endorses many of the unpleasant 'facts' of women's oppression which Martineau so bravely exposed and attacked in *Society in America*."[33] Indeed, it would be difficult to argue that *Deerbrook* is not conventional in its representations of gender relations. After all, the highest aspiration that Margaret and Hester seek is to find a husband and to serve him faithfully. Maria Young works only because she cannot find fulfillment in love and entertains little hope of devoting her intellectual and sympathetic powers to any social or moral purpose beyond her limited domestic circle.

However, beyond the novel's marriage-plot and the conventional gender relations it seems to advocate lies a deeper investigation of domestic issues of concern to women. By integrating the conventions of domestic fiction with those of sociological analysis, Martineau attempts to enable readers simultaneously to experience and question the social conditions that narrowly define women's social and economic roles. In *Deerbrook*, Maria Young's story continually "interrupts" the progress of the marriage-plot, providing an outsider's perspective on issues of love and marriage. By asking readers to identify with the marginalized perspective of Maria Young, Martineau encourages them to develop an objective, yet sympathetic, perspective on conventional domestic morality. As in *How to Observe Morals and Manners*, Martineau uses seeing as a metaphor for the kind of politicized cultural criticism she hopes readers will adopt. Just as Maria observes the marriage plot from a personally distanced critical perspective, so should readers become more careful observers of conventional domestic morality.

Unmarried, homely, and intellectual, Maria Young plays the role of the "redundant woman," a literary trope that would later become a staple of domestic fiction.[34] Existing always at the margins of the novel's plot, Maria's point of view is at once objective and peripheral. Like an internal narrator, she seems to have a broad view of the moral and emotional issues that are being addressed in the novel but does not play an active, central role. She functions as a "chorus" or "conscience" who provides perspective on the actions of others. Social activism for Maria, as for Martineau, is a kind of sympathetic interference in the lives of others that is carried out without thought of personal gain. By providing the perspective that others lack, she engages in public service without self-righteously displaying her own intellectual and moral superiority.

Of course, unlike Martineau, Maria does not attempt to influence political and social affairs at a national and international level, nor does she attempt to enter into "masculine" discourse, but she does define "social activism" in similar terms, as a form of social intervention premised on politicized, gender-sensitive observation of others.

One of the reasons Maria's superfluity is so interesting is that at the beginning of the novel she seems almost to fulfill the role of protagonist. Though the Ibbotson sisters are introduced early in the novel, it is Maria who takes center stage. We learn that she is an educated, philosophical woman who would "rather study than teach" and who reads the latest German philosophy.[35] Though she is clearly exceptional, Maria seems to submit to a system of institutional relations that would require her to sublimate her intellectual talents as a provincial governess. "There's no need to be sorry for me," she tells the Ibbotson sisters. "Do you suppose that one's comfort lies in having a choice of employments?" However, this sort of commentary is interspersed with criticism of social institutions that oppress educated women:

There is a great deal said about the evils of the position of a governess – between the family and the servants – a great deal said that is very true, and always will be true, while governesses have proud hearts, like other people: but these are slight evils in comparison with the grand one of the common failure of the relation.[36]

In this way, Maria affirms and submits to her own marginal status while at the same time criticizing the system that assigns her a subordinate social position. Throughout her discussion of the governess role, she is careful to point out that she speaks "quite generally" about the issue, rather than seeming to complain about the difficulty of her own situation. In this way, she attempts to construct her views as objective and philosophical, rather than as an expression of self-pity.

Early in the novel, Maria uses her marginality as the means of gaining a broad perspective on the events around her. In one of the only passages of extended monologue in the novel, Maria reflects on her marginal social position. Left alone for a few precious hours without the demands of her students, Maria analyzes the world outside her study:

What is it to be alone, and to be let alone, as I am? It is to be put into a post of observation on others: but the knowledge so gained is anything but a good if it stops at mere knowledge, – if it does not make me feel and act. Women who have what I am not to have, a home, an intimate, a perpetual call out of

themselves, may go on more safely, perhaps, without any thought for themselves, than I with all my best consideration: but I, with the blessing of a
peremptory vocation, which is to stand me instead of sympathy, ties and
spontaneous action, – I may find out that it is my proper business to keep an
intent eye upon the possible events of other people's lives, that I may use slight
occasions of action which might otherwise pass me by.[37]

Maria presents her marginality as the source of alienation but also as a
source of power. By achieving a "post of observation," a broad view of
the social affairs of others, the single intellectual woman can "feel and
act" in a way that promotes overall social good. She sublimates her own
desire for romantic fulfillment – her unrequited love for Philip Enderby
– as a way of increasing her "usefulness" to others. Like Martineau
herself, Maria assumes a narrative position that allows her to rise above
the personal, thereby exerting moral influence on issues of social and
moral concern.

Maria's sympathetic observation is contrasted with forms of voyeurism in the novel, the meddling of Mrs. Grey and Mrs. Rowland, who
peer at each other from behind the curtains as a means of gaining
ammunition for their social rivalry. They are presented as examples of a
general atmosphere of gossip and surveillance in the small town, where
there is little that escapes the eye and ear of public opinion. Hester and
Margaret soon discover that one of the major sources of entertainment
in Deerbrook is "to witness all the village spectacles which present
themselves before the windows of an acute observer."[38] Yet, even with
their ability to "see" the affairs of others, the gossips of Deerbrook never
achieve the kind of vision that would enable them to transcend their
limited points of view. Confined in the oppressive atmosphere of the
Grey household, the Ibbotson sisters, like "starlings in a cage," pine for
outdoor activity and thus a wider perspective on the world around
them.[39] Margaret, especially uncomfortable in Deerbrook society, continually chides Hester to rise above the "opinions of the people" in the
small community.[40] But Hester is too self-involved to be able to achieve
this emotional distance; only Maria Young seems to provide Margaret
with the broader, more sympathetic point of view she seeks.

One of the ways that Maria helps Margaret gain greater perspective is
to prepare her for the torment of romantic love. Though Maria entertains passionate feelings for Philip Enderby, she is able to overcome
these personal interests, presenting a more dispassionate view of love
and marriage. In a remark repeated almost verbatim from *How to Observe
Morals and Manners*, Maria says to Margaret,

all girls are brought up to think of marriage as almost the only event in life. Their minds are stuffed with thoughts of it almost before they have had time to gain any other ideas. Merely as means to ends low enough for their comprehension. It is not marriage – wonderful, holy, mysterious marriage – that their minds are full of, but connection with somebody or something which will give them money, and ease, and station, and independence of their parents. This has nothing to do with love.

But even those women who find "true love" still face the "agony of a change of existence" that they must endure "silently and alone."[41] Conditions are especially difficult for those women who must endure the "abyss" of unrequited love, which drives some to a "state of perpetual and incurable infancy" and leads others to "sacrifice themselves, in marriage or otherwise, for low objects." It is only by being "philosophical," that is, by resigning themselves to the "objects and conditions" of life, that they can transcend their individual circumstances and be of use to others.[42] Thus, Maria defines the excessive feeling associated with romantic love as a "problem" that must be overcome in order for women to achieve self-fulfillment and moral "usefulness."

The dangers associated with the self-indulgent expression of personal feeling take on larger social significance when an angry mob descends on Deerbrook, threatening to kill Margaret's brother-in-law, Edward Hope, who is accused of stealing corpses from pauper graveyards for scientific experimentation. Spurred on by superstition and gossip, the lower classes have lost their ability to tell truth from hearsay. The arrival of the local nobility – Lord and Lady Hunter – promises to quell the passion of the rioters by providing rational leadership, but their own selfishness prevents them from fulfilling this role. Lady Hunter's decision to go into town is premised by her desire to "catch a glimpse of the ladies in their terrors."[43] Her seeming concern for the social well-being of her community is revealed to be her thinly-disguised desire for public attention and adulation. As she departs Deerbrook with "Miss Nare's newest cap and story," she has succeeded in fanning – rather than dousing – the flames of gossip and rumor, further exacerbating the social crisis centered on the Hope household.[44]

Lady Hunter's voyeurism provides a contrast to Maria's sympathetic philosophical perspective. Though Maria is just as much of a voyeur as Lady Hunter, she uses her powers of observation to exert moral influence and to seek justice for those who are victimized by more unsympathetic forms of social interference. At the same time that Lady Hunter is retreating to her manor house, Maria breaks her leg as a result of being "thrown down by the crowd" during the riot. When her injury is discovered, all present suddenly forget their troubles and remember the self-effacing Maria: "How thankful were they all now, that some one had thought of Maria! She had been in extreme anxiety for them [Margaret and the Hopes]; and she would not certainly have sent for aid before the morning. It was indeed a blessing that some one had thought of Maria."[45] Even though circumstances make Maria's presence in the plot redundant, she is never completely forgotten; like a conscience, she is "remembered," brought back into the central focus of the novel just when she seems least important to its progress. A social anomaly in every way, her sympathetic, self-effacing presence is the only antidote to the vain emotionality and self-interested forms of social interference that absorb the common mind of Deerbrook.

Once the plague has run its course, Philip and Margaret are reconciled, and Edward and Hester regain their social status along with their mutual regard, Maria reenters the novel as a "loose end" that cannot be incorporated into the conventions of the marriage plot. The last scene in the novel is devoted to a conversation between Maria and Margaret just before Margaret's marriage to Philip. Margaret worries about Maria's future, pointing out that she is "infirm and suffering in body, poor, solitary, living by toil, without love, without prospect." While Maria views her own situation with some pathos, she refuses to see it as hopeless. She says to Margaret, "If I were without object, without hope, without experience, without the power of self-rule which such experience gives, you might well fear for me."[46] Though she laments that her solitude is "very hard to bear," it also provides her with "glimpses of heaven" that enable her to "look forward without fear of chance or change."[47]

Maria thus submits to providence, rising above her personal difficulties, social marginality, and romantic desire with her own sense of transcendent vision. While her future is unnarratable in terms of the conventional marriage plot, it is still a subject that cannot be let go. Even in the last line of the novel, when Philip and Margaret walk romantically in the twilight, they are "talking of Maria."[48] Both admirable and pathetic, Maria is never fully incorporated into a domestic novel focused on love and marriage; she remains a redundant, yet somehow vitally necessary, observer and moral commentator, who facilitates conventional romantic relations while at the same time interrupting and complicating the reader's understanding of them. Through the characterization of Maria Young, Martineau attempted to create a distanced, yet sympathetic, perspective on the woman question. In this way, she was able to discuss the need for women's educational and vocational opportunity while at the same time working within the conventions of domestic fiction. Of course, by communicating her viewpoints through the voice of a marginalized character, Martineau in some ways downplayed her own feminist messages. Likewise, by creating women characters who conformed to conventionalized gender roles, she provided no clear models of the kind of intellectual feminist activism she professed in her own career. However, by having Maria model the same kind of feminist process skills she defined in *How to Observe Morals and Manners*, she demonstrated how the development of a radical consciousness would enable readers to understand and question the morality of domestic relations within their own social spheres.

Martineau's contributions to the woman question in the 1820s and 1830s demonstrate the ways that conventional domestic narratives and marginal social roles could be reconfigured to serve the cause of women's emancipation. Martineau redefined and complicated "feminine" genres of writing, such as the domestic novel and the travel narrative, to include discussion of women's social, political, and economic roles. Likewise, she incorporated the self-effacement, reticence, and sympathy conventionally associated with the middle-class woman into a redefinition of the woman activist as a sociological observer. This definition requires that the woman activist assume a contradictory role that spans both public and private spheres. She must be dispassionate, yet sympathetic; objective, yet moralistic; domestic, yet political; reticent, yet outspoken; visible, yet invisible. In short, she must do the impossible: validate the patriarchal ideology of separate spheres, while at the same time challenging its underlying assumptions about women's "natural" roles and abilities.

This contradiction troubles many modern critics who object to her "inconsistent" feminist beliefs premised on a meliorist view of social change. Yet what many fail to realize is that Martineau's "inconsistent" feminism is an important precursor to modern feminist thought. As Gayle Graham Yates points out, Martineau's radicalism is a "true progenitor of the intellectual mode that reigns in Anglo-American liberalism today and provides the dominant informing paradigm of mainstream Western feminism."[49] Just as modern feminists contend with the contradictions of their roles within patriarchal institutions, so did Martineau struggle with her own relationship to liberal ideology. On one hand she sought to secure equal rights for women in a patriarchally controlled democratic society, that is, for women to be treated without regard to gender in educational, professional, and other social institutions. As she puts it in a letter to Henry Reeve, her ideal was not the promotion of "abstract doctrines of rights," but rather that gender not inhibit individuals from "giving their faculties fair play."[50] For a woman intellectual such as Martineau, this meant that her ideas, rather than her gendered identity, ought to be the subject of public attention and criticism.

However, beyond just promoting gender-blindness in social institutions, Martineau also laid the groundwork for a more militant feminism.[51] By encouraging women to engage in forms of gender-sensitive social observation and cultural criticism, Martineau helped to establish a feminist consciousness among middle-class women that not only led them to demand equality within a patriarchally defined public sphere but also facilitated the questioning of patriarchy itself. Martineau's contributions to debate over the woman question in the 1850s and 1860s demonstrate how her liberal feminism could be converted into more militant forms of social protest. As an anonymous leader writer for the *Daily News* (1852–66), Martineau played a key role in public debates on women's issues as diverse as divorce and rational dress. Perhaps the most important of these contributions was a series of letters on the Contagious Diseases Acts, which ignited public protests led by Josephine Butler in the 1870s.[52] As Judith Walkowitz points out, these protests were part of a larger social movement that "facilitated middle-class women's forceful entry into the world of publicity and politics, where they claimed themselves as part of a public that made sense of itself through public discourse."[53] However, while on one hand feminism was emerging as an increasingly "visible" movement, on the other hand it was becoming increasingly "invisible" as women activists such as Martineau maneuvered behind the scenes. Thus feminist consciousness developed not only in highly public cultural "moments" but also in innumerable private acts that do not easily conform to modern categories of liberal and radical feminism.

Throughout her long career as a feminist activist, Martineau demonstrated how women could embrace the contradictions inherent in their positions as insiders and outsiders in debates over the woman question. Instead of imagining feminism as an either/or proposition – that women must choose between domesticity and public life – she demonstrated how women could achieve both simultaneously through subversive forms of writing and seeing. She showed how women writers –

through a number of narrative strategies designed to create an objective, yet politicized, perspective – could speak out on issues of concern to women while still avoiding being labeled according to socially construc-ted stereotypes of "public women." Though these activities were in some sense "contained" by patriarchally defined institutions and narra-tive media, they were also subtly revolutionary, gradually altering the terms by which women's issues would be presented and discussed.

NOTES

1 For a broad overview of Martineau's contributions to the woman question, the following sources may be consulted. Valerie Pichanick, "An Abomin-able Submission: Harriet Martineau's Views on the Role and Place of Women," *Women's Studies* 5 (1977), 13–32; Gayle Graham Yates (ed.), *Harriet Martineau on Women* (New Brunswick, NJ: Rutgers University Press, 1985), pp. 1–27; Valerie Sanders, *Reason Over Passion: Harriet Martineau and the Victorian Novel* (Brighton, Sussex: Harvester, 1986), pp.168–85.

2 My use of the term "feminists" here is of course anachronistic. See Barbara Caine, *Victorian Feminists* (Oxford: Oxford University Press, 1992), pp. 4–8. In this chapter, I use the term generally to refer to those actions taken by individual women on behalf of their sex, rather than to refer to members of an organized feminist movement.

3 Harriet Martineau, *Autobiography*, 2 vols. (London: Virago, 1983), vol. 1, pp. 400–01.

4 For example, Martineau receives only brief mention in Barbara Caine's *Victorian Feminists* and Philippa Levine's *Feminist Lives in Victorian England: Private Roles and Public Commitment* (Oxford: Blackwell, 1990).

5 Though Martineau had been a published author since 1821, writing articles on various subjects for the *Monthly Repository*, it wasn't until the late 1820s that she defined herself primarily as a professional writer.

6 Yates (ed.), *Harriet Martineau on Women*, p. 33.

7 *Ibid.*, p. 35.

8 Martineau, *Autobiography*, vol. 1, p. 400.

9 This is not to say that Martineau did not feel an affinity for some blue-stocking writers, especially Anna Laetitia Barbauld (see Martineau, *Autobi-ography*, vol. 1, p. 302).

10 See Sylvia Meyers, *The Bluestocking Circle: Women, Friendship, and the Life of the Mind in Eighteenth-Century England* (Oxford: Clarendon Press, 1990), pp. 290–303.

11 Martineau, *Autobiography*, vol. 1, p. 100.

12 Yates (ed.), *Harriet Martineau on Women*, p. 91.

13 *Ibid.*, p. 89.

14 *Ibid.*, p. 92.

15 Dierdre David, *Intellectual Women and Victorian Patriarchy: Harriet Martineau,*

Elizabeth Barrett Browning, George Eliot (Ithaca: Cornell University Press, 1987), pp. 27–93; Linda Peterson, "Harriet Martineau: Masculine Discourse, Female Sage," in Thaïs Morgan (ed.), *Victorian Sages and Cultural Discourse: Renegotiating Gender and Power* (New Brunswick, NJ: Rutgers University Press, 1990), pp. 171–86.

16 Harriet Martineau, *Society in America* (New Brunswick, NJ: Transaction, 1994), p. 48.

17 For an extended analysis of the feminist content of *Society in America*, see Susan Hoecker-Drysdale, *Harriet Martineau, First Woman Sociologist* (Oxford: Berg, 1992), pp. 49–77.

18 Harriet Martineau, *Selected Letters,* ed. Valerie Sanders (Oxford: Clarendon Press, 1990), p. 45.

19 Harriet Martineau, *How to Observe Morals and Manners* (New Brunswick, NJ: Transaction, 1989), p. 13.

20 Richard Stein, *Victoria's Year: English Literature and Culture, 1837–38* (Oxford: Oxford University Press, 1987), pp. 181, 180.

21 Martineau, *How to Observe*, p. 179.

22 *Ibid.*, pp. 184–85.

23 *Ibid.*, p. 179.

24 *Ibid.*, p. 172.

25 *Ibid.*, pp. 173–74.

26 *Ibid.*, p. 180.

27 Martineau, *Autobiography*, vol. II, p. 108.

28 See, for example, John Croker, "Miss Martineau's Morals and Manners," *Quarterly Review* 63 (1839), 61–72.

29 Martineau, *Autobiography*, vol. II, p. 108.

30 See Valerie Sanders, *Reason Over Passion*, pp. 1–29, for a discussion of Martineau's theory of fiction, particularly her techniques for integrating social criticism into the domestic novel.

31 See Rachel Blau DuPlessis, *Writing Beyond the Ending: Narrative Strategies of Twentieth-Century Women Writers* (Bloomington: Indiana University Press, 1985), pp. 3–4.

32 Sanders, *Reason Over Passion*, p. 70.

33 David, *Intellectual Women*, p. 77.

34 See Sanders, *Reason Over Passion*, pp. 59–60, for a discussion of this trope in Victorian fiction.

35 Harriet Martineau, *Deerbrook* (Garden City: Dial Press, 1984), p. 20.

36 *Ibid.*, p. 22.

37 *Ibid.*, p. 35.

38 *Ibid.*, p. 25.

39 *Ibid.*, p. 27.

40 *Ibid.*, p. 102.

41 *Ibid.*, p. 159.

42 *Ibid.*, p. 164.

43 *Ibid.*, p. 311.

44 *Ibid.*, p. 317.
45 *Ibid.*, p. 324.
46 *Ibid.*, p. 521.
47 *Ibid.*, pp. 521, 522.
48 *Ibid.*, p. 523.
49 Yates (ed.), *Harriet Martineau on Women*, p. 5.
50 Martineau, *Selected Letters*, p. 164.
51 For an analysis of the liberal roots of radical feminism, see Zillah Eisenstein, *The Radical Future of Liberal Feminism* (Boston: Northeastern University Press, 1986), pp. 3–11.
52 The Contagious Diseases Acts (1864, 1868, 1869) required that women suspected of prostitution be detained and inspected for venereal disease. Martineau criticized the sexual double standard inherent in this legislation by publishing several letters of protest in the *Daily News*. See Hoecker-Drysdale, *Harriet Martineau*, pp. 143–47, Pichanick, "An Abominable Submission," pp. 24–26, and Yates (ed.), *Harriet Martineau on Women*, pp. 239–45.
53 Judith Walkowitz, *City of Dreadful Delight: Narratives of Sexual Danger in Late-Victorian London* (Chicago: University of Chicago Press, 1992), p. 7.

WORKS CITED

Caine, Barbara, *Victorian Feminists,* Oxford: Oxford University Press, 1992.
Croker, John, "Miss Martineau's *Morals and Manners,*" *Quarterly Review* 63 (1839), 61–72.
David, Deirdre, *Intellectual Women and Victorian Patriarchy: Harriet Martineau, Elizabeth Barrett Browning, George Eliot,* Ithaca: Cornell University Press, 1987.
DuPlessis, Rachel Blau, *Writing Beyond the Ending: Narrative Strategies of Twentieth-Century Women Writers,* Bloomington: Indiana University Press, 1985.
Eisenstein, Zillah, *The Radical Future of Liberal Feminism,* Boston: Northeastern University Press, 1986.
Hoecker-Drysdale, Susan, *Harriet Martineau, First Woman Sociologist,* Oxford: Berg, 1992.
Levine, Philippa, *Feminist Lives in Victorian England: Private Roles and Public Commitment,* Oxford: Blackwell, 1990.
Martineau, Harriet, *Autobiography,* 2 vols., London: Virago, 1983.
  Deerbrook, Garden City: Dial Press, 1984.
  Harriet Martineau: Selected Letters, ed. Valerie Sanders, Oxford: Clarendon Press, 1990.
  How to Observe Morals and Manners, New Brunswick, NJ: Transaction, 1989.
  Illustrations of Political Economy, 9 vols., London: Charles Fox, 1832–34.
  Society in America, New Brunswick, NJ: Transaction, 1994.
Meyers, Sylvia, *The Bluestocking Circle: Women, Friendship, and the Life of the Mind in Eighteenth-Century England,* Oxford: Clarendon Press, 1990.
Peterson, Linda, "Harriet Martineau: Masculine Discourse, Female Sage," in

Thaïs Morgan (ed.), *Victorian Sages and Cultural Discourse: Renegotiating Gender and Power*, New Brunswick, NJ: Rutgers University Press, 1990, pp. 171–86.

Pichanick, Valerie, "An Abominable Submission: Harriet Martineau's Views on the Role and Place of Women," *Women's Studies* 5 (1977), 13–32.

Sanders, Valerie, *Reason Over Passion: Harriet Martineau and the Victorian Novel*, Brighton, Sussex: Harvester, 1986.

Stein, Richard, *Victoria's Year: English Literature and Culture, 1837–38*, Oxford: Oxford University Press, 1987.

Walkowitz, Judith, *City of Dreadful Delight: Narratives of Sexual Danger in Late-Victorian London*, Chicago: University of Chicago Press, 1992.

Yates, Gayle Graham (ed.), *Harriet Martineau on Women*, New Brunswick, NJ: Rutgers University Press, 1985.

CHAPTER 6

Maximizing Oliphant: begging the question and the politics of satire

Monica Cohen

In one of Margaret Oliphant's most popular novels, *Phoebe Junior: A Last Chronicle of Carlingford* (1876), Reginald, the high-minded older son of a widowed clergyman with a large and impoverished family refuses a "sinecure" on the grounds that it means pay without work, that is, a generous stipend without any duties attached to it.[1] His sister, Ursula, the daughter saddled with the bulk of the household work and poignantly wishing that there were sinecures for girls, argues convincingly, "'They pay you for that which is not work, but they will find you plenty of work they don't pay for'" (*Phoebe Junior*, p. 112). Ursula intends merely to persuade Reginald to accept familial financial responsibility, a theme Oliphant repeatedly varies: her fiction is punctuated by a brood of feckless and insolvent fathers just as her autobiography turns on her struggle to support an increasingly large family in the wake of her financially encumbered husband's death and her brother's alcoholism.

Ursula's wish for sinecures for girls articulates an interesting fantasy about female work and its relationship to earnings. In being an object of envy for both Northcote, the Dissenting minister who has a salary but no poor people in his comfortable congregation to tend, and for Ursula, for whom a salary would provide her father with irrefutable proof of her contribution to the household he takes for granted, Reginald's vocational condition stresses the importance of work and the importance of pay without endorsing any notion of paid work. In this sense, Ursula's evocation of the sinecure as workless pay for payless work performs a strange reversal: rather than desire to work so as to have money, she seems to desire to have money so as to be free to work. Conceptualizing women's work along these lines and in this fashion, Ursula's phrasing represents domesticity as something like a neglected but rightful sinecure, a professional holding rather than a paid job. In this, her model of domesticity departs from conventional representations of the separate spheres, whereby men produce and women consume, and challenges

Marxist assumptions about class. In Ursula's fantasy, women's domestic work would enjoy both financial backing and freedom from the labor market. She would be a worker who could do a great deal of good by virtue of the financial independence her professional condition affords. In this, Ursula's homeworker presages Max Weber's professional politician as well as Virginia Woolf's woman writer: all three are paid in order to work in general and not for any work in particular.

The parallel here is worth explaining further in so far as it underlines the importance of Protestant concepts in northern European ethics and aesthetics. Weber differentiates between two professionals: "one lives 'for' politics [and] one lives 'off' politics"[2] in order to condition effective political leadership in the terms of economic independence. Psychological soberness – "*matter-of-factness*" ("Politics as a Vocation," p. 115) – accompanies a sense of responsibility in the financially secure and propertied breast of Weber's ideal politician (p. 86). Interestingly enough, a financially secure breast, in the shape of a room of one's own, and a small legacy, condition the cultivation of Woolf's ideal woman writer as well. According to Woolf, women's intellectual impoverishment stems from their material deprivations and distractions: the British Library cannot yield any glimpse of a female literary tradition because women are traditionally too poor and too busy to write; even an elite women's college serves up stringy beef, prunes and distracted conversation.[3] When women are not too busy, their material preoccupations limit their artistic range: Brontë, Woolf laments, is just too angry to produce great art. Good politics for Weber and good art for Woolf are conditioned by a prior financial independence rather than by the promise of rewards from a competitive consumer marketplace. Structurally, this bias mirrors the way in which salvation in Protestantism poses as a prior condition proved by a lifetime of good work rather than bought by the individual works of a Catholic marketplace. Weber and Woolf, an unlikely pair to be sure, articulate at the waning of a long nineteenth century, not only anxiety about marketplace exchanges, but a congenital anxiety about a Catholic structuration of works, which bears on how literature is valued and evaluated. This anxiety is important in nineteenth-century domestic fiction and is especially evident in stories revolving around domestic women and their lifetime work. Like all cultural constructs and contexts, this hostility toward a Catholic structuration of works poses a unique set of challenges for novelcraft.

Reginald's sinecure and his sister's praise for it introduce into the novel an idea of paid unpaid work. In the Anglican church, Oliphant identifies a professional institution that, in its practice of paying individuals to do unpaid work, provides a locus of value for the narrative generation of a courtship plot. Cast in the light of Anglican sinecures, domesticity assumes the task of absorbing female vocational desire. Romance, and consequently Oliphant's success in the literary marketplace, are enabled by a financial arrangement traditionally cited as evidence of clerical corruption and so her reconstruction of them can be seen as part of a strategy whereby an ostensibly conservative position can be put to rather revisionist purpose, if not revolutionary use. That sinecures can be praised by virtue of the *de facto*, if not *de jure*, social work they perform suggests that Oliphant's novel is positioned to intervene in Reform politics in so far as what is really at stake in her defense of the sinecure is a plea for the social, if not political (and I think the distinction is an important one for Oliphant), recognition of female labor and female desire for labor.

The "woman question" occurs in Oliphant's fiction then as a set of problems that middle-class "domestic" women face and learn to approach with a rhetorical caginess that perhaps precludes political pigeonholing. In a certain sense, Oliphant fits into the "Tory women's tradition," that Marilyn Butler describes as proto-feminist: aware of the gender inequalities characteristic of public life, Butler's Tory feminists insisted on the religious sanctity of women's service both to the family and to the larger community in an effort to promote greater equality for women.[4] Denise Riley has expanded this notion of women as social improvers by arguing that natural sociality, having already been saturated by eighteenth-century concepts of femininity, cleared new terrain for public action: "If women's sphere was to be the domestic, then let the social world become a great arena for domestic interventions" runs Riley's representation of what will become the nineteenth-century argument.[5]

But Oliphant's rhetorical witticisms imply a political ambivalence that aestheticizes such themes while still giving them a currency in the world of a historically specific literary marketplace. In other words, the style in which she confronts the question of how middle-class women are to make a living when their menfolk fail them and the formal techniques she devises to represent this question and this experience, contributed to the popularity of her novels while divesting them of the universal appeal we are taught to associate with the "canonical." This is not to say that there may not be other, equally compelling reasons for studying her novels, but it is my conviction that they cannot be studied for either their

transcendent attributes or, as I will argue, for their seeming verisimili-
tude; rather, there are formal and structural conflicts confronted in
Oliphant's novels that make them fascinating case studies of the relationship between genre construction and cultural moment.

Although Oliphant claims that the purpose of her novels was to
entertain, not to preach, and that the purpose of her writing them was to
earn a living, not to create art, the political implications of working at
entertaining and entertainment as work collapse the trope of separate
spheres by making the personal not simply political but peculiarly
professional. That the figure of the sinecure, of "paid unpaid work,"
should enable a romantic resolution that commanded a great deal of
financial clout in the literary marketplace suggests that Oliphant's artful
wordplay represents a fantasy of female professional compensation. By
intervening in debates that split the female, personal, amateur sphere
from the male, political, professional arena, Oliphant's figure of lucra-
tive unpaid work suggests that the emplotment of the separate sphere
doctrine in popular women's fiction records a somewhat different story
from that which some social history and some canonical novels (*Mill on
the Floss*, for example, or *Middlemarch*) have told us about Victorian
domesticity: the sharp divide between work and leisure, publicity and
privacy, men and women no longer so sharp, the ironies of an expansive
domesticity emerge. For when Ursula wishes for "sinecures for girls" is
she wishing for a concrete share in patriarchy or is she setting up the
institution of marriage as patriarchy's false imitation? Is it patriarchy
that is being questioned or only its fake?

The phrase that represents the "sinecure for girls" conveys the
slipperiness of the novel's politics. "They pay you for that which is not
work, but they will find you plenty of work they don't pay for" is
stylistically classic Oliphant: two ostensible opposites, being paid and
not being paid, equated through a rhythmic repetition of words (pay,
work, for) in inverted syntactic parallel. Heralded by a string of evenly
cadenced iambs, each clause's concluding dactyl, "is not work" and
"don't pay for," suggests that non-work and non-pay can be artful
means of inscribing precisely that which the terms are ostensibly positioned to deny, work and pay. The syntax implies that there is an
epistemological problem inherent in the relationship between work and
pay: because pay makes work culturally legible, pay is often taken as a
metonymic representation of work, when in truth, pay is only a condition that makes work recognizable, not evidence of its being. The
implied metonym misleads in the sense that although work and pay may

coincide, one cannot be taken as evidence for the existence of the other.

In this sense, Oliphant's characteristic use of chiasmus – that is, her inverted repetition of causal phrases in axiomatic fashion – imparts a tacit social critique. The hypothesis here then is that Oliphant's axiomatic inversions produce a fictional space where play politics can carry real resonance. But by abrading the distinction between the play and the real, Oliphant runs the risk of mocking the real rather than politicizing the play. The risk, of course, inheres in the politics of satire itself: at what point can satire become politically prescriptive? When is a send-up more than diverting bravado? Does Lucilla Marjoribanks' use of mock heroic, for instance, confine *Miss Marjoribanks* unwittingly to the misogyny of *The Rape of the Lock*, as Linda Peterson has argued[6] or does it coin an entirely new idiom of female middle-class empowerment, as Elizabeth Langland has suggested?[7]

In contrast to George Eliot's characteristic gestures toward a universal "we" who all can acknowledge the moral truths she lays out, Oliphant's "we" emerges from the axiomatic inversions she employs in capturing a gender-specific social experience. Written during her most successful period and serialized in the popular *Macmillan's Magazine* from August 1875 to January 1876, *The Curate in Charge* shares with *Phoebe Junior* the same predilection for aphoristic discourse. Having become teachers in the boarding school they attended as pupils, two sisters descend the social scale "from the level of those paying to be taught, to the level of those who are paid for teaching – curious though the paradox seems to be."[8] The move from paying to be taught to being paid for teaching is a common nineteenth-century female experience that Oliphant's syntactical symmetry and reflective structuration encompass with a sense of bemused distance. What would have been experienced as a traumatic turn of events, the fall from active subject (who pays) to passive object (who is paid) occurs as a pair of gerunds whose durative aspect reflects the nonlinear continuities of female experience. While the overt formal structure of the phrase aestheticizes and hence softens the sisters' hardship, it also provides the distance whence to view female experience as a social phenomenon.

We may recall here Riley's argument. According to Riley, the expansion of the domestic sphere to include the social world produced a new sociality that culminated in a systematized formalization of the goodness of women under the auspices of the social sciences ("*Am I That Name?*" pp. 53–54). In a sense, we can see Oliphant's axiomatic discourse working to this effect. The artistic project transforms into a sociological one. This gives pause to a feminist scholarship poised between theorizing a feminine aesthetic and retrieving long-interred female authors; the link between the two professional trajectories emerges in the recognition that the new sociality at the center of Oliphant's fiction is connected to the sociology at issue when the topic of women's work opportunities enters the public discourse as published fiction.

But if there is a job for a woman writer like Oliphant in describing and publishing female misfortune, the substance of political critique itself remains inchoate. The very artfulness of the phrase, "from the level of those paying to be taught to the level of those who are paid for teaching," seems to imply that the social significance of pay is as arbitrary as the easily exchangeable designations of linguistic signs: if private education – paid teaching – is socially desirable, what difference should the shift from payer to payee make? The implied objection to the double standard is of course more rhetorical than real: obviously it is more desirable to be able to pay for a service than to have to be paid for providing it. In this sense, Oliphant's epigrammatic ironies are seductive in a La Rochefoucauld tradition. For the metrics and formal reversals of each artful phrase collude to manufacture a maxim. But because the social realities faced by unmarried women still haunt the discourse, the reader is forced to speculate whether Oliphant's maxims themselves are real maxims or parodies of maxims, and then what it would mean to parody a maxim.

In this sense, it becomes possible to see that the feminine emplotment of the maxim, what Nancy Miller has said is problematic in the French novel, may work in the English novel as a politically elusive representational strategy. Miller has argued that we can read difference in the "demaximization" wrought by women writers when they "italicize" their heroines' "extravagant wish for a story that would turn out differently."[9] The example is Maggie Tulliver's wish to make "a world outside of love, as men do."[10] But this register of difference becomes difficult to read in an author like Oliphant, or even like Jane Austen, women writers who, rather than resisting the "maximized" languages of social convention, use maximized language as the basis for ironic critique. For these writers, italicization occurs, not as a wish for a story that would turn out differently (as Miller has illustrated it), but as a stylistic tick whereby conventional authority is parodied and thereby both opposed as well as usurped. For Oliphant, epigrammatic ironies like the idea of a woman's fall "from the level of those paying to be taught to the level of those who are paid for teaching" are characteristic of a discourse she employs especially when her heroines face objectionable challenges and limitations. In this sense, the pleasure of unexpected reversal and the authority of poetic form conspire to express political challenge in a fundamentally conservative modality, perhaps placing Oliphant in Marilyn Butler's tradition of Tory feminist writers.

In narrating a young woman's move from pupil to teacher, Oliphant is of course contributing to a hotly debated topic of several decades earlier, the problem of how England's "surplus" women were to employ themselves, a discussion that generally revolved around the plight of the governess.[11] As her readers would have known, the "paradox" of descending the social scale was no more than the fact that an unmarried woman's status, unfixed by property and unfixable by occupation, was peculiarly vulnerable during the recurrent economic fluctuations of the century. This is to say that although Oliphant's writings are considered conservative in light of her lifelong association to *Blackwood's* and her fiction excluded until relatively recently from what is understood as a women's tradition of letters, her prose techniques presume a women's subculture in which conventional political holdings are ironized through the implicitly conservative authority of such stylized syntax.

Let us return to *Phoebe Junior* and the picture of female labor lurking behind Reginald's sinecure. For Oliphant, the absence of the wage clouds the home's visibility as a workplace. She turns to the idea of domesticity as a "sinecure for girls" as a means of inscribing work that deserves pay but does not get it through direct conventional channels. In doing so, she depicts her own domestic work situation, which was, as one reviewer acerbically implies, remarkably similar to holding a sinecure. Oliphant was, after all, a professional novelist. And as a novelist, one of her disgruntled reviewers in *Blackwood's* comments, she had access to what was essentially workless pay:

In what other calling would she have been so fortunate? Perhaps if she had been a painter, a picture-dealer might have advanced her a few guineas. But we know of no "profession" other than letters in which remuneration can be anticipated to the same amount and on the same terms. Solicitors do not finance barristers to the tune of several thousands. A struggling surgeon will probably fail to raise a five pound note on the strength of a promise to cut off the lender's leg if called upon to do so. When the countless iniquities of "the trade" are rehearsed by prosperous and well-fed authors, let not the recording angel fail to note that publishers have long done and still continue to do, what is asked and expected of no man in any other kind of business.[12]

Although the reviewer distinguishes novel-writing both from "professions" and "trades" by bracketing the terms in the patronizing punctuation of citation-less quotation marks, his comparison of the writer to the lawyer or the surgeon and the publisher to the businessman suggests that novel-writing both is and is not a professional business. His high-minded objection, like Reginald's, is to workless pay. But Oliphant would have argued that such workless pay culminated in doing a great deal of payless work: she acknowledges the generosity of her publishers, but complains that they were still considered her "benefactors" even when "the balance changed,"[13] thereby implying that she was often underpaid if paid at all. Indeed her Byzantine arrangements with publishers for future work often meant that she received in the end less than she might have, had she marketed each piece individually and closer to a projected publication date, as savvy strategists like Trollope often did. But Oliphant had so many extended advances going on at the same time that it is unlikely she made the best deals per item and this perhaps explains why she never made as much money as Trollope despite her popularity and productivity.[14] In so far as her publisher "bankers" provided her with use of their capital "for nothing," requiring no security other than her sound mind and body,[15] her business dealings departed from conventional capitalist arrangements. According to her own account, she was paid to do nothing so she could work for nothing, a situation that provides her with much reason to complain but which also allows her to rationalize a domestic woman's participation in the nation's workforce. She wants to represent herself as an exploited worker who is nevertheless not quite a worker and therefore, by implication, perhaps not quite so exploited.

As usual with Oliphant, she links female domestic labor – in the shape of Ursula's sinecure for girls – to literary work by means of an argument that proceeds by introversion, that is, by the unexpected exchange of conventional opposites. For example, Hester, the soon to be dead mother figure of *The Curate in Charge*, "was a woman of genius," Oliphant writes, invoking all the nineteenth-century magical, ethereal and *sui generis* connotations of the word "*genie.*" She was not, of course, a woman of "poetical or literary genius – but that which is as good, *perhaps better.*" And what, the reader might ask, could be better than literary genius? She was an expert household manager, a fantastic domestic economist: "She guided her house as well, as only genius can" – and here Oliphant omits the article, "as only genius can," thereby turning the "she" belonging to the individual homemaker into a spiritual quantity of bodiless genius. "I don't pretend to know," Oliphant confesses, "how she did it [that is, make a "kind, warm beneficent living house" and yet keeping within her income] any more than I can tell you how Shakespeare wrote *Hamlet*. It was quite easy to him – and to her; but if one knew how, one would be as great a poet as he was, as great an economist as she" (*The Curate in Charge*, p. 10). By conflating home economy and literary endeavor – domesticity and poetry – in the word "genius," Oliphant suggests that there is a hidden similarity between these two ostensibly different occupations. In Oliphant's imagined world, literature – once refracted through domesticity – poses as a profession that can realize the fantasy of *Phoebe Junior*'s sinecure for girls.

Wishing for a sinecure, Ursula, however, gets a marriage. Wishing to be "a comfort to her dear papa," the eponymous heroine of *Miss Marjoribanks* (serialized in *Blackwood's*, September 1861–62) conducts a parliamentary campaign by substituting for a platform the slogan that character is everything.[16] But her story still concludes with a marriage rather than a parliamentary win. Reading Oliphant's work through the claims she makes in her *Autobiography* about women's relationship to the literary marketplace and its protected exploitation of intellectual property, we need to speculate here whether these two popular novels politicize romance or romanticize politics, and what precisely is at stake in that distinction. Several critics have noted the mock heroics encoding Lucilla's political gamesmanship. As I have already mentioned, Linda Peterson has argued that the mock heroic language makes Lucilla's work seem trivial even as it also diminishes the male sphere: the deflation works both ways and that perhaps is part of the reason why it is so difficult to glean any kind of utopian vision for Oliphant's gifted female characters; the ironized language, however pointed at men initially, is, novelistically speaking, a loose canon, potentially harmful to anyone in its purlieu, even those women who at first seem to benefit from its mockery.

Arriving in Carlingford "like a young king entering in secret a capital which awaits him with acclamations" (*Miss Marjoribanks*, p. 48), Lucilla is congratulated for her "masterly ... conception of social politics," her "statesman-like views" (p. 112), her "faculty of government" (p. 142) and of course the "genius" with which she devises Mr. Ashburton's very real political campaign: the thing, she instructs, was not to consider Whigs or Tories or Reform or opinions at all because what matters is that "it is the Man that is wanted" (p. 347). Lucilla perceives that political success is

not all that different from social success: power – even political power –
resides in one's capacity to influence others, in the social impression one
makes rather than in a set of political convictions. Thus Mrs. Woodburn
can say that Lucilla has "influence, which is a great deal better than a
vote" and Lucilla can turn a hearth brush into "something sublime"
(p. 447), that is, something not unlike a scepter.

In this sense, the good-humored affection Oliphant generates for
Lucilla's political campaign pivots on the potential controversion of its
ostensible implausibility. In other words, when it seems that Mr. Ashburton might really win the election without having uttered a single
political position, Lucilla's own sense of importance seems less fantastic
and the seriousness of her play less play-like. Miller's "wish for things to
turn out differently," that is, a woman writer's wish for a destiny other
than the one prescribed by intra- and extra-paginal social conventions
occurs in *Miss Marjoribanks* as a whole genderless group's wish for a
popular man to represent them in parliament. The wish is not a private
one, confined to a heroine and her author, but a communal one, one
shared by the various individuals composing that group called Carlingford. Rather than say that women, whether you realize it or not, play an
essential political role regardless of whether they may or may not vote,
Oliphant seems to say that politics, whether you realize it or not, is not
about how a candidate will vote on the Reform Bill, but about how well
he makes an impression, how well he advertises himself. The maxim in
the plot is that politics is nothing but the "social semiotics" Langland
identifies, which is to say, politics is nothing but domesticity, as critics of
Victorian domesticity have been arguing for quite a while now. That
this presumably gender-neutral campaign is launched under a violet
and green cockade, the colors adopted by the suffragette movement,
indicates that Oliphant's critique of politics as social semiotics participates in a more generalized feminization of culture.

But the novel's sudden move from the social politics of Lucilla's
"mission" to Carlingford – that is, "the reorganization of society" (*Miss
Marjoribanks*, p. 114) – to the politics of romance discloses the fictitious-
ness of Lucilla's political acts. She begins the novel without acknowledging the difference between running for office and managing a run for
office, thereby eliding the vicariousness of her political participation:
"there was something in the very idea of *being* MP for Carlingford which
moved the mind of Lucilla. It was a perfectly ideal position for a woman
of her views, and seemed to offer the very field that was necessary for her
ambition" (p. 114). Her romance with politics becomes quite clear,

however, when the language of courtship infiltrates her political strategies: when rival love interests also become rival political candidates,
Lucilla laments, "And the horrible thing was, that she had pledged
herself to another and put her seal upon it that Mr. Ashburton was the
man for Carlingford!" (p. 360).

Lucilla's retreat from the public world of parliamentary politics to a
private one of marriage to her cousin Tom does not clearly return
Lucilla to a separate sphere. Tom does not want to buy an estate on the
grounds that it would be a poor investment: "land doesn't pay" (p. 484),
he protests. He makes an exception, however, for the one estate that
would emblematize an emotional rather than financial yield: March-
banks, the lost family property that phonetically replicates both Lucilla
and his name. In the property of her own name, Lucilla envisions a
"new sphere" in which she "would find herself at home" (p. 488). In a
new conception of property, that is nevertheless rooted in an older
landed tradition, Lucilla sees "a larger sphere open before her feet"
(*Miss Marjoribanks* 497). My hypothesis here is that Oliphant posits a
fundamentally new conception of property by allowing Lucilla to keep a
maiden name that becomes a signifier of landed property. The legal and
philosophical expansion of the definition of property to include Locke's
notion of "having property in oneself" occurs here as the repetition of
Lucilla's name. The circularity of a romance plot that begins and ends
with the assertion of a woman's individual status results in the restora-
tion of the family estate. In this sense, Lucilla's individualism is encoded
twice: once by the eponymous property of a landed estate and once by
the eponymous property of the novel's title itself. Landed and intellectual property thus combine in the emplotment of female individualism.
That Lucilla's "own" name, however, remains her father's attests to
Oliphant's willingness to play both with and within the conventions of
traditional patriarchy.

Are we to understand Lucilla's fate as tragic accommodation to a world
in which a woman with such political "genius" is confined to managing
her domestic sphere or as a deeper social critique that unmasks the
fatuousness of male political endeavor in the first place? Is Oliphant's
irony pitched to produce protest or does it merely complicate the
binaries subtending the infamous separate sphere doctrine? Oliphant's
strategy emerges when the issue of women's work becomes a discursive
part of plot formation. *The Curate in Charge* again offers Oliphant's
readers some direction. Toward the end of the novel, one of the

heroines chooses to fall out of the respectable middle classes: her father
having died leaving the family homeless and penniless, Cicely would
rather stay in her home town as the parish schoolteacher than maintain
her class position as a governess among strangers in another county.
Had Cicely "been a lad of nineteen instead of a girl, something might
have been possible" (*The Curate in Charge*, p. 192), says the parson,
Mildmay, who is also Cicely's undeclared lover. "But nothing was
possible now," the narrative ventriloquizes.

And here Oliphant interrupts with one of the most strange utterances
in her fiction: "The reader will perceive that the arbitrary and fictitious
way of cutting this knot, that *tour de force* which is always thought of in every
young woman's story, the very melodramatic begging of the question,
still, and perennially possible, nay probable, in human affairs, had not
occurred to Mildmay" (p. 192). The sentence employs several rather
peculiar turns of phrase that straddle the threshold separating the reality
of limited work opportunities for women and the limited narrative
choices faced by novelists writing about such women: there is a "knot"
that needs to be cut fictitiously, the "*tour de force*" that associates this
biographical turning point with an author's aesthetic showmanship, and
the "begging of the question" that, however realistic, is too melodramatic
for realist fiction. The knot that needs to be fictitiously cut is imagining
respectable work for an unmarried young woman in financial need. And
the *tour de force*, the show of skill and ingenuity that would cut such a knot is,
of course, marriage. As a *tour de force* that solves the problem of imagining
work opportunities for nice girls, marriage is presented as a matter of
artistry, as a show of skill and ingenuity. And in the context of Cicely's
unchallenged innocence, it can be a show of skill and ingenuity only on
the author's part. In other words, the phrase "*tour de force*" suggests that the
fantasy of marriage as a viable work opportunity for women, which is
what Oliphant seems to imply about Lucilla's marriage to Tom, can be
only one of two things: a cynical reflection on the conniving of a
manipulative female character (which applies neither to Lucilla nor
Cicely) or an artistic resolution to a more complicated real conflict.

However much Oliphant's figurative language coyly obfuscates this
real conflict, that conflict returns in the striking double entendre: the
melodramatic "begging of the question." Oliphant designates the *tour de
force* marriage that will cut the fictitious knot of women's work by using
the idiom, "to beg the question." Begging the question can mean
popping the question, that is, begging for a hand in marriage, but it can
also mean avoiding the question, evading the issue at hand – that is,

abandoning a thoughtful discussion about Cicely's work opportunities. That a young woman's vocational moment of crisis idiomatically slips into a young woman's romantic moment of truth occurs as a linguistic crossing, a confusion of metaphors. Begging the question in the context of a proposal is context-determined and a prelude to performative speech. But the scene here is as much about plot construction as it is about Mildmay's possible proposal. As the context is two-sided, it is not clear which idiomatic meaning is appropriate. By straddling two worlds, that of the fiction and that of the fiction making, Oliphant produces a crossing of signals by which Mildmay's hypothetical proposal can be construed as a strategy of evasion: in other words, begging the question is begging the question.

This is important in that Oliphant's invocation of a border territory between female experience and its emplotment allows her to intone her lament as a lament about formal restraints rather than political ones, about literature and not about society, about art and not about culture. It is as a narrative craftsman that she objects to the narrowness of Cicely's choices, not as a woman. And it is through her perspective as a gender-neutral storymaker that she envisions an alternative female destiny. Here I quote in full:

the sudden "good marriage," which is the one remaining way in which a *god out of the machinery* can change wrong into right . . . comes dreadfully in the way of heroic story . . . That Cicely's brave undertaking ought to come to some great result in itself, that she ought to be able to make her way nobly, as her purpose was, working with her hands for the children that were not hers, bring them up to be men, having that success in her work which is the most pleasant of all recompenses, and vindicating her sacrifice and self-devotion in the sight of all who scoffed and doubted – this, no doubt, would be the highest and the best, the most heroical and *epical development of story*. To change all her circumstances at a stroke, making her noble intention unnecessary, and resolving this tremendous work of hers into a gentle domestic necessity, with the *"hey presto!" of the commonplace magician*, by means of a marriage, is simply a contemptible expedient. But, alas! it is one which there can be no doubt is much preferred by most people to *the more legitimate conclusion*; and what is more, he would be justified in knowing the accidental way is perhaps, on the whole, the most likely one, since marriages occur every day which are perfectly improbable and out of character, mere *tours de force*, despicable as expedients, showing the poorest invention, a disgrace to any romancist or dramatist, if they were not absolute matters of fact and true. (*The Curate in Charge*, pp. 193–94) (my emphasis)

Irony gives way to overt protest as Oliphant's social critique masquerades as convoluted literary criticism. Marriage as the resolution of a

woman's occupational perplexity occurs as a "deus-ex-machina" translated into the modern day "machinery" of anti-industrial sentiment and
Aristotelian bias. However common the deus-ex-machina device is in
classical fiction, it is for Oliphant antithetical to "heroic story" – again,
an article-less lofty spiritual quantity that, like Lukács' notion of epic,
eludes exemplification. Marriage in the passage belongs to the cheap
theater of facile "hey prestos" and here Oliphant mimics vocalized
stage-speech to underscore the alleged artificiality of a rite she allows
occurs everyday. The measure of a "good" ending then is neither a
matter of abiding by the dictates of past literature nor a matter of
mimesis. In this sense, the grounds according to which she rejects
marriage are the literary grounds according to which she rejects marriage *as a good ending*. Marriage is not a "legitimate conclusion" even if
tradition and experience endorse it because and only because marriage
does not make for an exciting story.

Now this may or may not be true. But I think in the final analysis,
Oliphant is being disingenuous. For surely there are all sorts of marriages that do make good story endings and even good story beginnings.
The imaginative (if not financial) impoverishment of the romance plot
is, for Oliphant, no matter how she might pretend otherwise, a political
and not an aesthetic question in so far as she consistently shakes her fist
at the cultural conditions that presumably refuse its reinvention.

Margaret Oliphant received the letter accepting her first novel on the
morning she was married. She tells this in an effort to capture both the
significance and insignificance of her profession as a writer by using the
terms of her domestic life: the novel was a trifle, she can barely remember its plot, news of its publication an aside on such a momentous day.
But such joy! The *Autobiography* barely contains it. Public success merges
with personal achievement, a serendipitous coinciding, to be sure. The
story of Margaret Oliphant's life as a writer, as she herself tells it, begins
on her marriage day. Let us place this anecdote next to the conclusion of
Middlemarch: Eliot's acknowledgment that marriage is still "a great
beginning" introduces her elegy for the great heroic modern women
who, forced by their times to live in private obscurity, lie silent in
unvisited tombs. In a sense, Oliphant presents herself in the *Autobiography*
as an Eliotian heroine who, having spent her energies in all the small
rivulets of unnoticed novels and articles, dies a "mother childless," with
no one left to visit her own silent tomb. Oliphant's life, however, as she
imagines it and as she writes about it, reminds us that behind Eliot's

lament, and even behind her own heart-wrenching one, is a great deal of fiction-making. For what is *Middlemarch* – the place and the book – after all but a great paean to Dorothea?

The point here is that if we accept that any given society invents different ways of producing social knowledge, we can see the Victorian novel in its epistemological role as a means of publicizing what small communities, communities that by their very nature are significantly female, know. That knowledge changes of course in the act of publication, and so the novel as a form becomes the site for evolving discourses of the everyday. Satire enables this translation – from neighborhood talk to sociological knowledge. By veiling the act of translation, Eliot invites drawing conclusions about Victorian experience that may not have been accurate: Dorothea was a great woman, she tells us in one voice, indeed a saint, but due to her sex and her historical moment she was deprived of a field of action and of public notice. But we all know that Dorothea is one of the most famous heroines of English literature and that her deeds as a character are well known. Part of our pleasure in the text is knowing "the truth" about Dorothea's greatness, but the truth is that we would be hard pressed to identify anyone in or outside the story who has not also been initiated into this secret. This is part of what great literature is about.

Oliphant dispenses with this kind of open secret. She draws attention to the tension between what is said and what is known in a way that places her with great satirists (and perhaps sheds some light on why some women writers should lean toward satire in the first place). The question as to why Oliphant's novels have been excluded from the canon has nothing and everything to do with her position on the question of women's role in English public life. In the end, social critique muffles artistry. But we can learn perhaps more about both.

NOTES

1 Margaret Oliphant, *Phoebe Junior* (London: Virago Press, 1989), p. 112.
2 Max Weber, "Politics as a Vocation," in *From Max Weber: Essays in Sociology*, ed. and trans., H. H. Gerth and C. Wright Mills (New York: Oxford University Press, 1958), p. 84.
3 Virginia Woolf, *A Room of One's Own* (San Diego, New York, London: Harcourt Brace and Company, 1979).
4 Marilyn Butler, *Jane Austen and the War of Idea* (Oxford: Clarendon Press, 1987), p. xxii.
5 Denise Riley, *"Am I That Name?" Feminism and the Category of "Women" in History* (Minneapolis: University of Minnesota Press, 1988), p. 48.

6 D. J. Trela (ed.), *Margaret Oliphant: Critical Essays on a Gentle Subversive* (London: Associated University Presses, 1995), p. 72.

7 Elizabeth Langland, *Nobody's Angels: Middle-Class Women and Domestic Ideology in Victorian Culture* (Ithaca and London: Cornell University Press, 1995), pp. 154–71.

8 Margaret Oliphant, *The Curate in Charge* (Gloucester: Alan Sutton, 1985), p. 40.

9 Nancy K. Miller, "Emphasis Added: Plots and Plausibilities in Women's Fiction," in *The New Feminist Criticism* (New York: Pantheon, 1985), p. 352.

10 George Eliot, *The Mill on the Floss* (Boston: Houghton Mifflin Company, 1961), p. 361.

11 Mary Poovey, *Uneven Developments: The Ideological Work of Gender in Mid-Victorian England* (Chicago: University of Chicago Press, 1988), p. 126.

12 "The Record of a Life," review of *The Autobiography* of Margaret Oliphant, *Blackwood's Edinburgh Magazine*, 165 (May 1899), 895–904.

13 Margaret Oliphant, *Autobiography*, ed. Elisabeth Jay (Oxford: Oxford University Press, 1990), p. 90.

14 Elisabeth Jay, *Mrs. Oliphant: A Fiction to Herself. A Literary Life* (Oxford: Clarendon Press, 1995), p. 280.

15 "The Record of a Life."

16 Margaret Oliphant, *Miss Marjoribanks* (London: Virago, 1988).

WORKS CITED

Blackwood's Edinburgh Magazine.

Butler, Marilyn, *Jane Austen and the War of Ideas*, Oxford: Clarendon Press, 1987.

Eliot, George, *Middlemarch*, New York: Viking Penguin, 1986.

The Mill on the Floss, Boston: Houghton Mifflin Company, 1961.

Jay, Elisabeth, *Mrs. Oliphant: A Fiction to Herself. A Literary Life*, Oxford: Clarendon Press, 1995.

Langland, Elizabeth, *Nobody's Angels: Middle-Class Women and Domestic Ideology in Victorian Culture*, Ithaca and London: Cornell University Press, 1995.

Miller, Nancy, "Emphasis Added: Plots and Plausibilities in Women's Fiction," in *The New Feminist Criticism*, New York: Pantheon, 1985.

Oliphant, Margaret, *Autobiography*, ed. Elisabeth Jay, Oxford: Oxford University Press, 1990.

The Curate in Charge, Gloucester: Alan Sutton, 1985.

Miss Marjoribanks, London: Virago, 1988.

Phoebe Junior, London: Virago, 1989.

Poovey, Mary, *Uneven Developments: The Ideological Work of Gender in Mid-Victorian England*, Chicago: University of Chicago Press, 1988.

Riley, Denise, *"Am I That Name?" Feminism and the Category of "Women" in History*, Minneapolis: University of Minnesota, 1988.

Trela, D. J., (ed.), *Margaret Oliphant: Critical Essays on a Gentle Subversive*, London: Associated University Presses, 1995.

Weber, Max, *The Protestant Ethic and the Spirit of Capitalism*, New York: Charles Scribner's Sons, 1958.

"Politics as Vocation," in *From Max Weber: Essays in Sociology*, ed. and trans. H. H. Gerth and C. Wright Mills, New York: Oxford University Press, 1958.

Woolf, Virginia, *A Room of One's Own*, San Diego, New York, London: Harcourt Brace and Company, 1979.

CHAPTER 7

Literary women of the 1850s and Charlotte Mary Yonge's Dynevor Terrace

June Sturrock

The issue of work was central to discussion of the "woman question" from the 1850s onwards. Books and periodicals commented frequently, variously, and at length on women's work in this period,[1] employment registers and employment societies for women, including the Society for the Promotion of Employment for Women, were founded, and the *English Women's Journal* was established in 1858 largely to discuss "the present industrial employments of women" and the "best mode of judiciously extending the sphere of such employments."[2] Literary work, however, was a special case. As Frances Power Cobbe observed, in her 1862 overview of women's employment opportunities, there was "little need to talk of literature as a field for woman's future work. She is ploughing it in all directions already" ("What Shall We Do," p. 375). Indeed, women had for many years been active in the literary world, working as editors, reviewers, and publishers' readers as well as poets, essayists, dramatists, and, preeminently, novelists.[3] For literary women, then, employment issues involved not so much establishing new opportunities as exploring the relationship between femininity and literature – the connection between gender and the nature and reception of the literary product, and the difficulty of combining a literary career with a woman's domestic responsibilities. Cobbe's survey addresses a dramatic recent change in the status of women in the arts, caused by an influx of "women ... distinguished for one quality above all others – namely strength" ("What Shall We Do," p. 366). "Strength," a word with traditional masculine connotations, raises directly the question of gender in literature, and indirectly the conflict between the domestic and the literary: a "strong" or "inspired" woman writer might well face – or be perceived as facing – endless domestic distractions with reluctance.

These perennial questions became especially prominent in the mid-1850s, partly because of the mixture of pleasure and anxiety engendered by a series of highly visible literary women, and a number of much-reviewed publications directly concerned with the woman writer. Charlotte Brontë's death in 1855 led to an intensified interest in the life and works of the Brontës, and to the publication of Elizabeth Gaskell's best-selling *Life of Charlotte Brontë* (1857); Elizabeth Barrett Browning in *Aurora Leigh* (1856–57) devoted thousands of lines to the conflict between art and love in a woman poet's life. Besides the effect of these well-known figures on concepts of the literary woman of the period, the inauguration of the *English Women's Journal* by members of the feminist Langham Place Group is also significant, in providing an outlet for a new kind of literary reviewing, with a deliberate focus on women's writing, as Solveig Robinson argues ("Amazed at Our Success," pp. 160–62). All this activity, within a few years, suggests a new and more public phase in the ongoing attempt to define the woman writer. This struggle is a crucial part of the agitation over the importance of women's work in general, in that it involved the question of women's freedom of expression as well as related concerns about the private and public obligations of the woman writer.

This newly invigorated discussion about women and work, especially women and literary work, forms the context for this chapter. The chapter aims not at contributing new material to the vigorous ongoing critical debates about Brontë, Gaskell, and Barrett Browning as individual writers, but rather at suggesting more fully the complexity and topicality of the concept of the literary woman in these years. It focuses on a text precisely contemporary with those of Gaskell and Barrett Browning, *Dynevor Terrace* (1857) by the popular religious novelist, Charlotte Mary Yonge (1823–1901), which, in the character of Isabel Conway, includes one of the earlier fictional representations of the woman writer.[4] Yonge is rarely considered in the company of the "canonical" women writers as Eliot, Barrett Browning, Gaskell, or the Brontës, but demonstrably she was seriously concerned with many of the same issues. Her work is generally highly responsive to current social and literary concerns;[5] in *Dynevor Terrace* she exploits fully one aspect of the widespread current public interest in the literary woman while studiously ignoring the other. A large part of her plot depends on the conflict between literary and domestic demands, and most of her central characters are defined largely by their histories as readers and writers. In fact, the relation to the written word becomes a token of a correct (that is, traditional) power balance within marriage – another matter disturbing feminists of the period. Yet, both here and in several later novels involving women writers as characters, Yonge refuses to raise implicitly or explicitly the question of gender characteristics in women's writing. All her writers are unquestioningly in the mainstream of literary femininity, as she was herself. Her traditional approach to the literary woman partly explains the distance that other women writers, seeking various degrees of freedom from the tacit censorship of their work based on their gender, placed between themselves and Yonge. This discussion of Yonge's work in the context of the various representations of the literary woman of the period ends, therefore, with a brief note on Yonge's reception among a specific and relevant group of literary women – her fellow popular novelists.

"The most alarming revolution of modern times," according to the disapproving and sardonic Margaret Oliphant in 1855, was proclaimed in *Jane Eyre*:

> Nobody perceived that it was the new generation nailing its colours to the mast. No one would understand that this furious lovemaking was but a wild declaration of the "Rights of Woman" in a new aspect. The old-fashioned deference and respect – the old-fashioned wooing – what were they but so many proofs of the inferior position of the woman, to whom the man condescended with the gracious courtliness of his loftier elevation... The man who presumed to treat her with reverence was one who insulted her pretensions; while the lover who struggled with her ... was the only one who recognized her claims of equality... Here is your true revolution. (Allott, *The Brontës*, pp. 312–13)

While Oliphant, as an experienced novelist herself, is perhaps exceptionally shrewd in her perception of the gender implications of *Jane Eyre*, in general terms her response is not unique. Most of the contemporary critical response to the work of the Brontës raised directly or indirectly the question of gender and the relation between literature and femininity. The Brontës were notoriously praised and blamed alike in language more often associated with the masculine than the feminine.[6] Their reviewers reiterated such terms as "strength," "power," "vigor," and "coarseness." G. E. Lewes, for instance, praises in *Wuthering Heights* "an extraordinary power of vigorous delineation," while condemning it as being (like *The Tenant of Wildfell Hall*) "coarse in language and coarse in conception" (Allott, *The Brontës*, p. 292). He uses the same gendered diction in discussing *Shirley*, which he describes as possessing a "vigour" that "often amounts to coarseness and is certainly the very antipode of 'ladylike'" (Allott, *The Brontës*, p. 163). Such contemporary accusations of coarseness and tributes concerning strength are well enough known to need no further repetition here.

In writing her biography of Charlotte Brontë, Elizabeth Gaskell wanted to correct the unwomanly image presented by the reviewers, or at least to make sure that Brontë was not condemned as a woman on the basis either of her own writing or of her sisters'. Gaskell aimed to establish the femininity of her friend, "to make the world ... honour the woman as much as they have admired the writer" (Letter to George Smith 1856, quoted in Fraser, *Charlotte Brontë*, p. 487). Her subject is the novelist as relative creature, "Charlotte Brontë – the friend, the daughter, the sister, the wife" (Letter to Ellen Nussey 1856, quoted in Fraser, *Charlotte Brontë*, p. 489), so that Lewes' response to Gaskell's work must have been particularly gratifying as a token of her success in her aims: "What a bit of the true religion of home is the whole biography," he writes (Allott, *The Brontës*, p. 330). Similarly, another contemporary reviewer notes that in Gaskell's account of Brontë, "we see the woman not the authoress" (Easson, *Elizabeth Gaskell*, p. 378).

Gaskell described her task as a biographer as providing a corrective to such impressions as Oliphant's, and as involving a careful choice of examples of "womanliness (as opposed to the common ideas of her as a 'strong-minded emancipated' woman)" (Letter to George Smith 1856, quoted in Fraser, *Charlotte Brontë*, 492). Accordingly, in connection with the projected publication of *The Professor*, Gaskell strongly opposes allowing "another syllable that could be called coarse to be associated with her [Bronte's] name" (Letter to George Smith 1856, quoted in Barker, *The Brontës*, p. 791). She emphasizes the skillful balance between woman and writer: after the publication of *Jane Eyre*, "henceforward Charlotte Brontë's existence became divided into two parallel currents – her life as Currer Bell the author and her life as Charlotte Brontë the woman. There were separate duties belonging to each character, not opposing each other, not impossible but difficult to reconcile" (Gaskell, *Life*, p. 384). Lyndall Gordon describes Gaskell's *Life* as "a woman's record of a woman, with its emphasis on private life, domesticity, obscurity, rather than public achievement" (Gordon, *Charlotte Brontë*, p. 331); others see it rather as a novelist's version of a novelist.[7] It is, of course, both – *The Life of Charlotte Brontë* is a woman writer's version of a woman writer. The strategic adjustments Gaskell makes to the image of Brontë carefully represent the woman writer as feminine and domestic as well as articulate and talented.

Contemporary feminist critics saw *Jane Eyre* as a watershed in the history of the novel, as Robinson suggests ("Amazed at Our Success," p. 162); Gaskell's *Life of Charlotte Brontë* was doubly a landmark for women's biography, as a distinguished woman's life of a distinguished woman. This period also saw another milestone in the development of the literary woman. For many women readers *Aurora Leigh* (1856–57) signaled a turning point in the development of women's poetry. Frances Power Cobbe, in writing about the new strength which she perceives in the work of recent women artists, refers with especial admiration to *Aurora Leigh* as "miles away from the received notion of a woman's poetry" ("What Shall We Do," 366). Barrett Browning's novel-epic, with its presentation of the woman poet as an inspired prophet-figure, with "work to do / The heavens and earth have set" (2. 455–56), for many years profoundly affected how women, at least, thought about women's writing (Stone, *Elizabeth Barrett Browning*, pp. 191–93). Barrett Browning annexes for Aurora's work terms associated with the intensity of the privileged masculine poetic genres; it involves "life-blood" (5. 353: *Aurora Leigh*, ed. Reynolds, p. 474) and "a special central power" (5. 368: *Aurora Leigh*, ed. Reynolds, p. 474).

Yet Barrett Browning portrays her heroine not only as dedicated to her work but also as learning with some difficulty to negotiate between art and love, her role as artist and her needs as woman. Suitably enough the epigraph to Gaskell's *Life of Charlotte Brontë*, stressing as it does the precarious adjustment between the domestic and the professional in the life of a woman writer, is provided by *Aurora Leigh*:

> O my God
> Thou hast knowledge, only Thou,
> How dreary 'tis for women to sit still
> On winter nights by solitary fires
> And hear the nations praising them far off.
> (5.434–38: *Aurora Leigh*, ed. Reynolds, pp. 376–77)

Yet if Gaskell's heroine is shown as finding a balance between the personal and the public, Barrett Browning's is shown for most of the poem as enduring the conflict between the two roles. Aurora sees the poet – and despite her pronouns she is especially concerned with the woman poet – as placed

> 'Twixt two incessant fires – his personal life's,
> And that intense refraction which burns back,
> Perpetually against him from the round
> Of crystal conscience he was born into,
> If artist born? O sorrowful great gift
> Conferred on poets of a twofold life
> When one life has been found enough for pain.
> (5. 376–82: *Aurora Leigh*, ed. Reynolds, p. 375)

The resolution of the poem comes in part with Aurora's realization that

> No perfect artist is developed here
> From any imperfect woman...
> Art is much, but...love is more.
> O Art, my Art, thou art much but Love is more!
>   (9. 645–59: *Aurora Leigh*, ed. Reynolds, p. 577)

Barrett Browning's explicit and implicit concern with issues of literature and gender is reflected in the contemporary reception of her poem. Positive and negative reviews alike address the work primarily in terms of gender. George Eliot, in the *Westminster Review*, describes Barrett Browning as "perhaps the first woman who has produced a work which exhibits all the peculiar powers without the negations of her sex; which superadds to masculine vigour, breadth, and culture, feminine subtlety of perception, feminine quickness of sensibility and feminine tenderness" (quoted in Mermin, *Barrett Browning*, p. 223). John Nichol's comments in the same periodical, however, are more hostile. He perceives Barrett Browning's complex maneuvers in crossing gender boundaries, but dismisses them as "straining after strength" (*Aurora Leigh*, ed. Reynolds, p. 403). Yet, despite the invective of reviewers whose comfortable preconceptions were disturbed by Barrett Browning's attempt "to prove her manhood" (Nichol, "Aurora Leigh," p. 401), *Aurora Leigh* in fact finally provides a similar, if idealized, kind of resolution to the conflict between the literary and the domestic to that provided by Gaskell's account of Charlotte Brontë. Dorothy Mermin reads the ending thus: "*Aurora Leigh* offers passionate testimony to a woman's right and sacred obligation to do her own work, but the ideal situation toward which the poem moves is that of a married woman plying her pen within a reformed domestic sphere" (*Godiva's Ride*, p. 56).

Thus in the mid-1850s exceptionally visible women in publications that aroused considerable general interest raised directly and indirectly profound concerns about their own profession.[8] In 1857, the year in which both the *Life of Charlotte Brontë* and *Aurora Leigh* were published, Charlotte Yonge, an enormously successful writer since *The Heir of Redclyffe* (1853), provided her version of the literary woman, Isabel Conway, in *Dynevor Terrace*. Her emphatic silence on one aspect of the question of the literary woman, both in this novel and in her later works, is as significant as her open concern with other aspects. Unlike the writers discussed previously, she avoids dealing explicitly with the issue of gender and authorship and never transgresses the prescribed boundaries of a woman's art either in person or through her characters. Her distinguished woman painter, Geraldine Underwood (in *The Pillars of the House*), unquestioningly keeps both to watercolors and to religious and domestic subjects, and her women writers work comfortably in genres traditionally associated with the feminine. They publish stories for children (Elizabeth Merrifield in *Two Sides of the Shield*), journalism (Elizabeth Merrifield and Arthurine Arthuret in "Come to her Kingdom," Ermine Williams in *The Clever Woman of the Family*), or religious verse (Isabel in *Dynevor Terrace*, Ethel in *The Daisy Chain*). In no way – except in the very fact that they are women writers – do they challenge the powerful censorship operating through literary conventions of gender.

Yet this conservative and antifeminist writer[9] does deal directly and repeatedly with women as successful, paid, and published writers, rather than displacing questions of women's creativity on to public performers, as George Eliot does with her great women singers, Armgart or Al Charisi, or as Charlotte Brontë does with her impassioned Rachel-figure, Vashti.[10] Indeed she resembles Barrett Browning rather than the novelists in creating fictions about characters driven by her own literary concerns. Yonge writes directly about women's urgent need to read and write and discusses how literary women should manage the tensions between their professional and their personal lives. As a self-proclaimed Church propagandist (Battiscombe, *Charlotte Mary Yonge*, p. 14), Yonge responds predictably to the changing concept of the literary woman and the new emphasis on the role of work in a woman's life with a reaffirmation of traditional duties and hierarchies. However, she was also a dedicated, almost addictive, literary woman herself, publishing about two hundred volumes and spending fifty years as editor of various Church periodicals. As a matter of biographical fact she interwove her own personal and professional life very closely, submitting her manuscripts to her father for criticism (which she did not necessarily use), gossiping about her novels in correspondence with her family, friends, and admirers, and reading submissions to her magazine, *The Monthly Packet*, to her mother by the fireside in the evening.[11] In the first of several novels in which she represents a woman with literary ambitions, *The Daisy Chain: or, Aspirations* (1856), the heroine's poetic aspirations are abandoned for domestic responsibilities.[12] The energetic and brilliant Ethel May gives up her literary, academic, and marital ambitions for the sake of her father and ten siblings. However, *Dynevor Terrace*, which was produced in the next year, while presenting a similar conflict, marks a radical change from its predecessor. Isabel's literary career, unlike Ethel's, is neither abandoned or disparaged but rather subordinated; Isabel's rewards for acceding readily to such subordination are both familial and professional. Literature remains a significant part of her life; in fact, writing and reading mold the lives of all the characters in this novel, men as well as women, servants as well as employers, as they did Yonge's own life and the lives of her friends and family.

Isabel Conway is portrayed as a dreamy intellectual beauty, using her literary talents initially as a form of escape from "the cramped round" of the London society life to which she is condemned by a foolish step-mother, and writing verse as a means of "relieving and giving expression to [her] yearnings for holiness and loftiness" (*Dynevor Terrace*, p. 126). Her long poem, a pious romance about the Crusades, *The Chapel in the Valley*, absorbs most of her energies not only in her girlhood but long after her marriage, in fact until well after the birth of three daughters. She remains throughout these years serenely indifferent to household man-agement: "the few domestic cares that she perceived to be her duty were gone through as weary tasks and her mind continued involved in her own romantic world where she was oblivious of all that was troublesome or vexatious" (p. 356). Eventually, in a financial crisis, after her husband loses his position as a schoolmaster, her first reaction is to plan to use her literary abilities to support her family. However, the Viscount Fitz-jocelyn, her cousin and the novel's hero, presents to her what is a central argument of this text: "it does not answer for the wife to be the breadwinner" (p. 382). He forces her to ask herself whether "to [her] home ... any remuneration" would "be worth [her] own personal care" (p. 382). Isabel rapidly comes to understand her own shortcomings as a wife: "I have been absorbed in my own pursuits, and not paid attention enough to details of management and so I have helped to fret and vex my husband," she confesses instantly (p. 383). She recognizes that her literary compulsion has been "a great tempter," and asks Fitzjocelyn to take the manuscript of her poem away from her so that she is forced to concentrate on domestic duties, as she "can have only one thought now – how to make James [her husband] happier and more at ease" (p. 383).

The conflict once recognized is soon resolved. Yonge's narrative includes no lingering difficulties or hesitations, with the effect that the problems of the woman writer, though they are presented here, are also minimized. Isabel's traditional femininity is confirmed by the speed with which she learns to enjoy childcare and domestic management; her literary ability is indicated by her readiness in contriving to work on her writing in the brief interludes between her various tasks. Her rewards for this enviable adaptability are professional as well as domestic – like Aurora Leigh, she "has it all." Her writing improves, becoming "more terse and expressive than anything she used to write when composition was the order of the day" (p. 419). Her long poem is published, is a success, and sells "very well" (p. 474). Not only is her fifth child the awaited son, but this son is immediately made the heir to the estates of a rich relation. In the conflict which Yonge acknowledges between the literary and the domestic in the life of a woman writer, she accords a clear priority to the domestic. Like Barrett Browning and Gaskell in their very different narratives she is compelled to stress the womanly in her version of the woman writer. All the same, Yonge manipulates her narrative so that literary ambitions are represented as permissible, even laudable, in a woman if they are duly subordinated. Moreover she presents honor and success in both fields as not only attainable but desirable.

Isabel readily learns to balance the different claims on her time and attention, giving priority to the practical without ignoring the intellectual. Yonge's narrative involves three couples, all experiencing similar tensions between intellectual and practical activities, Isabel and James, Viscount Fitzjocelyn (Louis) and Mary Ponsonby, and Charlotte Arnold (Isabel's maid) and Tom Madison (Louis' protégé). In this novel, Yonge repeatedly presents adjustments of gender roles as essential to a successful marriage, and expresses these adjustments in all classes through the tension between the intellectual and the practical. Louis Fitzjocelyn – a brilliant and charming dilettante and a skilled writer himself – must learn practicality and perseverance, while his "honest" and "downright" Mary (p. 106) needs intellectual stimulus. Yonge presents Louis as innately feminine in character and as acquiring masculine characteristics conscientiously, just as in *The Daisy Chain* Ethel May's femininity was acquired through the exercise of will and conscience. Louis closely resembles his pretty mother (*Dynevor Terrace*, p. 62) and "gentleness, affection, humility and refinement were in his nature... Indolence of will, facility of disposition, unsteadiness of purpose, inconsiderate impulses without perseverance, had all betokened an inherent weakness... but ... *religion ... had made a man of Louis*" (p. 470, my emphasis). Despite his distaste for political ambitions and preference for more intellectual pursuits, he becomes a distinguished Member of Parliament and an able "man-of-business" (p. 473) as well as a trustworthy support for Mary, whom he marries in the course of the novel. She, in turn, has to undergo a transformation in reverse. Naturally practical, she is "the one person who can see clearly and keep [Louis] steady" (p. 195), yet her mother anxiously postpones their engagement in the fear that Mary will be Louis' protective "husband" rather than his dependent "wife," as she expresses it (p. 196). Through reading and talking with Louis, Mary acquires a literary understanding that increases her feminine sensibility: "if her steadfast spirit had strengthened [Louis'] wavering resolution, the intercourse and sympathy with him had opened and unfolded many a perception and quality in her . . . A wider range had been given to her thoughts; there was a swelling of heart, a vividness of sensation such as she had not known" (p. 281). "Sensation" and emotion ("swelling of heart") are conventionally associated with the feminine: thus as Louis becomes stronger and more manly, Mary becomes vulnerable and more womanly, and the gender balance is achieved when at last she can lean on him, as "not the mere lad she had loved with a guiding motherly love but *a man* to respect and rely on" (p. 458, my emphasis). The central narrative depends on their gradual acquisition of the appropriate gender characteristics, which enables them to conform to conventional patterns of authority within marriage. Yonge insists on traditional domestic roles; a wife must not take on the role either of mother or of husband to her spouse. In this novel the means of adjusting the traditional balance is represented as reading and writing.

Yonge's working-class characters are involved in a similar adjustment. *Dynevor Terrace* is remarkable for its period in that it treats the marriage-plot of the servants as seriously and at almost as great length as those of the employers: the novel indeed ends with their wedding.[13] The maidservant Charlotte is a working-class Isabel, a delicate beauty – a "perfect Lady of Eschalott," according to Louis (p. 39) – with considerable "refinement and imagination" (p. 5), given (again like Isabel) to escaping into literature from an unsatisfying daily life – in her case, endless housework and domestic drudgery rather than parties and morning visits. Under stress she resorts to "the most violent fit of novel reading that had ever been known" and chanting "dismal ballads" as she works (p. 260). Like Isabel, Charlotte must learn to curb her literary propensities. She gives up "novels and sentiment" as Isabel gives up her obsessive writing (p. 393).[14] Thus, though a literary butler attempts to seduce Charlotte with songs and magazine verses, she has learned enough self-restraint to remain true to Tom, whose intellectual attainments are less showy but more profound. He starts out as a gardener's boy with "a loutish air" (p. 1), but with Charlotte's encouragement manages to "educate [him]self like Edmund in *The Old English Baron*" (p. 2), and with Louis' guidance, he acquires both religion and learning. His reading eventually includes "Spenser, Shakespeare, 'Don Quixote,' Calderon, Fouqué and selections from Jeremy Taylor" (p. 331); literary taste here is used as a gauge of moral character. Tom and Charlotte are rewarded by a happy marriage on Tom's earnings of 180 pounds a year as a Spanish-speaking confidential clerk. In their narrative again, literary involvement is shown as a benign agent of social adjustment, and here the adjustment involves social class as well as gender.

The reiterated variations on the related themes of gender roles in marriage and the balance of intellectual and practical duties extend the range of this domestic novel, while retaining its essentially domestic flavor. The domestic sphere here tends to be enlarged to include the practical in general: large landowners like Louis have management responsibilities that resemble the middle-class housewife's, so that both Louis and Isabel must learn to restrain their literary tastes and cultivate management skills in order to fulfill the duties of their stations, which depend on social class and gender. In fact, this novel domesticizes society, representing various interacting social worlds as operating most successfully through a domestic morality based on an immediate and practical concern with the economic and physical as well as spiritual welfare of other people.[15] The literary plays a significant part in this domesticized society for men and women alike: if Charlotte and Isabel must wean themselves partly from the written word in order to be more practical, Mary must learn to be less exclusively practical by developing her literary sensibilities. If Louis must learn to work, Tom must learn to think. Yonge presents a feminized and domesticized world, but in this world her characters must define themselves not only as men and women but as readers and writers.

As a novel about readers and writers, *Dynevor Terrace* must be read in the context of contemporary treatments of the literary woman; but its interlaced marriage plots also implicitly respond to another aspect of the developing debate over the position of women. *Dynevor Terrace* repeatedly insists on the traditional financial roles of men and women – traditional in fiction if not in life. The cases of wives, sisters, daughters, and mothers in mid-Victorian Britain who provided for their families through literature are well known, and include Mary Molesworth, Mary Elizabeth Braddon, Margaret Oliphant, and Elizabeth Sewell. All the same, Isabel is made to learn that "it does not answer for the wife to be the breadwinner" (p. 382), Louis finally marries the once well-to-do Mary with "nothing ... but Mary herself" (p. 474), and Tom earns Charlotte (and Charlotte's retirement into a financial dependence) with his 180 pounds per annum. Yonge's treatment both of power roles and of financial arrangements in marriage suggests her conservative attitude toward proposed changes in the laws affecting marital relations. Barbara Leigh Smith Bodichon's useful *Brief Summary in Plain Language of the Most Important Laws concerning Women* had been published in 1854, making the implications of the relative legal positions of husband and wife plain even to those who had not followed the arguments arising from the Norton affair.[16] In 1856 the House of Commons received more than seventy petitions supporting changes in the Married Woman's Property Law (Holcombe, *Wives and Property*, pp. 237–38), and the Married Woman's Property Bill was put forward in the House of Commons and rejected in 1857, the year which also saw the passing of the Divorce Act, which made divorce slightly less difficult. At a later stage in the debate Yonge expressed her support for the *status quo* at greater length in *The Three Brides* (1876); here it is merely worth noting that her three narratives of a supportive male and a dependent female depict a convention that was a matter of current political argument.

Yonge's interest in writing that reflects on writing continues throughout her career. While *Dynevor Terrace*'s Isabel Conway is Yonge's most developed version of the woman writer, she is by no means her last. Yonge's later women writers include Ermine Williams in *The Clever Woman of the Family* (1865), a successful columnist and the assistant editor of a magazine; Geraldine Underwood, who although she is primarily a painter also contributes to and helps to edit her brother's small town paper (*The Pillars of the House*); Elizabeth Merrifield, a children's novelist, as well as a journalist and public speaker ("Come to Her Kingdom," *The Two Sides of the Shield, Modern Broods*); and Arthurine Arthuret, who writes satirical sketches ("Come to Her Kingdom"). All these women, like Isabel, are involved in narratives that stress either the domestic or the moral responsibilities of the woman writer. For instance *The Two Sides of the Shield* provides a version of the *Female Quixote / Northanger Abbey* plot, in which a young woman is temporarily misled by her reading. This novel, however, is a variant on the type in dealing with the woman writer as well as the woman reader – women are not merely consumers of literature but also producers in Yonge's world. Dolores and the family of the aunt who is her guardian are made unhappy because "barbarous

aunts have come in" to fashion in the popular fiction that Dolores avidly
reads (*The Two Sides*, vol. II, p. 157). Elizabeth Merrifield, who in an early
publication has carelessly contributed to this fictional vogue, is overcome with shame and vows in future to write "conscientiously" (p. 158)
and to take "all the pains I can to make [fiction] useful" (p. 159). She
advises an aspiring woman writer "always to think of the impression for
good or evil produced on the reader as well as the effectiveness of the
story" (p. 159–60) and to ignore widespread critical disapproval of
didactic fiction. Yonge rationalizes the literary ambitions of her women
writers by representing them as sharing their author's avowed sense of
mission. At the beginning of her career, she had justified her own
novel-writing to a dubious and terrifying father by describing her aims
in writing as being moral rather than creative – as directed to "being
useful to young girls like myself" ("Lifelong Friends," p. 183). Her
women writers are thus justified either as didactic in their purposes –
"useful" – or as in need of money for their families, or both. They fulfill
their religious duties through their professional as well as their domestic
activities.

This limited and utilitarian view of her vocation determined in part
the changing response to Yonge's fiction during her own lifetime. All the
evidence suggests that she acquiesced readily in the "rigorous censorship of what [women] could read or write" (Kaplan, "The Right to
Write," p. 454) and the women writers she portrays share in this acquiescence. Nicola Thompson is surely right in arguing that the generally
favorable reception of such early works as *The Heir of Redclyffe* was largely
facilitated by this conformity to mid-Victorian conventions of gender in
literature. Yet in her acquiescence to censorship Yonge aligns herself
with traditions of women's writing that by the late 1850s were being
questioned, as I suggested at the beginning of this chapter, and that
would also rapidly become largely outmoded. By 1862, Cobbe could
credibly distinguish the "weak and washy" female artists of former times
with the "true and powerful" artists of her own day. She emphasizes the
need for women to treat their writing both seriously and independently,
and to reject the conventional gender-based muffling of their voices:

Writing is an art and as an art it should be seriously pursued. Female artists
hitherto always started on a wrong track; being persuaded beforehand that they
ought only to compose soft verses and soft pictures they set themselves to make
them accordingly, and left us Mrs. Hemans' works and Angelica's paintings. *Now*
women who possess any real genius apply it to what they (and not society for
them) really admire. A woman naturally admires power, force, grandeur. It is

these qualities then which we shall see more and more appearing as the spontaneous genius of woman asserts itself. (Cobbe, "What Shall We Do," p. 370)

Cobbe here, in expecting "power, force, grandeur," distinguishes her critical stance sharply from earlier theorists of women's writing, such as Mary Ann Stodart, who had in 1847 argued that women "cannot ... ascend to the height of great argument," or "dive into the deep recesses of the human heart," although they are capable of expressing "light and delicate moments" ("Female Writers," p. 389). Yonge makes a tacit assumption, evident in her representation of Isabel, of other female writers, and of her own career, that women writers would voluntarily restrict themselves to "light and delicate moments." This assumption aligns her with a code that is not only repressive but also largely outdated.

Other popular women novelists chose to dissociate themselves explicitly from such an unquestioning acceptance of professional limitations. They pointedly refer to Yonge's novels, but invariably with a touch of satire or condescension that distances her work from their own. Oliphant, for instance, who is herself hardly a radical at any stage of her career, makes it clear that her representations of middle-class families are to be regarded as more scrupulously realistic than Yonge's. She names the clerical family in *Phoebe Junior* (1873) "May," like the family in *The Daisy Chain*, only to allow her characters to deny firmly any resemblance to their predecessors. When Phoebe notes that the Mays' name is memorable "because of a family in a novel that I used to admire very much in my girlish days," young Janey May responds indignantly, "We are not a set of prigs like those people. We are not goody whatever we are" (*Phoebe Junior*, p. 141). The situation of the Mays in *Phoebe Junior* in fact parodies that of the Mays in *The Daisy Chain*: Ursula May is left like Ethel May to manage the house for her widowed father and her brothers and sisters, but unlike Ethel she resents the task, avoids it when possible, and has little respect for her father, who is in turn a far less attractive character than Yonge's Dr. May. And Yonge, in turn, indicates that the misplaced cynicism of a schoolboy character arises from the fact that he is "better read in Trollope and Mrs. Oliphant than his sisters."[17]

Similarly, Mary Elizabeth Braddon uses allusions to Yonge's fiction to establish her own characters, though in a more simple way than Oliphant's. In *Aurora Floyd* (1863) the fair, biddable Lucy – much like Lucy in *The Mill on the Floss* – or Lucille in *Corinne* – is a foil for her dark and more energetic cousin, the wildly attractive Aurora, and Lucy's

essential passivity, timidity, and conventional femininity – her inferiority to Aurora, in fact – is indicated by a taste for Yonge's fiction. Louisa
May Alcott, whose success was founded largely on a portrayal of a
young woman – Jo March – fired with literary ambition which has a
strong relationship with Yonge's earlier portrait of Ethel May, is also
quite dismissive. In her story, "Pansies" (1887), Alcott uses an addiction
to Yonge to indicate not passivity so much as immaturity. The childish
Eva speaks with enthusiasm of "dear Miss Yonge, with her nice large
families and their trials and their pious ways and pleasant homes full of
brothers and sisters and good fathers and mothers. I'm never tired of
them and have read 'Daisy Chain' nine times at least" ("Pansies,"
pp. 81–82). The wise old woman who provides the literary advice in this
story sees Eva as in need of discovering "new and better helpers for the
real trials of life" (p. 85) and directs her toward biographies, once more
implying that Yonge's works romanticize and sweeten the realities of
female existence.[18]

Oliphant, Braddon, and Alcott use Yonge to suggest limitation and
falsification, by implication differentiating their various brands of popular fiction from hers. As Kate Flint suggests in discussing the "self-
referential" use of such allusions to reading practices:

> To draw attention to what is involved in certain types of reading ... acts as a
> comment on the status of the text in which such a reference is to be found. It
> thus emphasizes the compliance, or otherwise, of this text with established
> conventions concerning both fictional form and the response of readers, and
> alerts the reader to pay attention to the implications of her own practice, and to
> be aware of her own expectations of a novel. (*The Woman Reader*, p. 256)

Other popular women novelists, in associating Yonge with less realistic
or less dynamic modes, claim a different status for their own fiction and
for their readers. And Yonge lent herself to such a portrayal, by her
careful avoidance of what might be perceived as coarse or unfeminine.
From *Dynevor Terrace* in 1857 onwards Yonge is remarkable in continuing
steadily to represent successful and dedicated women writers. Yet in
ignoring the transgressive claims to power and freedom voiced in
precisely contemporary representations of the woman writer, she aligns
herself with the more restricted gender codes of her own youth.

NOTES

1 Cora Kaplan's preface to *Aurora Leigh* comments on the importance of this
issue to "a male-dominated ruling class, increasingly threatened from below

by an organizing proletariat" ("The Right to Write," in Elizabeth Barrett Browning. *Aurora Leigh*, ed. Margaret Reynolds [New York: Norton, 1996], p. 455).

2 "Domestic Life" in the *English Women's Journal* 2 (1858), 73–82, quoted by Candida Ann Lacey in her introduction to *Barbara Leigh Smith Bodichon and the Langham Place Group* (New York and London: Routledge, 1987). The Society for the Promotion of Employment for Women was founded in 1859; see Joan N. Burstyn, *Victorian Education and the Ideal of Womanhood* (Totowa, NJ: Barnes and Noble, 1980), p. 127; Sheila Herstein, *A Mid-Victorian Feminist, Barbara Leigh Smith Bodichon* (New Haven, CT: Yale University Press, 1985), pp. 125–48; and Frances Power Cobbe, "What Shall We Do With Our Old Maids," in Candida Ann Lacey (ed.), *Barbara Leigh Smith Bodichon and the Langham Place Group* (New York and London: Routledge, 1987).

3 Dorothy Mermin's *Godiva's Ride: Women of Letters in England, 1830–1880* (Bloomington: Indiana University Press, 1993) discusses this question at length.

4 Margaret Oliphant's *The Athelings*, published in the same year, includes a woman writer, but does not explore the theme as fully.

5 See Margaret Mare and Alicia C. Percival, *Victorian Best-seller: the World of Charlotte M. Yonge* (London: Harrap, 1947), 207 for Yonge's response to historical fiction. For her response to the sensation fiction vogue, see June Sturrock, "Sequels, Series and the Sensation Novel: Charlotte Yonge's *The Trial*," in B. Schellenberg and P. Budra (eds.), Part II: *Theorizing the Sequel* (University of Toronto Press, 1998).

6 Nicola Thompson discusses *Wuthering Heights* as an especially interesting case in *Reviewing Sex: Gender and the Reception of Victorian Novels* (London: Macmillan; New York: New York University Press, 1996), pp. 42–65.

7 See, for instance, Juliet Barker, *The Brontës* (London: Weidenfield and Nicolson, 1994), p. 829.

8 At the same time George Eliot was beginning her own career as a novelist. She wrote: "September 1856 made a new era in my life for it was then that I began to write fiction" ("How I Came to Write Fiction," p. 322). See also "Women in France: Madame de Sable" (1855), a comparison of Margaret Fuller and Mary Wollstonecraft (1855), and, notably, "Silly Novels by Lady Novelists" (1856), all in *Selected Essays by George Eliot* (Oxford: Oxford University Press, 1992).

9 The admittedly anachronistic epithet "antifeminist" is based on such direct statements as "I have no hesitation in declaring my full belief in the inferiority of women, nor that she brought it upon herself" (*Womankind* [London: Mozeley and Smith, 1877], p. 1).

10 For women as public performers see Mermin (*Godiva's Ride*, pp. 17, 143).

11 See Mare and Percival (*Victorian Best-seller*, pp. 143, 208) for Yonge's delight in chatting about her work.

12 In the earlier *Scenes and Characters* Lilias Mohun writes poetry but makes no attempt at publication.

13 See Bruce Robbins, *The Servant's Hand: English Fiction from Below* (New York: Columbia University Press, 1986), p. 6 for the normal parodic treatment of servants in the novel of the period.

14 See Kathleen Tillotson for discussion of the roles of Isabel and Charlotte ("Charlotte Yonge as a Critic of Literature," in G. Battiscome and M. Laski (eds.), *A Chaplet for Charlotte M. Yonge* [London: Cresset Press, 1965], pp. 56–57).

15 Other novels by Yonge show a similar blurring of gender boundaries, notably *The Pillars of the House*; see June Sturrock, *"Heaven and Home": Charlotte Mary Yonge's Domestic Fiction and the Victorian Debate over Women* (Victoria: University of Victoria Press), pp. 104–07, where other contemporary instances are cited.

16 Caroline Norton left an abusive husband, who refused her an allowance; her property had all become his automatically, in accordance with the current law on property and marriage. Caroline Norton's literary career was quite profitable, but her husband asserted the right, which was his in law, to all his wife's earnings. He later abducted her three sons and refused to let her see them. Her three pamphlets on her situation helped to change laws about custody, and, much later, about married women's property.

17 *Beechcroft at Rockstone* (London: Macmillan and Co., 1893), p. 263.

18 However, in *Jo's Boys* (1886) she refers to "our dear Miss Yonge" and "her interesting tales" (Harmondsworth: Penguin, 1986), p. 223.

WORKS CITED

Alcott, Louisa May, "Pansies," in *A Garland for Girls*, New York: Grossett and Dunlap, 1942.

Jo's Boys, Harmondsworth: Penguin, 1986.

Allott, Miriam, *The Brontës: The Critical Heritage*, London: Routledge and Kegan Paul, 1974.

Barker, Juliet, *The Brontës*, London: Weidenfeld and Nicolson, 1994.

Battiscombe, Georgina, *Charlotte Mary Yonge: The Story of an Uneventful Life*, London: Constable, 1944.

Braddon, Mary Elizabeth, *Aurora Floyd*, London: Virago, 1984.

Browning, Elizabeth Barrett, *Aurora Leigh*, ed. Margaret Reynolds, New York: Norton, 1996.

Burstyn, Joan N., *Victorian Education and the Ideal of Womanhood*, Totowa, NJ: Barnes and Noble, 1980.

Cobbe, Frances Power. "What Shall We Do with Our Old Maids," in Candida Ann Lacey (ed.), *Barbara Leigh Smith Bodichon and the Langham Place Group*, New York and London: Routledge, 1987, pp. 354–77.

Easson, Angus, *Elizabeth Gaskell: The Critical Heritage*, London: Routledge and Kegan Paul, 1979.

Eliot, George, "Women of France: Madame de Sable," *Selected Essays by George Eliot*, Oxford: Oxford University Press, 1992.

"Silly Novels by Lady Novelists," in *Selected Essays by George Eliot.* Oxford: Oxford University Press, 1992.

Flint, Kate, *The Woman Reader 1837–1914*, Oxford: Clarendon Press, 1993.

Fraser, Rebecca, *Charlotte Brontë*, London: Methuen, 1988.

Gaskell, Elizabeth, *The Life of Charlotte Brontë*, Harmondsworth: Penguin, 1975.

Gordon, Lyndall, *Charlotte Brontë: A Passionate Life*, London: Chatto and Windus, 1994.

Herstein, Sheila, *A Mid-Victorian Feminist, Barbara Leigh Smith Bodichon*, New Haven, CT: Yale University Press, 1985.

Holcombe, Lee, *Wives and Property: Reform of the Married Women's Property Law in Nineteenth Century England*, Toronto: University of Toronto Press, 1983.

Kaplan, Cora, "The Right to Write," in Elizabeth Barrett Browning, *Aurora Leigh*, ed. Margaret Reynolds, pp. 453–56.

Lacey, Candida Ann (ed)., *Barbara Leigh Smith Bodichon and the Langham Place Group*, New York and London: Routledge, 1988.

Mare, Margaret and Alicia C. Percival, *Victorian Best-seller: The World of Charlotte M. Yonge*, London: Harrap, 1947.

Mermin, Dorothy, *Godiva's Ride: Women of Letters in England*, 1830–1880, Bloomington: Indiana University Press, 1993.

Elizabeth Barrett Browning: The Origins of a New Poetry, Chicago: Chicago University Press, 1989.

Nichol, John, "Aurora Leigh." in Elizabeth Barrett Browning, *Aurora Leigh*, ed. Margaret Reynolds, pp. 402–04.

Oliphant, Margaret, *Phoebe Junior*, London: Virago, 1989.

Robbins, Bruce, *The Servant's Hand: English Fiction from Below*, New York: Columbia University Press, 1986.

Robinson, Solveig C., "Amazed at Our Success: The Langham Place Editors and the Emergence of a Feminist Critical Tradition," *Victorian Periodicals Review 29* (1996), 159–72.

Stone, Marjorie, *Elizabeth Barrett Browning*, New York: St. Martin's Press, 1995.

Stodart, Mary Ann, "Female Writers," in Elizabeth Barrett Browning, *Aurora Leigh*, ed. Margaret Reynolds, pp. 387–91.

Sturrock, June, *"Heaven and Home": Charlotte Mary Yonge's Domestic Fiction and the Victorian Debate over Women*, Victoria: University of Victoria Press, 1995.

"Sequels, Series and the Sensation Novel: Charlotte Yonge's *The Trial*," in B. Schellenberg and P. Budra (eds.), *Part II: Theorizing the Sequel*, University of Toronto Press, 1998.

Thompson, Nicola Diane, *Reviewing Sex: Gender and the Reception of Victorian Novels*, London: Macmillan; New York: New York University Press, 1996.

Tillotson, Kathleen, "Charlotte Yonge as a Critic of Literature," in G. Battiscome and M. Laski (eds.), *A Chaplet for Charlotte M. Yonge*, London: Cresset Press, 1965, pp. 54–62.

Uglow, Jenny, *George Eliot*, London: Virago, 1987.

Yonge, Charlotte Mary, *The Daisy Chain, or Aspirations: A Family Chronicle*, London: Virago, 1982.

Dynevor Terrace: or, the Clue of Life, London: Macmillan, 1908.

The Clever Woman of the Family, London: Virago, 1985.

The Pillars of the House: Or Under Wode, Under Rode, 2 vols., London: Macmillan and Co., 1889.

Womankind, London: Mozeley and Smith, 2nd edn., 1877.

The Two Sides of the Shield, 2 vols., London: Macmillan and Co., 1885.

Beechcroft at Rockstone, London: Macmillan and Co., 1893.

"Come to Her Kingdom," in *More Bywords*, London: Macmillan and Co., 1890, pp. 188–244.

"Lifelong Friends." in G. Battiscome and M. Laski (eds.), *A Chaplet for Charlotte. M. Yonge*, London: Cresset Press, 1965, pp. 181–84.

Modern Broods: Or, Developments Unlooked For, London: Macmillan, 1900.

CHAPTER 8

Portraits of the artist as a young woman: representations of the female artist in the New Woman fiction of the 1890s

Lyn Pykett

> When you grow up, I think you will want to do something that only
> a few people can do well – paint a picture, write a book, act in the
> theatre, make music – it doesn't matter what; it if comes to you . . .
> just do it . . . And don't ask anybody if they think you can do it;
> they'll be sure to say no; and then you'll be disheartened. (Beth
> Caldwell's father addressing his daughter in Sarah Grand's *The
> Beth Book*)[1]

In a recent attempt to categorize a distinctive genre of New Woman
fiction and, in particular, to distinguish it from those *fin-de-siècle* novels
(often written by men) which are merely *about* the New Woman, Ann
Heilmann writes: "[I]n its most typical form, New Woman fiction is
feminist fiction written by women, and deals with middle-class heroines
who in some way re-enact autobiographical dilemmas faced by the
writers themselves . . . [it is] a genre at the interface between auto/
biography, fiction and feminist propaganda."[2] In this chapter I shall
explore the "feminism" of the New Woman fiction – a feminism so
fraught with contradictions, and apparently so preoccupied with narratives of female failure, that it sometimes appears to be antifeminist – by
examining the "interface", in a number of nineties fictions by women,
"between auto/biography, fiction and feminist propaganda," or, to use
terms which are probably more useful than the latter in this context,
feminist debate and polemic. I shall focus on an important aspect of the
New Woman fiction's engagement with the woman question in the
1890s: the uses made of the figure of the female artist in *fin-de-siècle*
variants of the semi-autobiographical *Kunstlerroman*, a narrative form
which was to become an important aspect of modernist writing.[3]

Most commonly the female artist represented in the work of the New
Woman novelists is the woman writer (or aspiring writer), as for
example in George Egerton's stories in *Keynotes* (1893) and *Discords* (1894)

and her novel *The Wheel of God* (1898); in Ella Hepworth Dixon's *The Story of a Modern Woman* (1894); C. E. Raimond's (Elizabeth Robins) *George Mandeville's Husband* (1894); George Paston's (Emily Morse Symonds') *A Modern Amazon* (1894) and *A Writer of Books* (1898); Sarah Grand's *The Beth Book* (1987); and Mary Cholmondeley's *Red Pottage* (1899). Occasionally the female artist is a musician, as in Mona Caird's *The Daughters of Danaus* (1894), whose heroine is a pianist and aspiring composer; or a painter, as in Dixon's *The Story of a Modern Woman*, and in *A Daughter of Today* (1894), by the London-based Canadian novelist, Mrs. Everard Cotes. In each of these latter works the heroine abandons her ambition to be a painter in order to earn her living as a journalist and writer of fiction.

It is not difficult to see why the figure of the female artist (and especially the woman writer) should have featured so prominently and so frequently in the work of the New Woman novelists and short story writers. It is an example of their turn to autobiography and of their claims for the authority of a distinctive women's experience "[n]ow that woman is conscious of her individuality as a woman."[4] The use of the female artist figure is also a component of the self-reflexivity that characterizes much New Woman writing: as I have suggested elsewhere, by making writing women its subject New Woman fiction foregrounds the conditions of its own production.[5] Perhaps most important of all, as the quotation at the head of this chapter indicates, the female artist serves as a compound figure for the exceptional or aspiring woman and for the obstacles that she will inevitably encounter in attempting to realize her aspirations in the face of dominant social definitions of femininity. It is one of the many paradoxes and contradictions of New Woman fiction of the 1890s, that at a time in which women writers were so numerous, commercially successful and much discussed in the newspaper and periodical press, their books should have focused so frequently and minutely on the conflicts, frustrations, and the compromised or thwarted careers and/or vocations of the professional woman writer and the aspiring woman artist. New Woman fiction is littered with would-be literary artists, painters, and musicians who break down or give in under the pressures of the various circumstances which conspire against them, and end up as lonely spinsters, or happily – or, more usually, unhappily – married wives and mothers, whose aesthetic ambitions have declined (if they survive in any form at all) into the weary labor of the hack writer or journalist.

In sharp contrast to the fictional plot of artistic ambition thwarted by inimical conditions, many of the women writers of the 1890s published memoirs or autobiographical essays, or gave interviews in which they told a very different story about their sense of their artistic vocation, the circumstances in which they wrote, and their experiences of becoming published writers. These autobiographical works are often significantly different in tone from their authors' fictional representations of the female artist, who generally (although by no means uniformly) has less fun, is more tortured, and less successful than her creator. Ella Hepworth Dixon provides one of the most striking examples of this discrepancy between the life and the work. It is tempting to assume that Dixon's sharply observed portrait of the aspiring woman artist in her novel of 1894 is fictionalized autobiography. It is possible that this portrait may indeed derive from Dixon's own experience. However, nothing could be further removed from the claustrophobic and self-confessedly "gloomy study of the struggles of a girl alone in the world and earning her own living"[6] by writing in *The Story of a Modern Woman*, than the colorful descriptions of the gregarious life of its author among the glitterati of the "Gay Nineties," which is found in her collection of autobiographical sketches, *As I Knew Them: Sketches of People I Have Met on the Way*. Compare, for example, the fictional Mary Erle's embarrassed and humiliating attempts to enter the literary marketplace in chapter ten of *The Story of a Modern Woman* ("In Grub Street"), and the rejection of her novel by the editor of *Illustrations*, on the grounds that "the public ... want thoroughly healthy reading" and "won't stand" a book such as her own in which "there's a young man making love to his friend's wife,"[7] with Dixon's description of her own initiation to the literary life.

In the 'nineties, I "commenced author" – first with a book under a pseudonym, the illustrations by Mr. Bernard Partridge, contributing much to its success, and, in 1894, with *The Story of a Modern Woman*, a somewhat gloomy study of the struggles of a girl alone in the world and earning her own living. To my great surprise, it caught at once. Mr. T. P. O'Connor, ever generous to young authors, devoted the whole front page of his *Sunday Weekly* to it; Mr. W. T. Stead made much of it in the *Review of Reviews. (As I Knew Them, p. 136)*

Just as striking is the difference between the way in which the act of writing (or any other form of aesthetic production) is represented in fiction and in published autobiography and interviews. Women writers *in* fiction not only find it difficult to place their work, they also find it difficult to produce it, as in this description of the toils of an unnamed woman writer in George Egerton's "Wedlock."

She is writing for money, writing because she must, because it is the tool given to her wherewith to carve her way; she is nervous, overwrought, every one of her fingers seems as if it had a burning nerve-knot in its tip ... she is writing furiously now, for she has been undergoing the agony of a barren period for some weeks, her brain has seemed arid as a sand plain.[8]

Women writers *of* fiction, on the other hand, tend to focus – at least in their public pronouncements – on their creative spontaneity, and fecundity. Margaret Diane Stetz cites the examples of Jean Middlemass, Charlotte Riddell, and Helen Mathers (Mrs. Reeves), each of whom claims, in interview with Helen C. Black, that writing comes easily and rapidly. Mathers, for example, asserts that "ideas seem to run out of my pen," and Riddell claims to reproduce with ease and rapidity in the morning, novels which had shaped themselves in the "border-land of sleep and waking."[9]

What are we to make of the difference between Dixon's representation of the female author in her fiction and in her autobiographical writing? What are we to make of the difference between the trials and usually gloomy fictional fate of the would-be woman writer or artist, and the accounts given to Helen Black by the "Notable Women Authors of the Day" whom she interviewed for the *Lady's Pictorial?* Clearly the New Woman writers of the 1890s were using the woman artist as a complex figure with multiple significations. First, and rather paradoxically given the nineteenth-century tendency to represent culture as a feminized space, the female artist is represented as an invader of a masculine (or, at least, male-controlled) domain; moreover, whatever her avowed position *vis-à-vis* the woman's cause, the female artist is represented as a feminist or proto-feminist, since artistic expression and the life of the artist are seen as in themselves both liberated and liberatory activities. Secondly, the female artist is used as a device for figuring a conflicted feminine interiority, and for exploring some of the contradictions involved in dominant definitions of (middle-class) femininity, and in the social and material conditions in which middle-class women lived their lives. Thirdly, she is deployed as an intervention in a variety of contemporary debates about the nature and function of art in the modern world: debates about the relationship of high art to commodified cultural production, and about aesthetic representation – about what can be represented, in what manner, by whom, and for whom.[10] Finally, in some cases (most notably in *The Beth Book*) the female artist is used as a way of exploring, from a woman's perspective, the relationship of the aesthetic and the political, and the competing claims of the life of the artist and that of the activist.

The New Woman fiction repeatedly focuses on the difficulties experienced by women who sought to enter the institutions of literature and art practice on their own terms. Those who guard the gates of entry into these institutions – teachers in art schools, members of the Royal Academy, publishers and editors of books and magazines, and professors of music – are, in fiction if not always in fact, male. Women can enter all three domains, but only on the circumscribed terms of what is considered to be suitable to their gender: they are accepted as journeywomen who may (possibly) do decent work in the foothills of literary and artistic production, but they are not expected to conquer the mountains of excellence: Hadria Fullerton's (male) music teacher, for example, regards women's maternal instinct as "the scourge of genius," and a barrier to artistic achievement. As Ella Hepworth Dixon's *The Story of A Modern Woman* indicates, the circumscribed terms on which women are permitted to enter cultural production have been fully internalized by middle-class women as well as by men. Thus Mary Erle's announcement that she wishes to realize her "long-cherished ambition" to become a painter is greeted in very similar terms by both her best female friend and her suitor. Her friend, the otherwise feminist-inclined Alison Ives, opines that "No woman ever made a great artist yet . . . but if you don't mind being third-rate, of course go in and try" (p. 42). Her view that, for a female artist, South Kensington and the Royal Academy will be followed inevitably by "portraits of babies in pastel or cottage gardens for the rest of your life," is complacently echoed by Vincent Hemming (Mary's suitor), who considers painting "especially in water colours . . . an eminently lady-like occupation" (p. 54).

As I have already noted, when Mary abandons painting and seeks to become a professional writer instead, she has to negotiate the masculine and sexist world of the journal office, and the condescending view of women's literary production proffered by the editor of *Illustrations*: "with practice you may be able to write stories that other young ladies like to read" (p. 107). Non-fictional corroboration of this fictional editor's jocular condescension can be found in Arnold Bennett's *Journalism for Women: a Practical Guide* (1898) which implies that all women journalists or aspiring journalists are ill-trained, ungrammatical, fanciful, whimsical, undisciplined, unbusinesslike, and full of excuses for their failures and failings.

As well as using the female artist to emphasize the degree to which, even at the turn of the century, able and (relatively) well-educated middle-class women were still excluded from, or consigned to the margins of, the public sphere of cultural institutions and the professions, several New Woman writers use the woman artist as a means of representing and exploring female subjectivity and "feminine" affectivity. The woman artist is also a vehicle for exploring and (in some cases) celebrating female desire. Mona Caird and Sarah Grand, for example, both use their artist-protagonists, Hadria Fullerton and Beth Caldwell, to represent women as actively desiring and experiencing subjects rather than as merely the passive victims of "feminine" affectivity. Caird, in particular, anatomizes the empowering aspects of the heightened emotional states associated with Hadria's particular suscep-tibility to dance and music. This susceptibility is evidence of her singu-larity: "She, more than the others, seemed to have absorbed the spirit of the northern twilights... Every instinct that was born in her with her Celtic blood ... was fostered by the mystery and wildness of her surroundings."[11] Hadria's susceptibility to music and dance is both a symbol for and a means of self-transcendence, and of transcending the limitations of the social world. Thus her celebrated reel-dancing is a symbol and symptom of her free spirit: "Some mad spirit seemed to possess her. It would appear almost as if she had passed into a different phase of character. She lost all caution and care and the sense of external events" (*The Daughters of Danaus*, p. 136). At the same time, however, Hadria's singularity and susceptibility to aesthetic experience are also represented as disabling, and a source of danger. By making her "more ready to sway on the waves of emotions" they expose her to the sexual advances of predators such as Professor Theobald (p. 384).

The protagonist of Sarah Grand's *The Beth Book* is also represented as an exceptional woman (or, perhaps, several kinds of exceptional woman in succession), as the subtitle of the novel emphasizes – *Being a Study of the Life of Elizabeth Caldwell Maclure, A Woman of Genius*. The first part of this novel (an interesting anticipation of James Joyce's representation of the young Stephen Dedalus) is Grand's portrait of the artist as a young woman, which represents Beth's coming to consciousness in and of language as she emerges from being "as unconscious as a white grub" (*The Beth Book*, p. 10) into an awareness of words and world, and of her relationship to and separateness from her natural and social surround-ings. Beth is depicted as "a fine instrument, sensitive to a touch" (p. 43), with unusually acute senses and a memory which, "from the first," involuntarily associated "incongruous ideas" (p. 17). She is a dreamer and visionary, possessing a "further faculty" which makes her "calm, strong and confident," and gives her access to a vision of life "as if from a height, viewing it both in detail and as a whole" (p. 28). An apparently instinctive poet, she hears poems in her natural surroundings, such as "the song of the sea in the shell" (p. 68).

Mary Cholmondeley's Hester Gresley is also portrayed as "a woman of genius," who writes, not (as so many professional women writers did in the nineteenth century) merely for occupation and for financial reward, but rather because she must. Her writing is a "power," which she recognizes in an epiphanic moment of woman-to-woman identification.

And as Hester leaned against Rachel [her closest friend, and the woman who accompanies her on her travels after she has broken down and abandoned writing] the yearning of her soul towards her suddenly lit up something which had long lain colossal but inapprehended in the depths of her mind. Her paroxysm of despair at her own powerlessness was followed by a lightning flash of self-revelation. She saw, as in a dream, terrible, beautiful, inaccessible, but distinct, where her power lay, of which restless bewildering hints had so often mocked her... The strength as of an infinite ocean swept in beneath her weakness, and bore it upon its surface like a leaf... A year later Hester's first book, "An Idyll of East London," was reaping its harvest of astonished indignation and admiration.[12]

All three of these female artists – the musician, the poet (for Beth is a kind of poet in her childhood and youth), and the novelist – are represented at some point in terms of the discourse of the romantic artist or genius; they each display aspects of the egotistical sublime; they possess innate genius and negative capability, and they have an instinctive yearning to see into the life of things. Penny Boumelha has recently argued that the New Woman writers' preoccupation with the woman of genius is indicative of their evasion of key issues of power and choice, since: "the concept of innate genius enables the representation of achievement without conscious ambition – then, as now, a problematic quality in feminist reconstructions of the feminine. If the power of genius simply resides within, then it becomes only another form of destiny to which women must assent, without challenge to the conventional womanliness of self forgetfulness."[13] Boumelha makes a persuasive case for her interpretation of this late nineteenth-century instance of the contradictory nature of feminist reconstructions of the feminine, linking the female genius represented in the New Woman writing to contemporary gendered discourses on genius and on degeneration. However, I would suggest that the New Woman writers' representation of the female genius is more self-conscious than Boumelha's argument might seem to allow. The New Woman *Kunstlerroman* does not simply reproduce a gendered post-romantic or *fin-de-siècle* discourse of genius as a way of avoiding feminist issues of choice, but rather it engages with contemporary feminist polemic in the way that it explores and exposes (as well as sometimes reproducing), the complexities and contradictions of the relationship between post-romantic conceptions of the artist (or, indeed, of the individual), and dominant conceptions of self-sacrificial domestic femininity. Typically the female artist figure in the New Woman novel is engaged in a complex negotiation of various forms of self-sacrifice: the sacrifice of the self to or for art; the accommodation of her aesthetic ambitions to the demands of the marketplace (so that she may provide for herself or for dependent relatives); the subsuming of her own aesthetic or professional ambitions to those of a male relative; the abandonment of them for domestic duties.

As well as using the female artist figure to explore female desire, and feminine genius, the New Woman writers also use this figure as a way of exposing the contradictions of female desire, and the tensions between women's desires and aspirations, and the nineteenth-century gender system in both its ideological and social and material forms. The plot of thwarted or abandoned genius and aesthetic ambition is replayed in one form or another in each of the novels or stories discussed in detail here, as if to echo and underline Hadria Fullerton's refutation of Emerson's "beaming optimism" (*The Daughters of Danaus*, p. 6) on the question of whether circumstance can always be conquered. The occasion of this refutation is a debate held by the aptly named "Preposterous Society" in the opening chapter of Caird's *The Daughters of Danaus*.

Given (say) great artistic power, given also a conscience and a strong will, is there any combination of circumstances which might prevent the artistic power (assuming it to be of the highest order and strength) from developing and displaying itself, so as to meet with general recognition? . . . There seems to be a thousand chances against it . . . Artistic power, to begin with, is a sort of weakness in relation to the everyday world . . . I think Emerson is shockingly unjust. (pp. 6 ff.)

The injustice is particularly serious, Hadria argues, in relation to "the conditions of a girl's life of our class". These are "pleasant enough", but "they are stifling, absolutely stifling; and not all the Emersons in the world will convince

me to the contrary. Emerson never was a girl . . . If he had been a girl, he would
have known that conditions do count hideously." (p. 14)

Caird's narrative (in common with virtually all of the novels I refer to
here) is constructed so as to demonstrate the extent to which the
material circumstances of a woman "of our class" do indeed count
hideously against aesthetic ambition, or "genius."

Helen Black's interviewees (referred to above), like earlier "womanly" writers such as Elizabeth Gaskell and Margaret Oliphant, repeatedly
represent themselves as reconciling the conflicts between their writing
and their feminine, domestic vocations with cheerfulness and equanim-
ity. Helen Mathers' report of her "laughing" response to habitual
interruptions is typical:

Often, just as I have settled down to do a good morning's work, and have
perhaps finished a page . . . my boy Phil rushes up and lays his air gun or his
banjo on the table, or my husband brings in some little commission or a heap of
notes to be answered for him. I always tell them, "laughing," that everyone
combines to put out of sight the story which is being written, and often it is not
touched again for a week.[14]

In the New Woman fiction this conflict between the self-sacrificial
womanly vocation on the one hand, and the self-expressive artistic
vocation or the productivity demands of the professional career on the
other, is more usually a source of tension, frustration, rebellion and/or
failure than of laughter. A couple of examples must suffice. Unlike
Helen Mathers, Mary Cholmondeley's fictional novelist, Hester Gresley, is so distraught at her inability to cope with the interruptions of the
domestic round (she bursts into tears at being distracted when "in a very
difficult place" in her novel) that she destroys her health by getting up at
5 a.m. in order to write without interruption before the rest of the family
rises. Mona Caird also analyzes the causes and consequences of her
artist-protagonist's efforts to negotiate the pressures of the domestic
ideal:

[H]er greatest effort had to be given, not to the work itself, but to win an
opportunity to pursue it . . . [in the face of her mother's contention that] It was
not good for a girl to be selfishly preoccupied . . .

If Hadria yielded the point on any particular occasion, her mood and her
work were destroyed: if she resisted, they were equally destroyed, through the
nervous disturbance and the intense depression which followed the winning of
liberty too dearly bought . . . [This] process told upon her health . . . the injury
was insidious but serious. Hadria, unable to command any certain part of the
day, began to sit up at night. (*The Daughters of Danaus*, p. 109)

Later in the narrative, when Hadria flies in the face of convention, leaving her husband and child in order to pursue her ambitions to study musical composition in Paris, she still finds her energies dissipated by the social obligations imposed on a woman of her class. As Caird observed in her polemical collection of essays on *The Morality of Marriage*: "anyone [who] wishes to know why many women have not written Shakespeare's plays (as it is generally expressed)" might do well to consider the damaging constraints of "the weary detail of domestic duties, of the unending petty responsibilities, the constant call 'to give small decisions and settle minute emergencies.'"[15]

The New Woman writers, no less than their male contemporaries (for example, William Pett Ridge in *A Clever Wife*, 1895), habitually represent the female artist as succumbing to physical and/or mental breakdown. However, whereas the male writers of the *fin-de-siècle* tend simply to reproduce contemporary medical discourses on hysteria and on the problems of a female physique entirely determined by the reproductive function, the New Woman novelists rewrite those discourses. In the New Woman writing female creativity and aesthetic production are not the by-products of an excess of feminine affectivity or hysteria (as so many male reviewers of the New Woman writing stated or implied), rather it is the frustration of women's creative production by the circumstances of their lives which produces hysteria: women are not the victims of their affectivity and their inferior physical makeup, but of a specific ideology of femininity and specific social and material conditions.

However, if the New Woman writers interrogate the gendered discourse on hysteria, elsewhere they would seem to reproduce the dominant discourse on gender, for example, in the way in which they position their female artist figures in relation to feminine self-sacrifice and maternality. Thus Mary Erle sacrifices her health and her artistic ambitions (in part) in order to give her brother the sort of education that she herself was denied. Beth Caldwell performs similar sacrifices in order to nurse the man with whom she is eventually to be united. Hadria Fullerton is returned to her wifely and maternal duties after her attempts to free herself from them in order to pursue her musical ambitions, and in any case the "costs" of pursuing her aesthetic ambitions are persistently measured against those incurred by the successful "womanly" novelist Valeria Du Prel, whose literary success has entailed (as she sees it) the sacrifice of marriage and motherhood. Cholmondeley's Hester Gresley apparently rejects marriage and motherhood in favor of her writing vocation, but the novel's language suggests that the latter is merely a displaced version of her womanly vocation: she discusses her book "as a young girl talks of her lover" (*Red Pottage*, p. 80), and she likens her second novel, which is destroyed by her disapproving clergyman brother, to a murdered child: "when Regie [her brother's son] was ill ... I did what I could. I did not let your child die. Why have you killed mine?" (p. 276). The New Woman writers may thus be seen as challenging, but also as being contained by contemporary discourses of femininity. They are also caught up in contradictory feminisms. On the one hand they explore (and sometimes seem to propound) the equal opportunities of feminism which argued for the extension of education and employment to women, and for the right for women to live their lives as independently as men did. On the other hand, they espouse the *magna mater* strand of feminism which glorified the superior morality and spirituality of the maternal woman, and saw feminization as the means of saving the race.

The final aspect of the New Woman writers' use of the female artist which I want to examine is the role this figure played in their intervention in contemporary debates about the nature and function of art. I noted earlier that the New Woman *Künstlerroman* has a recurrent pattern in which the aspiring female artist begins or ends in New Grub Street, as a researcher, hack writer, or journalist. The woman artist and her *alter ego* the woman of New Grub Street are regularly deployed in their author's intervention in contemporary debates about the relationship of women and "the feminine" to the commercialization of art in a mass culture. In the New Woman writing the woman of New Grub Street is a multi-accented sign. As Penny Boumelha argues, she confirms the nineteenth-century "association of femininity with trash: with commerce ... with the values of the marketplace ... and inferior aesthetic values," but, at the same time, she also represents the goals of many late nineteenth-century feminists: "professionalisation, career, financial independence, and the opportunity to manifest talent."[16] However, this same figure of the aspiring (and usually failing) female artist is also frequently represented, at least at some point in her development or decline, as oppositional and avant-garde: she is opposed both to conventional social and gender roles and to the debased values of the commercial marketplace, and she is seeking an authentic aesthetic mode that will enable her to articulate the truths of modern experience. Thus Caird's Hadria aspires to produce a new kind of music, which, as her teacher, Professor Jouffroy, remarks will expose her to the painful possibility of being misunderstood, "derided for departure from old rules and conventions," and of having her work "despised and refused, till at last the dull ears shall be opened and all the stupid world shall run shouting to her feet" (*The Daughters of Danaus*, p. 319). The artistic failures and frustrations of Dixon's Mary Erle similarly derive from the stupidity of the world, and more particularly, from the market's inability to accommodate her aspiration to write a realist novel that would tell the truth of modern life. In short, in the figure of the female artist (notwithstanding her failure) the New Woman writers reverse the dominant discourse on the degeneration of contemporary culture which equates commercialization and inauthenticity with feminization.

Sarah Grand's *The Beth Book* introduces a different aspect of the debate about the nature and function of art in modernity. Grand departs from the dominant pattern of the New Woman *Kunstlerroman* by constructing a narrative in which her heroine self-consciously abandons (rather than simply fails to realize) aesthetic ambition. In this narrative the key opposition is that between art for art's sake and art for money's sake, on the one hand, and writing with a purpose, on the other. In other words aestheticism and commerce are bracketed together in opposition to social action or politics. To some extent this opposition is replicated in each of the novels on which I have focused in this chapter. In each of them the debates about the competing claims of art and the marketplace which center on the female artist/woman of New Grub Street, are positioned in relation to debates about social intervention and political action which center on another female character: Hadria's sister, Algitha, in *The Daughters of Danaus*; Hester's friend, Rachel, in *Red Pottage*; the philanthropist Alison Ives in *The Story of A Modern Woman*; Ideala and her circle in *The Beth Book*.

It is interesting to note that while contemporary male reviewers and critics (in reality as well as in fiction) attributed the failings of modern fiction to its domination by women and their (supposedly) narrow experience, the New Woman writers, through their female artist figures, associate both aesthetic value and authenticity in art not just with women, but specifically with women's experience of suffering, hence contriving to square the circle of the self-sacrificial feminine ideal by yet another route. Thus Dixon's Mary Erle asserts: "It is because they suffer so that women have written supremely good fiction" (*The Story of a Modern Woman*, p. 122). A concern with the relation of the sufferings of women to art (in this case a shifting relation) is also at the centre of Beth Caldwell's history, and the debates about art for art's sake in *The Beth Book*. Ultimately Beth grounds her writing in women's experience,

resolving "to write for women, not for men ... [who] entertain each
other with intellectual ingenuities and Art and Style, while women are
busy with the great problems of life, and are striving might and main to
make it beautiful" (p. 376). It is entirely typical of the spiritual or social
purity feminism espoused by Grand that her heroine should abandon a
devotion to the aesthetic in favor of a commitment to moral beauty.
Beth's history is the story of both the making and the unmaking of the
artist as a young woman. *The Beth Book* is a critique of aestheticism, a
rejection of style for style's sake and of the aestheticization of morality.
Time and again Beth's development is shown as being inhibited by the
burden of style and the tyranny of male stylists such as Macaulay and
Ruskin (p. 37). Ultimately Grand's narrative structures Beth's trajectory
not as a decline from aesthetic ambition into artistic failure and/or
commercial production, but rather as an ascent from a private world of
imagination and dreams to a public world of substance and action, as
she abandons "the mere pictorial art of word-painting" for philosophy
and ethics: "Art for art's sake she despised, but in art for man's sake she
already discovered noble possibilities" (pp. 357–58).

In common with several other female artist figures in the New
Woman writing, Beth undergoes a breakdown, but in her case breakdown is represented as both a scarcely avoidable consequence of the
circumstances of the life of "a girl of our class" (to return to the
formulation of Caird's Hadria Fullerton), and a necessary stage in the
remaking of the young woman artist as activist or inciter to action.
When Beth resumes writing after her breakdown she does so: "rather
with a view to making herself useful to her friends than to satisfy any
ambition or craving of her own ... Beth had stepped away from the old
forms by this time. She had escaped from the bondage of the letter that
killeth into the realm of the spirit that giveth life" (p. 522). Beth's escape
from the bondage of style and the letter paves the way for her discovery
of her vocation as a public speaker and activist. This is a vocation in
which the delusions of fiction, imagination, and culture are abandoned
(it is affirmed) in favor of truth, the body, and nature, and writing gives
way to the voice: "She had been misled herself ... by her pretty talent
for writing, her love of turning phrases ... The writing had come of
cultivation, but this [power of oratory] ... was the natural gift" (p. 525).
Moreover, in opting for the voice and public speaking rather than the
written word and publication, Beth also frees herself from the demands
and constraints of the literary marketplace and avoids the mediation of
(male) editors and publishers.

The New Woman *Kunstlerroman* (like other New Woman novels) were condemned by many contemporary critics as symptoms of the hysteria and degeneracy of their age, and examples of "erotomania," "ego-mania," and/or a feminine or feminist will-to-power. They have been viewed by some later feminist critics as defeatist narratives which ulti-mately reinscribe their artist-protagonists within traditional definitions of femininity.[17] I would suggest that these fictions cannot simply be written off as conservative narratives of the containment of the femi-nine, nor can they be read off as heroic stories of feminine or, as some would argue, feminist transgression and subversion.[18] Rather these complexly fissured narratives are vehicles for the exploration of the psychological as well as social and material contradictions of the situ-ation of women at the end of the nineteenth century. The female artist figure is used to represent "feminist" aspiration. Even (or, indeed, especially) in her "failed" artist or hack writer form she represents the realization of women's ambition to become financially as well as emo-tionally independent, and to make their own way in the world of professional work. The figure of the female artist is also used variously to represent and explore female desire: oceanic longings for self-transcen-dence as well as the desire for self-expression; the desire to speak up and speak out; the desire for a form of creativity other than the biological one of maternity. In their use of the female artist figure The New Woman writers anticipate Freud's question of what a woman is and what she wants, and they also attempt to think beyond the terms in which Freud was to pose those questions. In much New Woman writing the figure of the female artist is used both as a means of exploring the desire of late-nineteenth-century women to transcend the ideological and material conditions of middle-class femininity, and (both conscious-ly and unconsciously) as a means of demonstrating the determining power of those conditions.

NOTES

1 Sarah Grand, *The Beth Book* (1897) (London: Virago, 1983), p. 69.
2 Ann Heilmann "'New Woman' Fiction and *fin de siècle* feminism," *Women's Writing* 3 (1996), 197–216, p. 205.
3 John Kucich, *The Power of Lies: Transgression in Victorian Fiction* (Ithaca:Cornell University Press, 1994), p. 242.
4 Laura Marholm Hansson, *Modern Women*, trans. Hermione Ramsden (Lon-don: John Lane, 1896), p. 78.
5 See Lyn Pykett, *The "Improper" Feminine: The Women's Sensation Novel and the New Woman Writing* (London and New York: Routledge, 1992), p. 177.

6 Ella Hepworth Dixon, *As I Knew Them: Sketches of People I Have Met on the Way* (London: Hutchinson, 1930), p. 136.
7 Ella Hepworth Dixon, *The Story of a Modern Woman* (1894) (London: Merlin Press, 1990), p. 181.
8 George Egerton, *Discords* (London: John Lane, 1894) p. 123.
9 See Margaret Diane Stetz, "New Grub Street and the Woman Writer of the 1890s," in Nikki Lee Manos and Meri-Jane Rochelson (eds.), *Transforming Genres: New Approaches to British Fiction of the 1890s* (New York: St. Martin's Press, 1994), pp. 21–45. All quotations are from Helen C. Black's interviews in the *Lady's Pictorial*, collected in *Notable Women Authors of the Day: Biographical Sketches* (Glasgow: David Bryce and Son, 1893).
10 See Pykett, *The "Improper" Feminine*, chapter 6.
11 Mona Caird, *The Daughters of Danaus* (London: Bliss, Sands, and Foster, 1894), p. 17.
12 Mary Cholmondeley, *Red Pottage* (1899) (London:Virago, 1985), pp. 37–38.
13 Penny Boumelha, "The Woman of Genius and the Woman of Grub Street: Figures of the Female Writer in British *Fin-de-Siècle* Fiction," *English Literature in Transition* 40 (1997), 164–180, p. 172.
14 Helen Mathers in Black, *Notable Women Authors*, quoted in Stetz, "New Grub Street and the Woman Writer of the 1890s," p. 9.
15 Mona Caird, *The Morality of Marriage and Other Essays on the Status and Destiny of Women* (London: George Redway, 1897), pp. 5–6.
16 Penny Boumelha, "The Woman of Genius," 177.
17 See, for example, Elaine Showalter, *A Literature of Their Own* (London: Virago, 1978.)
18 See Rita Kranidis, *Subversive Discourse: The Cultural Production of Late Victorian Feminist Novels* (London: Macmillan, 1995).

WORKS CITED

Black, Helen, C., *Notable Women Authors of the Day: Biographical Sketches*, Glasgow: David Bryce and Son, 1893.
Boumelha, Penny, "The Woman of Genius and the Woman of Grub Street: Figures of the Female Writer in British *Fin-de-Siècle* Fiction," *English Literature in Transition* 40 (1997), 164–180.
Caird, Mona, *The Daughters of Danaus*, London: Bliss, Sands, and Foster, 1894.
  The Morality of Marriage and Other Essays on the Status and Destiny of Women, London: George Redway, 1897.
Cholmondeley, Mary, *Red Pottage* (1899), London: Virago, 1985.
Cotes, Mrs. Everard, *A Daughter of Today*, London: Chatto and Windus, 1894.
Dixon, Ella Hepworth, *As I Knew Them: Sketches of People I Have Met on the Way*, London: Hutchinson, 1930.
  The Story of a Modern Woman (1894), London: Merlin Press, 1990.
Egerton, George (Mary Chavelita Dunne) *Keynotes*, London: John Lane, 1893.
  Discords, London; John Lane, 1894.
  The Wheel of God, London: Grant Richards, 1898.

Grand, Sarah, *The Beth Book* (1897), London: Virago, 1983.

Heilmann, Ann, "'New Woman' Fiction and *fin de siècle* feminism," *Women's Writing*, 3 (1996), 197–216.

Hansson, Laura Marholm, *Modern Women*, trans. Hermione Ramsden, London: John Lane, 1896.

Kranidis, Rita, *Subversive Discourse: The Cultural Production of Late Victorian Feminist Novels*, London: Macmillan, 1995.

Kucich, John, *The Power of Lies: Transgression in Victorian Fiction*, Ithaca: Cornell University Press, 1994.

Lubbock, Percy, *Mary Cholmondeley: A Sketch From Memory*, London: Jonathan Cape, 1928.

Paston, George (Emily Morse Symonds), *A Modern Amazon*, London: Osgood and McIlvaine, 1894.

A Writer of Books, London: Chapman and Hall, 1897.

Pett Ridge, William, *A Clever Wife*, London: Richard Bentley and Son, 1895.

Pykett, Lyn, *The "Improper" Feminine: The Women's Sensation Novel and the New Woman Writing*, London and New York: Routledge, 1992.

Raimond, C. E. (Elizabeth Robins), *George Mandeville's Husband*, London: Heinemann, The Pioneer Series, 1894.

Showalter, Elaine, *A Literature of Their Own*, London: Virago, 1978.

Stetz, Margaret Diane, "New Grub Street and the Woman Writer of the 1890s," in Nikki Lee Manos and Meri-Jane Rochelson (eds.), *Transforming Genres: New Approaches to British Fiction of the 1890s*, New York: St. Martin's Press, 1994.

CHAPTER 9

Lady in green with novel: the gendered economics of the visual arts and mid-Victorian women's writing

Dennis Denisoff

"'A woman make an artist! Ridiculous!... Ha! don't come near my picture – the paint's wet. Get away!' ... [H]e stood, flourishing his mahl-stick and palette – looking very like a gigantic warrior guarding the shrine of Art with shield and spear."[1] As Michael Vanbrugh's outburst in this passage from Dinah Mulock's novel *Olive* demonstrates, professional women artists in nineteenth-century Britain were perceived by many to be a challenge to male hegemony. Michael's very suggestion that a defense of his authority is necessary, however, exposes the falsity of his own claim for the inherent superiority of men. A provoking counter-image to that of Michael's defense is Anne Brontë's heroine Helen Graham, in *The Tenant of Wildfell Hall*, using her palette knife not only to finance her liberation from an abusive marriage but also, in one scene, to protect herself from a seducer. Mulock and Brontë's two images capture the economic and sexual conflicts which permeated Victorian conceptions of women's relation to the visual arts. The predominant conviction that men were both naturally and culturally better suited than women to artistic professions led society to configure women who attempted to infiltrate the hegemony as a sexually deviant, masculine threat. Conversely, the circumvention of the hegemony through forms of affectionate female–female interaction such as the gift-exchange of artworks was deemed trivial, and therefore sanctioned. As Terry Castle has argued, however, same-sex female attraction also contests men's economic and sexual authority over women.[2] In addition, not all women who used their artistic talents as a source of employment were viewed as transgressive; respectable governesses, for example, were expected to earn their income by teaching such things as painting, sketching, and music. Although there was a cultural differentiation between women's proper amateur interests in the arts and improper professional participation, this differentiation was not a complete severance. There existed a continuum that ranged from amateurs to instructors to professional artists, a spectrum tinged with an "unnatural" sexuality that was deemed more threatening as the woman artist became more involved in the public sphere. In accord with this spectrum, women performers, whose very creation of art occurs in public view, were often associated with a sexual transgressivity akin to prostitution. Focusing on Geraldine Jewsbury's *The Half Sisters*, Mary Braddon's *Lady Audley's Secret*, and Dinah Mulock's *Olive*, I wish to consider some of the ways in which these novelists used this sexual fluidity that permeated the culture of the arts both to redirect against men the familiar accusation of sexual deviancy that was applied to professional women, and to empower their depiction of a woman-centered economy of the arts.

VICTORIAN WOMEN AND THE ECONOMICS OF PAINTING

Victorian women were encouraged to dabble in watercolors and sketches rather than the more valued medium of oils, and to prefer picturesque works to dramatic pieces that dealt with historical or classical themes. In an 1857 *Englishwoman's Review* article, the anonymous author concludes that "in the more heroic and epic works of art the hand of man is best fitted to excel; nevertheless there remain gentle scenes of home interest, and domestic care, delineations of refined feeling and subtle touches of tender emotion, with which the woman artist is eminently entitled to deal."[3] However, as the American anthologist Elizabeth Ellet speculated, the reason that women artists neglected historical and allegorical subjects was because they did not have access to the time and education required to become experts in these areas, while the painting of generally less respected genres "might be pursued in the strict seclusion of the home to which custom and public sentiment consigned the fair student. Nor were they inharmonious with the ties of friendship and love, to which her tender nature clung."[4] It is more than a coincidence that the career limitations imposed upon women coordinated with both the differing values placed on artistic genres and the celebration of the disempowered domestic female.

George Du Maurier's 1874 *Punch* cartoon "Female School of Art" (Figure 9.1) encapsulates this correlation.[5] The piece implies that male dandies, due to their frivolity, belong in a female context – signified both by the room full of women and by the man fulfilling what was seen as the more passive role of object of the gaze. The cartoon represents effeminacy and self-display as attractive in women but repulsive in men, just as these qualities are promoted in women and yet depicted as unworthy of

FEMALE SCHOOL OF ART.—(*Useful Occupation for Idle and Ornamental Young Men*).

9.1 "Female School of Art," from *Punch*, May 30, 1874.

respect *in anybody*. In keeping with women's encouraged self-debasement, the illustrator crams a small space with eighteen awkwardly positioned female artists (an extreme number despite the fact that studios were often crowded), thereby belittling any serious, career-based efforts by suggesting that the women choose to treat the role of artist as a hobby. The comic subject of their gaze, and the mixing of young girls with mature women further enhances the amateurish quality of all of their endeavors. In addition, the cartoon reflects the view that virtuous women are asexual, and therefore uninterested in painting the nude figure which was often central to works with historical or classical themes. The dandy is dressed for the outdoors, complete with baggy trousers and a knee-length coat that ludicrously obscures his physique. Even the classical statue in the background, depicted only from the waist down, wears an ankle-length robe. Although the young man is the main butt of the joke, the women artists – with their diverse poses and facial expressions, Pre-Raphaelite hair, and voluminous sleeves and skirts – draw the viewer's gaze away from the male poseur and suggest that "true" beauty resides in the young women whom Du Maurier has associated with idleness and ornamentation. This prettified representation makes a striking contrast with Mulock's own depiction of women artists in her descriptive essay "A Paris Atelier": "They did not look particularly tidy, having on their working clothes an apron and sleeves grimed with chalk, charcoal, and paint, but all looked intelligent, busy, and happy. The room was as full of easels as it would hold; and in the centre was a rostrum, where the model, a picturesque old woman, sat placidly eating her morning bread and I hope not garlic, but it looked only too like it."[6] Mulock confirms Du Maurier's suggestion that women artists worked in environments that were not conducive to serious development but, while his cartoon implies that the students did not really demand space for serious endeavor, Mulock emphasizes the earnestness and pleasure that women experienced from the opportunity to learn.

The best-known nineteenth-century visual depiction of the economic struggles of the female painter is *Nameless and Friendless* by Emily Mary Osborn, who herself had to put up with reviewers who claimed that her talents were not "female."[7] The painting – which garnered a fair amount of attention when it was exhibited at the Royal Academy in 1857 – depicts a young, modestly dressed woman attempting to sell an artwork to a male proprietor. Although she is apparently trained in the visual arts, the woman's bent head, troubled expression, and fidgety hands suggest that she has adopted the career out of necessity. The young boy at her side leads one to speculate on the reason for her namelessness, while the combination of a black dress and the lack of a wedding band suggest that she is an orphan. By depicting a second woman dressed much like the central figure and leading another boy out of the store, Osborn establishes a visual echo that implies that the heroine's situation is not unique. Except for herself and the departing woman, all the people in the store are men who appear relaxed and comfortable, giving the shop the distinct air of a private gentlemen's club. Two customers, having turned their gaze away from a print of a scantily clad female dancer (the only painting within Osborn's piece with a discernible subject), eye the female painter with expressions of curiosity. Indeed, almost every man in the shop and even one outside on the street is attracted by the spectacle.

This composition offers a complex delineation of representations of women as individuals worthy of respect and as objects inviting sexual-ized derision. Osborn represents the central female in the painting as being in the former category, but also as having fallen into the latter category in the men's eyes. The male characters suggest that the heroine, by entering the public art world, has invited their exploitation of what Laura Mulvey has called women's "to-be-looked-at-ness."[8] It is as if, by demonstrating agency, she has proclaimed no need for the protective cover of bourgeois respectability, thereby demanding to be viewed as an "unnatural" woman, a woman with "masculine" at-tributes of ambition, confidence, and self-determination. The facts of her history are less significant because she has turned to painting for a profession, a gesture to be read as proof of her "nameless" status. As the hypocritical Conrad Percy comments in Jewsbury's *Half Sisters*, "A woman who makes her mind public, or exhibits herself in any way, no matter how it may be dignified by the title of art, seems to me little better than a woman of a nameless class."[9] In Osborn's piece, the woman is seen to invite her sexualized objectification, even as she demonstrates gender and class transgressivity by displaying what were viewed as both male and female characteristics. The men are attracted not by an image of womanly perfection, but by a hermaphroditic semiotics. Their de-mand that women fulfill the apparently less interesting ideal arises not from their attraction to that ideal but from a desire to have women function as a control mechanism for men's own transgressive potential. As Deborah Cherry points out, Osborn's painting demonstrates the methods by which Victorian masculinity, couched in a discourse of protecting and aiding women, in fact functioned to exclude and to disempower them.[10] Rather than set up a contrast between the central figure and the semi-nude performer that the men are handling, the painting establishes a continuum which portrays women as constantly at risk of being pushed down toward the lower end of the scale of respectability, but never having the opportunity to push back. Although the number of professional women artists did grow during the Victorian era, it is not surprising that one of their main artistic channels remained non-professional women-centered networks that circumvented accusations of deviancy.

ABNORMALITIES AND *THE HALF SISTERS'* AFFECTIONS

Geraldine Jewsbury was fairly consistent throughout her life in claiming that men were naturally intended to be in charge of society. Yet, in an essay published a year before *The Half Sisters*, she observes that "men are afraid of women becoming less agreeable, less useful to them – lest they should become less relative in their existence, lead their own lives for their own soul's sake, and not with an eye to the pleasure and taste of men alone."[11] Her irritation with patriarchal constraints is also apparent in an erotically charged letter to Jane Carlyle in which she writes: "I love you my darling, more than I can express, more than I am conscious of myself, and yet I can do nothing for you."[12] Apparently Thomas Carlyle claimed that "Such mad, lover-like jealousy on the part of one woman towards another it had never entered into my heart to conceive."[13] *The Half Sisters* explores this tension between women's potentials and cultural constraints through a comparison of cultural attitudes toward women's involvement in the domestic arts and professional performance.

Jewsbury's novel follows the lives of the half-Italian performer Bianca and her housewifely half-sister Alice. The author's descriptions of the performer's experiences were grounded in her friendship with the actress Charlotte Cushman, who was often described as notably masculine by the press.[14] In the novel, the Italian artist and her mother are abandoned by Bianca's father, and this loss of economic stability leads the young heroine into destitution. However, it also releases her from the confines of conventions by forcing her, as it did Osborn's heroine, into a creative career that, in this case, ultimately proves strengthening and fulfilling. Jewsbury makes it clear that, although Bianca is initially forced to become a performer, the woman "continued in it from choice" (*The Half Sisters*, p. 33). As she explains to Alice, "I must realise myself in my own way, or not at all. I am already [stained] in the eyes of all the quiet, gentle, still-life people amongst whom you dwell" (p. 134), words like "stained" and "still-life" highlighting Jewsbury's contrast of the women's respectability according to art form.

In a strategy akin to Mulock's undermining of Michael's cultural authority, Jewsbury suggests that the performer's threatening masculinity is unstoppable because the image of deviancy is in fact the product of male anxieties. Conrad envisions Bianca as a beast whose career

has unsexed her, made her neither a man nor a woman . . . [Women in public life] may, and many of them no doubt do, keep virtuous in the broad sense of the term; but, in their dealings with men, they use their sex as a weapon; they play with the passions of men to some degree like courtesans . . . she strides and stalks through life, neither one thing nor another; she has neither the softness of a woman, nor the firm, well-proportioned principle of a man . . . She is a bat in the human species; when she loves, she loves like a man, and yet expects to be adored as a woman. (pp. 216–17)

This stalking vampire whose perceived gender transgression Conrad feebly attempts to reconstitute as an asexuality ultimately remains transgendered, in Conrad's eyes, through the heroine's attractive sexuality and her desire to be economically independent. The combination is only conceived of as monstrous greed, however, if this asexual bisexual is always also a woman, if the possibility of her passing as a heteronormative female continues to undermine the false essentialism and denied performances of individuals such as Conrad. For this reason, rather than focusing on the notion of woman as artist, Conrad's image of Bianca constantly reverts to a consideration of the way in which her career undermines his own position.

Jewsbury ultimately fulfills the transposition of the monstrous iconography onto the hegemony by depicting the man himself as a predatory sexual transgressor. Threatened by the successful woman artist, Conrad concludes that in fact his preference is for a woman "at anchor by her own fire-side, gentle, low-voiced, loving, confiding" (p. 218). Bianca's half-sister Alice, when first described, appears to fulfill this ideal:

In an extremely neat sitting-room, without one particle of taste visible in the arrangement of the grave substantial furniture, sat the wife and daughter of the late Phillip Helmsby of Newcastle, engaged on a large piece of household needle-work. A bookcase, filled with books of uniform size and binding, stood in a recess by the fire-place; but none were lying about. An engraving of the Princess Charlotte, and another of her husband, hung against one of the walls. (p. 13)

Jewsbury's narrator defines the women by the name of the dead patriarch, an echo of the family's self-definition through the more public,
higher authority signified by the portraits. As Jewsbury and the English
reading public knew, Princess Charlotte, the only child of the man who
was to become George IV, had died in 1817 after giving birth to a
stillborn boy. The engraving demonstrates a system of abnegation
which emphasizes the dependence of public order on women's *private*
responsibilities. The portraits, like the untouched books, serve not as
beauty or inspiration but as signifiers of traditional order. Completing
the docile harmony, the Helmsby women turn their skills not to new
creations but to mending. Alice is taught to draw and play the piano, but
her mother directs these talents as well toward marriage and domesticity; "I do not object to your practising an hour a day – nor to keeping up
your drawing," explains Mrs. Helmsby, "if you would only make it
practical, and paint me some screens for my drawing-room, or a cabinet
for the library, or a chess-table, or something that would be really
useful" (p. 15). Elsewhere she scolds Alice for not turning her creative
abilities toward making a dog collar.

Like Bianca, however, Alice has inherited her father's artistic sensibility; even as a child, she feels "a striving after some meaning she could
not express" (p. 22), what the narrator refers to as "the sensibility of
genius without its creative power" (p. 42). The widowed Mrs. Helmsby,
however, sells the majority of her husband's art collection, including the
one piece that most stimulated Alice's "vague yearnings and dim aspirations" and offered her "an opening through which she escaped from
the contact of the dull, harsh, common details by which she was
hemmed in on all sides" (p. 41). The matriarch replaces this particular
painting with a no doubt uninspiring portrait of herself. Later, Alice's
husband Bryant proves equally practical, voicing "a singular objection
to meeting with authors, actors, artists, or professional people of any
sort; except in the peculiar exercise of their vocation, which I am willing
to pay for" (p. 262). In contrast to Bianca's fulfilling artistic career, the
domestic arts are depicted as forcing Alice to identify with the "still-life
people" (p. 134) that have "hemmed [her] in on all sides" (p. 41).

Finding her marriage to Bryant constraining, Alice develops an
interest in Conrad, even though he, after his difficulties with Bianca,
sees the image forced onto Alice as ideal. Because of her marriage, Alice
and Conrad avoid acknowledging their mutual attraction until the
lover, agitated by his own desires, breaks a lamp and Alice cuts herself
while trying to pick up the pieces. Conrad reacts by laying the woman

on the sofa and sucking her blood because "it seemed to him like sacrilege to let any of the precious drops be lost" (p. 275). Alice is "terrified at the expression of his countenance; his lips were still marked with blood, traces of tears were on his cheeks, and his eyes were pale and almost extinct." Defining his love for Alice as the source of this transformation, the vampiric Conrad then disappears into the night, only to return soon after under the pretense of obtaining a drawing that she had promised him. The present, however, is quickly subsumed by the man's crazed restatement of his love, all couched in a discourse of purchase. The gift of artwork is not so much forgotten as reconstituted as an attempt to buy her love and devotion: "let me live as your slave... [T]his last precious month . . . would have been cheaply bought with an eternity of pain ... I will pay the penalty, if it be death or madness" (pp. 278–79). Conrad undermines his own apparent desire for an exchange of affection via the drawing by using financial terminology – "precious," "cheaply bought," "pay" – that highlights the economic assumptions that support his notion of love. But as it is Alice as embodiment of stability and control that Conrad admires and indeed requires, so too is it her control that allows her to banish him from her presence forever. She soon reconsiders her decision, but then her husband's sudden appearance causes her to faint and eventually die. "Utterly transformed" by his sense of guilt over the woman's demise (pp. 328–29), Conrad decides to give up all his worldly possessions. "The Conrad you knew is dead," he tells Bianca, "The last day of my old life closed yesterday – to-day my new life has arisen" (p. 331). He kisses the performer with lips "cold as death" and departs "never [to reappear] in the world," but leaving behind a miniature of himself (p. 396). By blaming his own ghastliness on Alice, Conrad shifts responsibility for his lack of control onto the object of his attention. The monstrously encoded exchange of affection is in fact a corporeal representation of the man's earlier attempts to blame his own weakness on Bianca's professionalism, an accusation that in both cases is part of an attempt to drain the vitality of the women in order to justify their subjugation.

In contrast to Alice's failed relationships with men, Jewsbury presents a fulfilling engagement between her and Bianca. Upon recognizing a portrait of their father hanging over Alice's mantelpiece, Bianca realizes that, in addition to their artistic urges, the two women are also joined by blood. Although this discovery fills the performer with an "ineffable yearning," the women's socioeconomic differences make her determined "to quell the mighty 'hunger of her heart' for natural

affection" (p. 132). Jewsbury reinforces the fusion of artistic and emotional affinity by having Alice reciprocate the love even though she
remains unaware of their family ties. In contrast to her apathy toward
Bryant, Alice tells Bianca: "I cannot let you go so soon – I care for
you, as I never cared for any one – you do me so much good" (p. 134).
Bringing to mind Jewsbury's own dream of leading a same-sex domestic life,[15] Alice's declaration of love is followed by a scene of emotional
harmony in which she briefly attains her marital aspirations by procur-
ing Bianca a flat and fulfilling her "labor of love" by furnishing the
home, right down to the artworks that adorns the walls (p. 135). Within
the limited economic realm of their societies, the creative potential of
both women meshes into an attachment temporarily satisfying a hunger for affection. When Alice assures Bianca that she will visit often,
the other woman replies "As often as you are allowed ... for you are
not a free woman: but absent, or present, I shall love you equally"
(p. 136). Bianca's necessarily pragmatic existence has made her keenly
aware of the constraints against sustained relationships based on female–female emotional fulfillment, as well as the restraints placed on
female mobility, desires, and independence once inside a conventional
bourgeois marriage. Echoing the contrasting perspectives in Osborn's
painting, Jewsbury presents the professional artist as a hermaphroditic
manifestation of Conrad's fear of his own potential transgressivity,
while offering an alternative reading in the female performer's emotionally fulfilling relationship with her artistic half-sister, although their
harmonizing interests and affections fail to overwhelm the cultural
teleology which encourages each woman to try to locate such fulfillment in a man.

THE LIVING DEAD AND *LADY AUDLEY*'S ARTISTIC SECRETIONS

Mary Elizabeth Braddon was sharply aware of the prejudices against
female performers, having supported herself not only as an author but
also as an actress. The heroine of *Lady Audley's Secret* also finds herself in
need of attaining financial security in a society that severely limits her
options. Although skilled in painting and employed for a time as a
governess, she ultimately transgresses the boundaries of acceptability
when she marries and attempts to murder for money. Despite the fact
that Lady Audley never turns to an artistic profession, her drive for
self-determination is connected to visual art, as well as same-sex attraction and monstrosity. As in Jewsbury's novel, however, it is ultimately

suggested that this matrix of associations is actually the transposition of patriarchal insecurities.

When George Talboys leaves his wife and child to look for work in Australia, the heroine decides that she warrants another chance as well. Removing her portrait from its position beside that of her first husband,[16] she fakes her own death and moves away with the intention of attaining financial security elsewhere. Having killed off her previous self, the new-born heroine now seems doomed to a visage of the living dead. When green and crimson light falls on her through a window displaying the Audley coat of arms, the woman's face remains a "ghastly ashen grey" (*Lady Audley's Secret*, p. 120). Elsewhere she is described as "more pale than winter snow," like Lot's wife "with every drop of blood congealing in her veins, in the terrible process that was to transform her from a woman into a statue" (p. 310). Noting his wife's "poor white face" and "the purple rims round [her] hollow eyes," Sir Michael Audley laments that he "had almost a difficulty to recognize [his] little wife in that ghastly, terrified, agonized-looking creature... Thank God for the morning sun" (p. 76). The chapter in which Lady Audley is condemned to an insane asylum carries the appropriately vampiric title "Buried Alive." In contrast to her frequently deathly pallor, however, there also exists a series of artistic signifiers whose decay and bloodiness seemingly publicize her duplicity and unwillingness to remain framed by cultural regulations. An engraving of some "lovely ladies" is found "yellow and spotted with mildew" (p. 158), while other pieces in the estate grow a blue mold (p. 446). When Lady Audley, nervous about being discovered, drops a paintbrush onto her work, the paint blots out the subject's face "under a widening circle of crimson lake" (p. 117). Likewise, when she has a new portrait painted of herself, her complexion comes off as "lurid," her eyes as "strange" and "sinister," and her "pretty pouting mouth" as "hard and almost wicked" (p. 70). Notably, the explanation that the narrator offers for this image of a "beautiful fiend" is not the heroine's transgressivity, but the possibility that the painter might have gone partially mad from copying "mediæval monstrosities" (p. 71). The portrait – with its "crimson dress, the sunshine on the face, the red gold gleaming in the yellow hair, [and] the ripe scarlet of the pouting lips" (p. 71) – is virtually dripping red, assumedly exposing the heroine's monstrous desires. Winifred Hughes has noted, however, that Lady Audley is never directed by sexual passions;[17] it is her determination to gain control of her life that leads to her being constituted as sexually transgressive.

Braddon solidifies the connection between women's economic assertiveness and sexual deviancy through Lady Audley's influence over her
young maid, Phoebe. The erotic implications are especially obvious in a
scene where the heroine lies in bed covered in satin and fur amidst the
opulence of her jewelry-strewn private bedroom. Phoebe helps her
mistress prepare for bed, spending most of the time it seems combing
Lady Audley's profusion of golden blonde hair. The heroine recipro-
cates by smoothing "her maid's neutral-tinted hair with her plump,
white, and bejewelled hand" (p. 58). The young Phoebe even looks like
Lady Audley, so much so that "you might have easily mistaken her for
my lady" (p. 105). The heroine also describes her maid as a pale version
of herself: "Why, with a bottle of hair dye ... and a pot of rouge, you'd
be as good-looking as I" (p. 58). As part of the same evening, the heroine
arranges to pay the maid to assist in her subterfugal machinations. The
business deal and the mutual petting are then sealed with a kiss (p. 59).
The women's physical resemblance correlates with their similar economic concerns and their instructor/student relationship. We are informed that Lady Audley is guilty of putting new, strange ideas into her
maid's head, in part by exposing her to "yellow-paper-covered" French
novels (p. 104), which were characterized in Victorian society by risqué
and immoral scenes much like that which Phoebe and Lady Audley
themselves enact in the bedroom. Phoebe also listens to the older beauty
ask: "Shall I ever grow old, Phoebe? Will my hair ever drop off as the
leaves are falling from those trees, and leave me wan and bare like them?
What is to become of me when I grow old?" (p. 105). The same concerns
belong to the unwealthy Phoebe, who ultimately decides to marry a
laborer named Luke, despite his strong tendency to violence. On her
wedding day, the young protégée appears as a gothic specter: "a
superstitious stranger might have mistaken the bride for the ghost of
some other bride, dead and buried in the vaults below the church"
(p. 110). While the novel suggests that the reader should be anxious
about the heroine's influence on her friend, the maid's decision to follow
tradition by marrying results in an image not of wedded bliss but of
death, implying that it is not women's transgressivity, but the fact that
one of their few options for financial security is a domestic role, that kills
off the possibility of self-fulfillment.

The association of Lady Audley with monstrosity and sexual deviancy
is complicated in an extended showdown between the heroine and her
step-nephew Robert. As with Conrad in Jewsbury's *Half Sisters*, Robert's
sexual anxieties are most obvious in his misogynistic rants against

women. The young man argues that he hates women because they are "bold, brazen abominable creatures, invented for the annoyance and destruction of their superiors" (p. 207). However, he then criticizes them for being "the stronger sex, the noisier, the more persevering, the most self-assertive sex" (p. 207), thereby undermining his own claim to preordained social dominance. Meanwhile, Robert is himself consumed by a growing realization of the depth of his love for George Talboys. Indeed, Sir Michael, the heroine's husband and family patriarch, concludes that Robert is himself "unnatural" because of his lack of heterosexual attraction and his obsession with George rather than Sir Michael's daughter: "because Alicia was a pretty girl and an amiable girl it was therefore extraordinary and unnatural in Robert Audley not to have duly fallen in love with her" (pp. 331–32). As with Conrad and Michael Vanbrugh, Robert's decision to perceive Lady Audley as an insane, monstrous threat is based less on the heroine's scheming than on personal anxieties regarding his ability to fulfill his society's predefined gender-based expectations.

The title of *Lady Audley's Secret* appears on a first read of the novel to refer to the heroine's fear that she has inherited or will inherit her mother's insanity. Nevertheless, while Lady Audley and Robert both try to convince Sir Michael that the other is mad, neither of the two ultimately ever offers any definitive proof. The doctor who is brought in to check the mistress' mental state concludes that she does not suffer from madness but an "insanity which might never appear" (p. 379). According to him, the heroine actually has a combination of cunning, prudence, and intelligence – traits one would expect to be valued but which instead, in this woman, he deems "dangerous" (p. 379). *Lady Audley's Secret* is thus less about what the heroine hides, than about what she, like some moldering portrait, secretes – what she threatens to expose intentionally or not regarding the duplicity and false essentialism of the system within which she struggles. As Pamela Gilbert has noted, Braddon's novel offers a "subversive portrait of alienated patriarchy," in which so many of the male characters fail to fulfill their societal roles but escape punishment regardless.[18] The bloody, rotten artworks that seem to signify the heroine's sinister soul actually manifest the conflict, which the men must deny exists, between a woman struggling for security and the patriarchal framework which demands that she conform to an image that disarms her. Although Robert sees the heroine as threatening to bleed the dominant hegemony dry, he cannot reveal her history without risking a seepage of social inequities. Therefore, rather than having her taken to court, the family, under the auspices of benevolence, sends her off to a Belgian insane asylum. Braddon makes sure, however, that her heroine packs her art supplies, signaling the possibility of Lady Audley even now continuing to struggle to convert her cultural confines into a site of self-affirmation (p. 363).

DEFORMITY AND *OLIVE*'S DEVOTION

Olive agrees with Braddon's novel on the issue of women's rights to self-determination, but rather than embodying the conflict in sensational images of erotically vampiric heroines and decomposing artworks, Dinah Mulock uses a hyper-virtuous heroine to argue that physical, emotional, and artistic anomalies do not reflect an immoral individual. Having studied drawing at the Government School of Design at Somerset House in 1843, Mulock was familiar with the contemporary arts scene, as suggested by works such as *Olive*, "The Story of Elizabetta Sirani," and "A Paris Atelier." In *Olive*, Meliora Vanbrugh is aware of a number of women artists: "Oh yes, plenty. There was Angelica Kauffman, and Properzia Rossi, and Elizabetta Sirani. In our day, there is Mrs. A—— and Miss B——, and the two C——s. And if you read about the old Italian masters, you will find that many of them had wives, or daughters, or sisters, who helped them a great deal" (*Olive*, p. 156). While naming historical figures from previous centuries, Mulock erases her contemporaries through the use of the ABCs to suggest the lack of recognition proffered on women artists in her time. Notwithstanding the fact that Mulock believed that women should prefer employment as wives and mothers, she realized that, "whether voluntarily or not, one-half of our women are obliged to take care of themselves – obliged to look solely to themselves for maintenance, position, occupation, amusement, reputation, life."[19] For Mulock, "it is not necessary for every woman to be an accomplished musician, an art-student, a thoroughly educated Girton girl; but it is necessary that she should be a woman of business."[20] While she felt that women met men "on level ground" when it came to literature, she still believed that, for various reasons including "the not unnatural repugnance that is felt to women's drawing from 'the life'," women could not be men's equals as painters.[21] She then comments, however, that, if a woman did choose a profession in the arts, she could still be respectable because she need not leave the domestic sphere in order to succeed.[22]

Olive's narrator reiterates Mulock's concerns, arguing that, even though a woman prefers to "sit meekly by her own hearth ... sometimes chance or circumstance or wrong, sealing up her woman's nature, converts her into a self-dependent human soul" (p. 167). The eponymous heroine is one such unnatural woman because of a deformation in her spine that, although slight, makes her conclude that marriage is an unlikely prospect. Her inability to attract the male gaze obviates her being categorized as a woman. In addition to her hunchback, Olive is also described as having her father's hands (p. 200) and an "almost masculine power of mind" (p. 167). Such deformity and gender ambiguity are directly connected in the text to the question of artistic potential. Michael Vanbrugh claims that creative genius is of no sex, but still callously informs Olive that genius "scorns to exist in weak female nature; and even if it did, custom and education would certainly stunt its growth" (p. 162). Michael himself is "gigantic and ungainly in height" (p. 147), but while his deformity might be expected to reflect his talent, Mulock undermines the equation by emphasizing his mediocrity and his dependence on various women in order even to attempt to paint well. For Olive, however, her physical uniqueness functions as a liberating catalyst: "That personal deformity which she thought excluded her from a woman's natural destiny, gave her freedom in her own" (p. 168). As with Bianca's poverty, the assumed unlikelihood of Olive entering into a respectable marriage sanctions her shift of attention away from heterosexual prospects and toward a career as a painter, both gestures threatening to constitute the heroine as a deformation of essentialist heteronormative bodily and performative signification.

The general cultural desexualization of the deformed is in part the reason why Olive's friend Marion apparently need not be taken seriously when she confides to the heroine that, "if I were a man, I should fall in love with you ... Aye, in spite of–of–. . . . any little imperfection which may make you fancy yourself different to other people" (pp. 322–23). Nor do Olive's same-sex options end there. While her picture-perfect mother, "a Venus de Medici transmuted from the stone" (p. 13), poses for portraits painted by male artists, the deformed, artistic daughter develops an interest in "[her] beauty next door" (p. 76), a young woman whom she finds so attractive upon first sight that she spends the entire evening drawing pictures of her from memory. The labor involved in artistic creation establishes such an act as one of the strongest sanctioned modes of communicating affection between women. In "A Paris Atelier," Mulock notes that the female art students have no adventures with men, and yet, by the same token, there is nothing threatening about

these women becoming same-sex couples. The students frequently paint
pictures of each other and exchange them as gifts. A character describes
two students who, foreshadowing a scenario in Radclyffe Hall's *Well of
Loneliness* (1928), "for seven years ... have never been separated, and
seem quite indispensable to each other. It is the clever one who is the
most devoted, who carries the canvas, washes the brushes, arranges the
easel, and, in short, does everything for her companion."[23] If an art
student should never find a man, concludes Mulock, "she learns to do
without him, and will be all the happier and better woman for having
put her life to useful account."[24] Acknowledging her awareness both of
the fact that many saw an artistic career as a risk to a woman's
respectability and of its association with unconventional sexuality,
Mulock ensures her readers that "these young students seem to go
through the ordeal [of studying art in Paris] unscathed, and, so far as I
could judge, without being unfeminized."[25] In Mulock's view, careers in
the visual arts repel heterosexual dalliance, while encouraging women
to develop healthy emotional and cultural bonds with each other and
offering them access to greater socioeconomic liberty.

  Lest readers should choose to brush aside Olive's artistic signification
of affection for the girl next door as nothing more than the desperate
infatuation of an ostracized abnormality, Mulock goes out of her way to
establish the equivalency between this attraction and heterosexual desire:

There is a deep beauty – more so than the world will acknowledge – in this
impassioned first friendship, most resembling first love, the foreshadowing of
which it truly is ... How they used to pine for the daily greeting – the long walk,
fraught with all sorts of innocent secrets. Or, in absence, the almost intermi-
nable letters – positive love-letters, full of "dearests," and "beloveds," and
sealing-wax kisses . . .– embraces sweeter than those of all the world beside.
(p. 77)

In this passage, Mulock's narrator is not describing the passionate love
between the seemingly less attractive female artist and another woman
but, shifting into a philosophizing tone, appears to be reminiscing about
her own experiences as she expounds on a type of relationship portrayed
as familiar to all women. The narrator ultimately normalizes these
affections by inserting them into an acceptable teleology of maturity.
The heroine's masculinizing deformities thus put her out of the loop of
heterosexual relations, ironically making it safer for Mulock to depict
unconventional attractions (couched within a discourse of artistic cre-

ation and exchange) which then seductively transform into ideal affections by which, the narrator informs us, all women's lives are in fact partially defined and from which men are excluded. Like Jewsbury, Mulock realized that the economy of women's amateur art, while existing within a constructed spectrum of deviant sexuality, nevertheless offered a context that sanctioned women's enjoyment of intense same-sex affection. Throughout *Olive*, Mulock reiterates that the heroine's physical deformity is far less relevant than her outstanding character and humanitarian spirit. Ultimately, she does marry and discards her artistic career, having earlier concluded that, when she is not painting, she feels "less of an artist, and more of a woman" (p. 243). While this conclusion concedes to generic heteronormative closure, as Jewsbury and Braddon's novels seem less jubilantly to do as well, it also complicates the demonization of women artists by presenting a person who spends part of her life as a professional painter and part of it as a traditional wife, while her perfect character remains unchanged.

In their novels, Mulock, Jewsbury, and Braddon each use the visual arts to address the hegemony's anxieties regarding women's circumventions of male-centered systems in their efforts to fulfill their own economic and emotional desires. The authors retain the cultural equation of this challenge with unnatural sexuality, but redirect the accusation against anxious male characters such as Conrad Percy, Robert Audley, and Michael Vanbrugh. The cultural gestures and metaphors of gender, genius, and genre which these men depend on ultimately collapse under the strain of their own contradictions. The efficacy of this strategy is registered most emphatically by the fact that the authors managed their revisions of the misogynistic conflation of economic self-determination, non-heteronormative pleasures, and art without disavowing women's rights to participate in all three.

NOTES

This research was made possible through a Social Sciences and Humanities Research Council of Canada Postdoctoral Fellowship at Princeton University. I would also like to express my gratititude to the staff at the Princeton University Rare Books Department and at the British National Portrait Gallery.

1 Dinah Mulock, *Olive* (New York, nd.), p. 160. All future page references to this novel will appear in the main body of the essay.
2 Terry Castle, *The Apparitional Lesbian: Female Homosexuality and Modern Culture* (New York, 1993), p. 62. Lillian Faderman has demonstrated that, despite the

fact that nineteenth-century sexological, juridical, and other institutional terminology did not reify what we now define as a lesbian identity, the very absence of such a controlling discourse meant that there existed "a latitude of affectionate expression and demonstration that became more and more narrow with the growth of the general sophistication and pseudo-sophistication regarding sexual possibilities between women" (*Surpassing the Love of Men: Romantic Friendship and Love between Women from the Renaissance to the Present* [London, 1982], p. 152). This observation encourages the study of female–female desire prior to the institutionalization of lesbianism as it was manifested through existing discourses which, only in certain combinations, conflated acceptable female–female affections with deviant sexuality.

3   Quoted in Whitney Chadwick, *Women, Art, and Society* (London: 1990), pp. 170–71.

4   Elizabeth Ellet, *Artists in All Ages and Countries* (New York: 1859), p. 3.

5   George Du Maurier, "Female School of Art – (*Useful Occupation for Idle and Ornamental Young Men*)," *Punch* (May 30, 1874), 232.

6   Dinah Mulock, "A Paris Atelier," in *About Money and Other Things* (New York: 1887), pp. 184–85.

7   Pamela Gerrish Nunn, *Victorian Women Artists* (London: 1987), p. 22.

8   Laura Mulvey, "Visual Pleasure and Narrative Cinema," in *Visual and Other Pleasures* (London: 1989), p. 19.

9   Geraldine Jewsbury, *The Half Sisters* (1848; Oxford: 1994), p. 214. All future page references to this novel will appear in the main body of the essay.

10 Deborah Cherry, *Painting Women: Victorian Women Artists* (London: 1993), pp. 80–81.

11 Geraldine Jewsbury, "How Agnes Worral Was Taught to Be Respectable," *Douglas Jerrold's Shilling Magazine* 5 (1847), 258.

12 Quoted in Faderman, *Surpassing the Love*, p. 164.

13 Quoted in Virginia Woolf, "Geraldine and Jane," in *Collected Essays*, 4 vols. (London: 1967), vol. IV, pp. 27–39; p. 35.

14 Norma Clarke, *Ambitious Heights: Writing, Friendship, Love – The Jewsbury Sisters, Felicia Hemans, and Jane Welsh Carlyle* (London: 1990), pp. 178, 188.

15 Geraldine Jewsbury, *Selection from the Letters of Geraldine Endsor Jewsbury to Jane Welsh Carlyle*, ed. Annie E Ireland (London: 1892), p. 333.

16 Mary Elizabeth Braddon, *Lady Audley's Secret* (1862; Oxford: 1987), p. 40. All future page references to this novel will appear in the main body of the essay.

17 Winifred Hughes, *The Maniac in the Cellar: Sensation Novels in the 1860s* (Princeton, NJ: 1980), p. 127.

18 Pamela Gilbert, *Disease, Desire, and the Body in Victorian Women's Popular Novels* (Cambridge: 1997), p. 94.

19 Dinah Mulock, *A Woman's Thoughts about Women* (London: 1858), p. 24.

20 Mulock, "About Money," *About Money and Other Things* (New York: 1887), p. 7.

21 Mulock, *A Woman's Thoughts*, pp. 50–51.

22 *Ibid.*, p. 58.
23 Mulock, "A Paris Atelier," p. 194.
24 *Ibid.*, p. 197.
25 *Ibid.*, p. 196.

WORKS CITED

Braddon, Mary Elizabeth, *Lady Audley's Secret*, 1862, Oxford: 1987.
Castle, Terry, *The Apparitional Lesbian: Female Homosexuality and Modern Culture*, New York: 1993.
Chadwick, Whitney, *Women, Art, and Society*, London: 1990.
Cherry, Deborah, *Painting Women: Victorian Women Artists*, London: 1993.
Clarke, Norma, *Ambitious Heights: Writing, Friendship, Love–The Jewsbury Sisters, Felicia Hemans, and Jane Welsh Carlyle*, London: 1990.
Du Maurier, George, "Female School of Art – (*Useful Occupation for Idle and Ornamental Young Men*)," *Punch* (May 30, 1874), 232.
Ellet, Elizabeth, *Artists in All Ages and Countries*, New York: 1859.
Faderman, Lillian, *Surpassing the Love of Men*, London: 1982.
Gilbert, Pamela, *Disease, Desire, and the Body in Victorian Women's Popular Novels*, Cambridge: 1997.
Hughes, Winifred, *The Maniac in the Cellar: Sensation Novels in the 1860s*, Princeton, NJ: 1980.
Jewsbury, Geraldine, *The Half Sisters*, 1848, Oxford: 1994.
   "How Agnes Worral Was Taught to Be Respectable," *Douglas Jerrold's Shilling Magazine* 5 (1847), 16–24 and 246–66.
   Selection from the Letters of Geraldine Endsor Jewsbury to Jane Welsh Carlyle, ed. Annie E. Ireland, London: 1892.
Mulock, Dinah, "About Money," in *About Money and Other Things*, New York: 1887.
   Olive, 1850, New York: n.d.
   "A Paris Atelier," in *About Money and Other Things*, New York: 1887.
   A Woman's Thoughts about Women, London: 1858.
Mulvey, Laura, "Visual Pleasure and Narrative Cinema," 1975, in *Visual and Other Pleasures*, London: 1989, pp. 14–26.
Nunn, Pamela Gerrish, *Victorian Women Artists*, London: 1987.
Woolf, Virginia, "Geraldine and Jane," in *Collected Essays*, vol. IV, London: 1967, pp. 27–39.

CHAPTER 10

Ouida and the other New Woman

Pamela Gilbert

[T]here are conspicuous at the present two words which designate
unmitigated bores: The Workingman and the New Woman
Ouida[1]

Ouida's antifeminism was vocal; her denunciation of the New Woman
did as much to lend currency to the term as feminist apologists did.[2]
That antifeminism, combined with stylistic extravagance, has contributed to render Ouida invisible within today's canon, in which she can be
classified neither as canonical nor as a feminist foremother. Yet, Ouida's
fiction is not simply opposed to the interests of New Women novelists.
Certainly, for example, Ouida is a believer in aristocratic privilege; her
reasons, however, are embedded in notions of eugenics which inform
much New Woman writing.[3] Her hatred of socialism is curiously mixed
– though a resolute defender of private property, her main critique of
the redistribution of power appears in the Italian novels as a critique of
abuses which are liable to occur in the opportunism attending social
transition, particularly sexual abuse of women.[4] Her partisanship of
animal rights is specifically connected to women's abuse under patriarchy as it often is in New Woman fiction.[5] Ouida is wholly opposed to
Female Suffrage and the New Woman, but in part for reasons which are
aligned with the reasoning of New Women like George Egerton and
Victoria Cross, who see in women's sexuality a power distinct from the
power of men. In short, Ouida's conservatism is formulated through a
radical rhetoric.

Many of Ouida's characters anticipate the New Woman. Most importantly for our purposes here, her portrayal of women often licenses
extramarital sexuality as an expression of a higher ethical standard in a
world wherein marriage is corrupted by the profit motive.[6] Further,
many of her women reject traditional gender roles, being active, heroic,
able to fight men and win. Although these characters succumb to the

fate prescribed by mid-Victorian narrative – they die – they retain the sympathy of the reader and in so doing, sustain a critique of the conditions that necessitate their elimination.

Though the passage from "The New Woman" cited at the beginning of this chapter has been frequently quoted, others from the same essay are rarely quoted and are revelatory of a stance which places Ouida very far from Eliza Lynn Linton in her reasoning, if not in her conclusions. Ouida's sense of the hostility of men for the New Woman is unabashedly cognizant (and supportive!) of male homoeroticism; she warns,

In the finest intellectual and artistic era of the world women were not necessary to either the pleasures or passions of men. It is possible that if women make themselves as unlovely and offensive as they appear likely to become, the preferences of the Platonic Age may again become acknowledged and domi-nant, and women may be relegated entirely to the lowest plane as a mere drudge and child-bearer.[7]

In fact, she argues, the New Woman is most at fault because she imitates men, "and thus loses any originality she might possess" in her passion to "emulate . . . all his cruelties and follies."[8] She attacks the contemporary feminist position on prostitution as suggesting that women are passive victims of male seduction and not sexual beings themselves: "The youth and the maiden incline to one another as naturally as the male and female blossoms . . . It is nature which draws one to the other; and the blame lies less on them than with the hypocritical morality of a modern world which sees what it calls sin in Nature."[9] She calls marriage elsewhere "the tomb of love"[10], compares it to prostitution[11] and re-marks in "Female Suffrage" that the "prejudices and conventionalities of society, and the fictions of monogamy have stranded a vast number of women . . . who would imagine themselves disgraced if they enjoyed the natural affections of life."[12] Ann Ardis writes, "New Woman novelists . . . are interested in rewriting an aspect of nineteenth century realism – the idealized representation of 'Womanhood' – which the naturalists neither criticize nor correct."[13] New Women were also interested in "expos[ing] the contradiction of romantic love as they question the plausibilities of the marriage plot . . . and rethink[ing] the orthodox Victorian opposition between the 'pure' and the 'fallen' woman."[14] As we shall see, although riddled with contradictory messages, Ouida's work challenges this idealization of the non-sexual woman as early as the 1860's.

Gail Cunningham has observed that the focus of "the elevation of the New Woman into a symbol of all that was most challenging and dangerous ... was, inevitably, sex ... Feminist thinkers ... appeared to be redirecting their energies ... towards the formulation of a new ... sexual ethics."[15] Yet, many scholars have emphasized the difficulties of the New Woman in claiming sexuality. Though most New Women emphasized the rights of women to a sexuality free from the constraints of patriarchy, constructing female sexual desire as nature which had been perverted by masculine culture, others embraced the mid-Victorian perception of women as less sexual than men, arguing that women were more spiritually evolved and physically refined. These New Women argued for higher standards of sexual purity – rather than women being accorded the dubious sexual privileges traditionally held by men, men should be elevated to the standard women had long since taken for granted. Others still, such as Olive Schreiner and George Egerton, recognizing the power of the "sexual instinct," were concerned about the enslavement of women to their own biology, reading in the idealization of motherhood an attempt to subordinate women's subjectivity to an essentialist biology which was anything but progressive. The idealization of motherhood, its connection with eugenics and emphasis on the dangers of sexually transmitted diseases, complicated this replication of the traditional dichotomy in the perception of women's sexuality as both more voracious (as celebrated by such writers as Victoria Cross)[16] and more controlled than its degenerate masculine counterpart (as Sarah Grand's Evadne, by necessity, demonstrates).[17] In many of these novels, the woman protagonist ends unhappily, unable to live an ethical, satisfying sexual life in the context of overwhelming social constraints. Whether they are Women who Did or Women who Didn't, they end as Women who Lose against a stacked deck.

I do not wish to imply that Ouida novels of the sixties and seventies featured New Women. As we have earlier noted, she was overtly unsympathetic to the goals of the New Woman even in the nineties, and to "discover" a New Woman in the sixties would be anachronistic. But recent scholarship has recognized a connection between the sixties sensation novel and nineties New Woman fiction. Lyn Pykett has shown that both genres were "engaged in a general struggle about the definition of woman, and also about the nature, power and function of the feminine within the culture,"[18] and, most significantly, both "[chart] the conflict between 'actual' female experience and the domestic, private, angelic feminine ideal ... [and both] constructed plots and characters which registered or interrogated the contradictions of contemporary marriage and the domestic ideal."[19] Ouida's novels, fitting precisely into neither tradition, perhaps best exemplify some of the points of connections between the two genres. Ouida is something of a puzzle – the rare high Victorian author with a middle class readership (although her readership also extended to the lower classes) who "gets away with" sexually active, strong female characters who do not die decorously after a period of hideous suffering repudiating the errors of their ways.[20] Her description of a London dancer elevated by the hero to the overnight fame of the upper-class courtesan is instructive: "The Zu-Zu was perfectly happy; and as for the pathetic pictures that novelists and moralists draw, of vice sighing amid turtles and truffles for childish innocence in the cottage at home ... – the Zu-Zu would have ... told you to 'stow all that trash'... The Zu-Zu is fact; the moralists' pictures are moonshine."[21] In addition to courtesans, Ouida paints many jovial middle-to-upper class adulteresses, most of whom don't worry about lost pearls unless they are mounted as earrings. Although my interest here is not to rehabilitate Ouida as a lost feminist foremother (or even to recuperate her as a wicked step-foremother), it is salient to consider that many New Women writers must have grown up reading Ouida, and that Ouida's novels allowed, in however carefully mediated a context, identification with female characters whose notions about female sexuality ran counter to middle-class norms at mid-century.

These characters were, of course, often villains. However, one category of Ouida's female characters remains heroines even while marked by the disassociation of sex and love from marriage and the capability for "male" occupations. They tend to be racial hybrids, culturally displaced, of uncertain class origins, fated by their circumstances and "the doom of sex" to tragic ends, yet honored for their reliance on self-generated codes of behavior which preserve their integrity in situations wherein traditional gender roles lose their explanatory power.[22] Cigarette (*Under Two Flags* 1867) and Folle-Farine, the eponymous heroine of the 1871 novel, are important early examples of such characters. In these cases, racial/cultural hybridity both grants the women more freedom to act, and dooms them as tragic characters for whom no narrative is ultimately possible in the normative social world into which other characters must be integrated.

These characteristics must be understood in relation to anxieties stemming from England's imperial expansion and growing recognition of colonial subjectivity as separate from – and hostile to – English subjectivity. The role of the colonies as a proving ground for English masculinity has often been discussed,[23] but the problem posed by the figure of the racially hybrid woman is only now being adequately explored. It is in this woman that many characteristics of the New Woman – long before she was so described – are treated by Ouida with some approval. Paradoxically, though, these characteristics are used in the narrative to transfer power to male characters rather than to realize a goal of female empowerment. The men are then integrated or reintegrated into the social order on the basis of their successful absorption of "masculine" qualities from and through the "feminine" self-sacrifice essential even to a hybridized femininity.

The enactment of this drama of racial and gendered (dis)integration is imbricated in discourses on race, empire, gender, economics and the body, which would later be part of the broader New Woman cultural debate. By displacing anxieties about women's roles to the colonial context and the hybrid woman, Ouida both contains those anxieties and exposes the way both women and racial others are used to consolidate imperial masculinity. Through the refusal of these characters to fulfill traditional European gender roles as commodified female bodies, Ouida also critiques the cash nexus as an adequate basis for social relations.

Under Two Flags, the most enduring in popularity of all Ouida's novels, owes much of its memorability to Cigarette, *vivandière* to the North African French army. The daughter of a camp follower and a soldier, her origins are uncertain – Creole French? Franco-African? Like the later New Woman, her disregard for conventional gender roles is illustrated by her cigarette smoking and her policy of free love. Less directly comparable, but still consonant with the New Woman, is her status as an excellent shot, a military hero, and a pitiless warrior. However, she is not an "imitation man" – despite the hero Beauty's judgment of her as "unsexed," she is "feminine" in her sexuality and in her role as "maternal" caretaker of "her" troops.

Under Two Flags is set in Algeria, and draws its force from the oppositions of colonial encounter, of which Cigarette is the synthesis. Our first introduction to Algiers is a catalog of Orientalism:

Pell-mell in its fantastic confusion, its incongruous blending, its forced mixture of two races, that will touch but never mingle, that will be chained together but never assimilate, the Gallic-Moorish life of the city poured out . . . a single palm rose, at a few rare intervals, as though to recall amid the shame of foreign domination, that this was once the home of Hannibal, the African that had made Rome tremble.[24]

Cigarette herself is a remarkable medley of those "never mingling" races, and this fusion extends to gender as well. Cigarette is introduced as a "piquant" bit of exotica, a seductive bundle of contradictions:

> She was very pretty ... though her skin was burned to a bright sunny brown, and her hair was cut as short as a boy's, and her face had not one regular feature ... she would swear if need be like a Zouave, she could fire galloping, she could toss off her brandy or her vermout [*sic*] like a trooper ... yet with all that, she was not wholly unsexed ... though she ... had been born in a barrack and meant to die in battle.[25]

We are told, "she had had a thousand lovers ... and she had never loved anything, except the roll of the *pas de charge* ... She was more like a handsome, saucy boy ... Of a surety, she missed virtues that women prize; but, not less of a surety, had she caught some that they miss."[26] Later we read that she "had all the faults, as she had all the virtues, of the thorough Celtic race."[27] A "thorough Parisienne," she is "desert bred." In addition to this interesting and contradictory catalog of traits, she is explicitly connected with the Oriental woman: "Cigarette danced with the wild grace of an Almeh, a Bayadere, of a Nautch girl."[28] British readers were familiar with the figure of the Nautch girl as the emblem of Indian moral decay and its infectiousness; British men, it was thought, were vulnerable to the appeal of the Nautch girls who encouraged them to "go native."[29] Cigarette also moves freely among all classes and races: "Cigarette knew everybody; she chatted with a group of Turcos, she emptied her barrel for some Zouaves, she eat [*sic*] sweetmeats with a lot of negro boys."[30]

Ouida's omniscient narrative voice explicitly states that Cigarette is not "wholly unsexed," but there is much gender ambiguity in Cigarette's presentation. Beauty, the hero for whom Cigarette has an unrequited passion, pities her as unsexed, but is most concerned, not with her present moral state, but with her future economic status.

> "What a gallant boy is spoiled in that little Amazon!" he thought ... he was sorry a child so bright and brave should be turned into three parts a trooper as she was, should have been tossed up on the scum and filth of the lowest barrack life, and should be doomed in a few years time to become the yellow, battered, foul-mouthed, vulture-eyed, camp-follower that premature old age would surely render [her] ... Cigarette was making scorn of her doom of Sex ... But ... her sex would have its revenge one day and play Nemesis to her.[31]

However, an artist (Ouida's artists are always prescient) disagrees with Beauty. Always in Beauty's mind is Cigarette's projected fate as that "thing which is unsightly and repugnant to even the lowest among men," i.e., an aged whore. But the artist responds

Spare me the old world-worn, threadbare formulas. Because ... the garden flowers grow trained and pruned, must there be no bud that opens for mere love of the sun ... ? Believe me, ... it is the lives which follow no previous rule which do the most good and give the most harvest ... she will die ... at the head of a regiment ... There will always be a million commonplace women ... One little lioness here and there in a generation can not do overmuch harm?[32]

In fact, this analysis proves truer; Cigarette dies, having just been decorated with the Cross of the Legion of Honor for her heroism in battle, when she interposes her body between a firing squad and Beauty. Ouida's narrator also seems to indicate that Beauty rather misses the point of Cigarette: "[he] thought that a gallant boy was spoiled in this eighteen-year-old brunette of a campaigner; he might have gone further and said that a hero was lost."[33]

Although wounded by Beauty's evaluation of her femininity, Cigarette's response is telling: "she struck him across the lips with the cigar she hurled at him. 'Unsexed? Pouf! If you have a woman's face, may I not have a man's soul? It is only a fair exchange.'"[34] And indeed, Cigarette is not the only gender-bender in the narrative. Sara Suleri writes,

while the Anglo-Indian woman writer has much invested in maintaining standard Orientalist stereotypes to mystify the East, her work, far more than that of her male counterpart, engages in an incipient questioning that dismantles colonialism's master narrative of rape ... [she] seems to be at a better vantage point to assess how much the colonial encounter depends upon a disembodied homoeroticism ... [and] evinces a powerful understanding of the imperial dynamic as a dialogue between competing male anxieties.[35]

Although Suleri is writing about Anglo-Indian women living in India and writing about their lived experience there, Ouida, whose understanding of the colonies was gleaned principally from discussions with military men and newspaper accounts, encodes both of these narratives in her treatment of North Africa. Beauty, our hero, is often described as "womanly"; here one of many descriptions will perhaps suffice: "The appellative [Beauty], gained at Eton, was in no way undeserved ... a face of as much delicacy and brilliancy as a woman's ... His features were exceedingly fair – fair as the fairest girl's."[36] This does not impinge on his masculine abilities in fighting and sport, but there is a suggestion in his languidness and his love of French novels and cologne of degeneracy. Fortunately, despite the fact that he several times avers that the Arabs are right and the French wrong, his fighting on the French side masculinizes him. As he thinks back on years of rape and pillage, he muses that "[The Arabs] will never really win again ... it is the conflict of the races ... their day is done." He wonders if his life there has been wasted, but the narrative voice assures us that, "it might be doubted if ... any other [life] ... would equally have given steel and strength to his indolence and languor as this did. In his old world, he ... would have glided from refinement to effeminacy."[37] What finally masculinizes him sufficiently to be returned to England, to his dearest friend "the Seraph," and incidentally to marry the Seraph's sister (a familiar pattern in homosocial narrative, as Eve Sedgwick notes), is Cigarette's sacrifice. It is (conveniently) too late when Beauty learns to value Cigarette properly. As she lies dying in his place, he exclaims

"Oh God, how I have wronged you!" The full strength and nobility and devotion of this passion he had disbelieved in and neglected rushed on him as he met her eyes ... he saw ... All of which the splendid heroism of this untrained nature would have been capable under a different fate ... "What have I done to be worthy of such love?"

he wonders, and the reader wonders with him. Although Venetia is the substitute offered for Cigarette at the end of the novel, at the climax of the novel, the moment both of Cigarette's martyrdom and of Beauty's reunion with the Seraph, she is not even present. In fact, it is for the Seraph that Cigarette actually "stands in." He offers to cover Beauty's body with his own,

"If they send their shots through you, they shall reach me first in their passage ... Why have you been lost to me, if you were dead to all the world beside?" They were the words his sister had spoken ... Cecil's [Beauty's] eyes filled with slow, blinding tears; tears sweet as a woman's in her joy, bitter as a man's in his agony ... He knew that this love, at least, had cleaved to him.[38]

Yet it is Cigarette who actually interposes her body between the firing squad and Beauty. The logic of the substitutions is dizzying here: the Seraph speaks his sister's words, Beauty will consummate with Venetia the love he bears the Seraph, Cigarette stands in for both the Seraph and Venetia as protection and substitute for Beauty and also as the bridge that allows Beauty to return from her hybrid world to his own, cleansed and purified of his own gender hybridity.

Both Cigarette and Folle-Farine owe much to the discourse of the colonized woman circulating in this period. Although neither are "really" comparable to, say, the Indian woman, and Ouida is certainly not drawing from "real" experience, she articulates both characters within recognizable narratives of otherness drawn from colonial representation, both in their idealized exoticism and implicit critique of female objectification. Both women, as culturally and racially mixed characters, bridge the troubling distance between the ruling and subordinated race, allowing them both the sexual freedom denied to the proper European woman and at the same time a subjectivity which is recognizably European in many properties – and sympathetic. The placement of the women in non-English scenes in which the opposing cultures are in a relation of hostility safeguards Ouida from too obvious association with the volatile Indian situation, while still allowing comment, especially in *Under Two Flags*, on a colonial situation in which comparisons can certainly be drawn.

Folle-Farine takes the questions posed in *Under Two Flags* a level further. Here, the hybrid woman is the protagonist, instead of a supporting character; here also, the Oriental woman is brought into the European context (rural France) as a subject instead of being part of the exotic setting for a masculine adventure story. Instead of beginning, as Cigarette does, as a powerful adult character, Folle-Farine is introduced to us as a child on the defensive against the self-commodification which is the only form of power her society offers. The circulation of wealth, a minor theme in *Under Two Flags*, is the central metaphor of *Folle-Farine*. In partially domesticating the setting, Ouida takes an important, if small, step toward the realism of the New Women novelists.

Folle-Farine, like Cigarette, is racially ambiguous, the bastard child of a French peasant girl seduced by a very Africanized Spanish gypsy. She is "a starry eyed, Arab faced child," with "a face of Asia" or of "old Egypt," who "walked with the free and fearless measure of the country women of Rome or the desert born women of Nubia." After years of ill treatment by the French, who see her as a daughter of the devil, "She was a bronzed, bare-footed, fleet-limbed young outcast ... a curious sovereignty and savageness in her dauntless carriage ... a certain nobility ... like one of a great and fallen race."[39]

Her father fulfills the stereotype of the morally decadent African or Indian of mid-Victorian rhetoric. He is "like an Eastern prince," who had "the indolence, the passions, the rapacity, the slothful sensuality of the gypsy – who had retained all the vices of his race while losing their virtues of simplicity in living." Her father decides to sell the child, first as a street performer and later as a courtesan – a thing that offends "the proud liberty and wild chastity" of his compatriots' "race."[40] This dichotomy is reflective of contemporary British accounts of Indian gender relations: Indian men are so fiercely protective of their women's chastity that they shut them in the zenana, thus depriving them of intellectual growth and fostering a morally degenerate sensuality, yet at the same time, they prostitute their women (as Nautch girls, for example – it is significant that Folle-Farine's father decides to prostitute her after he sees her dancing), and by implication themselves, being feminine in their luxury loving deceitfulness (and in the subtext of Arab or Indian homosexuality).

But Folle-Farine, the hybrid, is the opposite of her father in that she combines the virtues of both races, "all the strength and swiftness of the nomadic race . . . nought of their indolence and dishonesty." Although she has the innate feminine "chastity" of her father's race (fallen women being represented in this novel largely as lower class French women becoming mistresses to wealthy European city dwellers), she is also a gender hybrid: although "she always toiled hard at such bodily labour as was set to her; to domestic work, to the work of the distaff and the spindle, of the stove and of the needle, they had never been able to break her." Like Cigarette, she can take care of herself: when a man attempts to beat her, she "seized the staff in her right hand, wrenched it with a swift movement from his hold, and catching his head under her left arm, rained blows on him from his own weapon, with a sudden gust of breathless rage which blinded him, and lent to her slender muscular limbs, the strength and force of man." She does not even realize she is a woman until told so at sixteen by an old man, who muses, "It was a pity to make you a woman . . . You might be a man worth something; but a woman! A thing that has no medium; no haven between heaven and hell." Even her appearance, oft cited as beautiful and womanly, suggests some androgyny; after her hair is cut in the hospital, Sartorian remarks, "Well, I am not sure but that you are handsomer, – almost. A sculptor would like you more now, – what a head you would make for an Anteros, or an Icarus, or a Hyacinthus."[41]

Folle-Farine and Cigarette are unquestionably sympathetic characters for both narrator and reader. The narrator never lets us forget that the characters are "doomed" by their sex – which perhaps affords the reader's sympathy more scope, being assured that the women are not going to "get away with" anything. However, although both indeed die, they do not die as conventional fallen women (though both technically are); they die as heroes and martyrs. As Antoinette Burton has recently noted, many feminist writers of the later nineteenth century were complicit in the discourses of empire, using the Oriental woman – as she had long been defined by European male writers,[42] as sexually decadent and uncivilized victim and child – strategically in order to claim their own rights. Ouida is certainly complicit in the rhetoric of exoticism, but may be more radical than many feminists in her use of the sexual freedom associated with the Oriental woman to critique the decadence and hypocrisy of European society. If Ouida's borrowing of imperial narratives of Oriental exoticism is important in allowing her characters' scope for their role-breaking behavior, she also critiques those narratives.

This practice is also reflected in her use and critique of the exotic picturesque in character description. Suleri remarks on the tendency (especially of British women authors in the colonies) to reify the bodies of the colonized into static "pictures," especially of the female body, which tends to then be elided in favor of its clothing and adornment: "the complex economies of race and religion ... are to the imperial eye essentialized into the literalism of figure and feature ... hysterically [insisting] ... on the static readability of physicality."[43] In Ouida's take on this tradition, however, it is men who turn women into static images for purposes of commodification. Folle-Farine especially is indeed presented as the still and suffering body, first of her grandfather's torture, then the object of Arslan's painting, and then of Sartorian's consumption and display as a reified image of a barbarian queen. Early in the novel, when her grandfather scourges the seven year old Folle-Farine to make her work harder, she "stood mute and immovable, her head erect, her arms crossed on her chest. A small, slender, bronze hued, half nude figure amongst the ruby hues of the gladioli and the pure snow-whiteness of the lilies." Later, both Arslan and Sartorian treat her as an object to be used and displayed. Arslan's interest is intellectual and artistic, but merciless: "[Arslan] liked to make her smile; he liked to make her suffer; he liked to inflame to wound, to charm, to tame her; he liked all these without passion, rather with curiosity than with interest." Sartorian ignores Folle-Farine's display of anger, but: "He was studying the shape of her limbs, the hues of her skin... 'All of these in Paris,' he was thinking, 'just as she is, with the same bare feet and limbs... The poor barbarian! she sells her little brazen sequins, and thinks them her only treasure, whilst she has all that!'"[44] Ouida presents Folle-Farine early in the narrative as a static image, but later invokes the reader's sympathy for Folle-Farine's quest to avoid being turned into a *tableau vivant*, both capitalizing on the erotics of the image and denouncing them simultaneously. When Folle-Farine attempts to elude Sartorian, he points out that "gold [has] a million eyes"[45] which transform her into a commodity as well as an object of surveillance. When Folle-Farine becomes his mistress in order to save Arslan from starvation, it is explicitly her transformation into a visual commodity which is the price, in addition to her sexual victimization. The world (here Paris, or "the great market"), the narrator tells us, is confronted with two phenomena simultaneously: the genius of an artist (Sartorian has secretly engineered this reception for Arslan at Folle-Farine's behest, although Arslan never knows of her sacrifice for him) and "The bodily beauty of a woman ... a creature barefooted, with chains of gold ... the woman whom it was a tyrant's pleasure to place beside him now and then in the public ways, as a tribune of Rome placed in his chariot the vanquished splendour of some imperial thing of Asia made his slave."[46] Her reactions to visual objectification are generally explained in racial terms, "It was ever painful and even loathsome to her to give her beauty to the merciless imitations of art; it stung the dignity and the purity that were inborn in the daughter of an outlawed people."[47] Ouida's complicity with the narratives of empire is complicated by a counternarrative of female subjectivity in which the colonial woman who is consumed as picturesque resists her reification and is finally murdered in the process of consumption.

Against the backdrop of French peasant life which is the social setting for the first two volumes of the novel, the imperial male is represented by the racial opposite of the African – Arslan, an ultra-blond Scandinavian who "had dwelt much in Asiatic countries." He is dedicated to art, but has little sympathy for humanity – "The quality of passionate imagination was in him welded with a coldness and stillness of temper born in him with his northern blood." He turns a "vivisector's" eye on Folle-Farine. Whereas the sensualist Sartorian is a clearly vitiated, degenerate specimen of European subtlety, "a small and feeble man, with keen and humorous eyes, and an elfin face, delicate in its form, malicious in its meaning," Arslan, physically beautiful and intellectually powerful, is the "natural" European conqueror – and he displays the conqueror's vices, in comparison to Folle-Farine's Rousseauian Savage Nobility. She admires his sketch for the scene of the crowd choosing Barrabas over Christ, knowing that he longs for wealth and fame:

"You care for the world – you? – who have painted *that?*"
Arslan did not answer her: he felt the rebuke.
He had drawn the picture in all its deadly irony, in all its pitiless truth, only
himself to desire and strive for the wine streams, and the painted harlotry, and
the showers of gold, and the false gods, of a worldly success.

On another occasion, he taunts her, "You are only a barbarian; how
should you understand that the attractions of civilization lie in its
multiplications of the forms of vice?" And indeed, the narrator tells us,

She had no conception of them [the nature of his desires for wealth and fame] –
of the weakness and the force that twine one in another in such a temper as his.
She was at once above them and beneath them . . . [but the desire for gold] was
a longing plain to her, one that moved all the dullest and most brutal souls of
the world around her. All her years she had seen the greed of gold, or the want
of it, the twin rulers of the only little dominion that she knew.

In fact, "She scarcely knew of the existence of the simplest forms of
civilization. . . Left to herself, and uncontaminated by humanity, because proscribed by it, she had known no teachers . . . [save natural
forces, which] had breathed into her an unconscious heroism, a change-
less patience, a fearless freedom."

The status of nature or essence, a staple of imperial discussions of
race, is vexed in the novel. When Folle-Farine admires the "freedom" of
the ocean, Arslan responds,

It is not free . . . It must obey the laws that govern it, and cannot evade them. Its
flux and reflux are not liberty; but obedience – just such obedience to natural
law as our life shows when it springs into being and slowly wears itself out and
then perishes . . . There is no such thing as liberty; men have dreamed of it, but
nature has never accorded it.[48]

This appeal to the laws of "nature" and "science" are familiar in the
context of Darwinist discussions of race and empire which follow the
Mutiny of 1857, and recall Beauty's ruminations on the "conflict of the
races." But the narrator also presents Folle-Farine's longing for freedom
as "natural" to any "young creature" and also to her "race." It is
unclear how much sympathy the narrator evinces for Arslan's position,
but it seems much less than in *Under Two Flags* – the narrator does not so
much contradict his point of view as suggest that it is beside the point
when dealing with the Other. Arslan never lacks confidence in his own
pronouncements, yet misreads everything about Folle-Farine, right
down to the end of the novel, when, unaware that she has become

Sartorian's mistress only to save his life, he comments "'So soon?' and only smiled to think – all women were alike." Yet, so far from being supported by his own talents, he is the unknowing beneficiary of Sartorian's monetary gifts (through Folle-Farine's intervention). He is the recipient, therefore, not only of a gift which "saps the strength of the receiver," but one that is "shameful" – it is he who is truly prostituted to Sartorian, not Folle-Farine. Significantly, the imperial male is no longer protagonist and hero, brave soldier needing the colonial experience to mature and define his masculinity, as in *Under Two Flags*. Here, the male is not only made the beneficiary of the colonial woman's sacrifice, but explicitly dishonored. Arslan never realizes, as Beauty is made to, the true nature of his relation to the hybrid woman, and therefore he is left unable to grow or to see clearly – a fatal flaw in an artist whose great gift is to see and represent "truth," as Ouida repeatedly states. Ouida also uses the "barbarism" of Folle-Farine to suggest that imperial views of gender have less to do with nature than with the degenerate aspects of civilization, a cornerstone of feminist argument articulated by Mary Wollstonecraft which later became a key theme of New Woman fiction. Perhaps also, imperial males' perceptions of Oriental women have less to do with the women than with the dynamic of desire that operates, in Sedgwick's terms, "between men."[49]

The integrity of the Other cannot be measured in European terms, which for Ouida are tied to capitalism and its impact on social relations, a view most fully articulated in *Folle-Farine*, wherein the argument "comes home" – at least as far West as France. Both Cigarette and Folle-Farine share a disinclination to link their sexuality with economic exchange.[50] That which separates Cigarette from the courtesans is also what unites the courtesans and the "fast" upper class wives – monetary rapacity. Cigarette, however greedy for gifts, is not interested in money for its own sake: "As much gold was showered on her as on Isabel of the Jockey Club; but Cigarette was never the richer for it. 'Bah!' she would say ... 'Money is like a mill, no good standing still. Let it turn ... and the more bread will come from it for the people to eat.' The vivandiere was by instinct a fine political economist."[51] Folle-Farine, the barbarian, understands gold only in terms of its use value. When she overhears Arslan soliloquizing on his desire for gold, she seeks out Sartorian to sell the sequins inscribed with "Arabic characters" which are the only remaining souvenir of her early life among the gypsies. But she learns from Arslan that gold has meanings attached to it beyond the pragmatic ones when he is furious with her for offering him such a gift: "Gifts of gold from man to man are bitter, and sap the strength of the receiver, but from woman to man they are – to the man shameful . . . It is for the man to give to the woman. You see?" Folle-Farine is perhaps understandably confused. "'I do not see,' she muttered. 'Whoever has, gives: what does it matter?'"[52] And since he will not take it, she throws the gold away as valueless. She realizes that Arslan must never know that she has already arranged for Sartorian to come and buy his sketches, freeing him to go to Paris and try his luck there. Yet when he leaves for Paris, he gives her a gift of half the coins he receives from Sartorian: "Her bloodless face grew scarlet with an immeasurable shame . . . He who denied her love to give her gold!"[53]

Folle-Farine is devoted to the quest of its doomed protagonist, not to preserve her physical "virtue" but her moral virtue by refusing to be treated as a commodity. Her grandfather is a miser, hoarding both gold and food (in an often starving community), and Sartorian is one who collects old coins, art, and women as commodities; in short, both value commodities not for their uses but for the power they represent and the value that accrues to them in an economy of scarcity, and both stop the circulation of wealth, reifying and fetishizing it, thus making it a destructive force. Like many other Victorian novelists, Ouida attacks the notion of marriage for wealth as prostitution; however, unlike most of them, and much like the New Women novelists later, she valorizes women's sexuality and love outside of marriage, and sees the social constraints placed on women's sexuality as contributing to their moral decay; her indictment of "gold" is readable as an indictment of the cash nexus itself.

It is love which destroys both women, but whereas Cigarette must merely take a bullet (or several), Folle-Farine must sacrifice her very self, living on in the realm of exchange to trade for Arslan's economic support. It is only in death that she finds respite from the "thousand eyes" of gold. In loving, both are drawn into the realm of commodification: Folle-Farine, like Cigarette, is made "womanly" and Europeanized by her love for Arslan and through the consciousness of shame which accrues to her through his imperial gaze. The narrator of *Folle-Farine* remarks, "Perfect love casts out fear, runs the tradition: rather, surely, does the perfect love of a woman break the courage which no other thing could ever daunt."[54]

In both cases, the women sacrifice themselves bodily so that the loved male can have access to power, wealth and status. But in so "selling" themselves, they simultaneously pass out of the realm of exchange through the economy of the gift; the wealth does not accrue to them, and so they remain untainted, and finally through death, untaintable, unable to be hoarded, sold, or used again. The penetration of their bodies, is, in Folle-Farine's case, an explicitly sexual one; in Cigarette's, bullets "pierced her bosom, and broke her limbs." Sartorian describes Folle-Farine's ascent (descent) to European status in specifically economic terms: "That sublime unreason – that grand barbaric madness – and yet both will fall to gold."[55] Thus, even though they are brought into the economy of exchange or substitution, feminized and Europeanized by their acceptance of the values the male characters dictate, they vanish as commodities in the very act of becoming so into the irrevocable Otherness of death, retaining their purity.

The themes of women exercising power in traditionally masculine roles, of women who exercise their sexuality freely, for their own pleasure and outside the boundaries of exchange implied by marriage or prostitution would become, in the nineties, key components of New Women fiction. Few authors at mid-century provide such powerful and popular models of sympathetic characters caught in the social conflict implied by the exercise of such rights and abilities as Ouida.

NOTES

1 Ouida, "The New Woman," *Views and Opinions*, 2nd edn. (London: Methuen, 1896), p. 205.
2 See Ellen Jordan, "The Christening of the New Woman: May 1894," *Victorian Newsletter*, 48 (Spring 1983), 19–21.
3 E.g. Haldane's – see Susan Squier, "Sexual Biopolitics in *Man's World*: The Writings of Charlotte Haldane," in Angela Ingram and Daphne Patai, (eds.), *Rediscovering Forgotten Radicals: British Women Writers, 1889–1939* (Chapel Hill and London: University of North Carolina Press, 1993).
4 E.g., Ouida, *A Village Commune*, 2 vols. (London: Chatto and Windus, 1881).
5 E.g. Shoshana Milgram Knapp on Victoria Cross, "Real Passion and the Reverence for Life: Sexuality and Antivivisection in the Fiction of Victoria Cross," in Ingram and Patai (eds.), *Rediscovering Forgotten Radicals*.
6 As in *Moths* (London, Chatto and Windus, 1880), wherein the heroine divorces her sadistic husband to join her lover.
7 Ouida, "The New Woman," p. 209.
8 *Ibid.*, pp. 211, 210.
9 *Ibid.*, p. 216.
10 Ouida, "O Beati Insipientes," in *Views and Opinions*, p. 73.
11 Ouida, "The New Woman," p. 217.
12 Ouida, "Female Suffrage," in *Views and Opinions*, p. 318.

13 Ann Ardis, *New Women, New Novels* (New Brunswick, NJ: Rutgers University Press, 1990), p. 318.

14 *Ibid.*, 61.

15 Gail Cunningham, *The New Woman and the Victorian Novel* (London: Macmillan, 1978), pp. 2–3.

16 See Knapp, "Real Passion."

17 E.g., Cunningham, *The New Woman*, pp. 54–55, and Ella Hepworth Dixon's Mary in *The Story of a Modern Woman* (London: Merlin Press Ltd.; Chicago: Ivan R. Dee Inc., 1990).

18 Lyn Pykett, *The "Improper" Feminine: The Women's Sensation Novel and the New Woman Writing* (London: Routledge, 1992).

19 *Ibid.*, p. 6.

20 This galled George Moore, who denounces the librarian Mudie's practice of excluding Moore's fictions and including Ouida's in *Literature at Nurse or Circulating Morals: A Polemic on Victorian Censorship* (Brighton, Sussex: Harvester, 1976).

21 *Under Two Flags* (Chicago and New York: Rand, McNally and Co. [1917?]), p. 83.

22 A characteristic typical, according to Kate Flint, of New Woman protagonists. See *The Woman Reader, 1837–1914* (Oxford: Clarendon Press, 1993).

23 See Patrick Brantlinger, *Rule of Darkness: British Literature and Imperialism, 1830–1914* (Ithaca: Cornell University Press, 1988); Edward Said, *Orientalism* (London: Routledge, 1978).

24 *Under Two Flags*, pp. 180–81.

25 *Ibid.*, p. 197.

26 *Ibid.*, pp. 202–03.

27 *Ibid.*, p. 287.

28 *Ibid.*, p. 218.

29 See Antoinette Burton, *Burdens of History: British Feminists, Indian Women, and Imperial Culture, 1865–1915* (Chapel Hill: University of North Carolina Press, 1994).

30 *Under Two Flags*, p. 209.

31 *Ibid.*, p. 293.

32 *Ibid.*, p. 350.

33 *Ibid.*, p. 294.

34 *Ibid.*, p. 230.

35 Sara Suleri, *The Rhetoric of English India* (Chicago: University of Chicago Press, 1992), p. 77.

36 Ouida, *Under Two Flags*, pp. 5–6.

37 *Ibid.*, pp. 244, 266.

38 *Ibid.*, p. 586.

39 *Folle-Farine*, 3 vols. (London: Chapman and Hall, 1871), vol. I, p. 102; vol. I, p. 129; vol. II, p. 176; vol. I, p. 123; vol. II, p. 269.

40 *Ibid.*, vol. I, p. 29; vol. I, p. 96.

41 *Ibid.*, vol. I, pp. 184–85; vol. I, p. 184; vol. I, p. 147; vol. I, pp. 171–72; vol. III, p. 190.
42 Burton, *Burdens of History*; see also Said, *Orientalism*.
43 Suleri, *The Rhetoric of English India*, p. 108.
44 *Folle-Farine*, vol. I, p. 9; vol. II, p. 268; vol. III, pp. 91–92.
45 *Ibid.*, vol. III, 258.
46 *Ibid.*, vol. III, p. 320.
47 *Ibid.*, vol. II, p. 293.
48 *Ibid.*, vol. II, p. 237; vol. II, p. 237; vol. III, p. 28; vol. II, p. 291; vol. II, p. 312; vol. III, pp. 8–9; vol. II, pp. 256–57.
49 Eve Sedgwick, *Between Men: English Literature and Male Homosocial Desire* (New York: Columbia University Press, 1985).
50 It is important to note that Folle-Farine's chastity is not avoidance of extramarital sex – Ouida makes it clear that Folle-Farine would have willingly offered that intimacy to Arslan – but a disinclination to prostitute her sexuality.
51 Ouida, *Under Two Flags*, p. 214.
52 Ouida, *Folle-Farine*, vol. III, pp. 56–57.
53 *Ibid.*, vol. III, p. 126.
54 *Ibid.*, vol. II, p. 187.
55 *Ibid.*, vol. III, p. 99.

WORKS CITED

Ardis, Ann. L., *New Women*, New Brunswick, NJ: Rutgers University Press, 1990.
Brantlinger, Patrick, *Rule of Darkness: British Literature and Imperialism, 1830–1914*, Ithaca: Cornell University Press, 1988.
Burton, Antoinette, *Burdens of History: British Feminists, Indian Women, and Imperial Culture, 1865–1915*, Chapel Hill: University of North Carolina Press, 1994.
Cunningham, Gail, *The New Woman and the Victorian Novel*, London: Macmillan, 1978.
De la Ramée, Louise (Ouida), *A Village Commune*, 2 vols., London: Chatto and Windus, 1881.
  Folle-Farine, 3 vols., London: Chapman and Hall, 1871.
  Moths, 3 vols., London, Chatto and Windus, 1880.
  Under Two Flags, Chicago and New York: Rand, McNally and Co. (1917?).
  Views and Opinions, 2nd edn., London: Methuen, 1896.
Dixon, Ella Hepworth, *The Story of a Modern Woman*, with an introduction by Kate Flint, London: Merlin Press Ltd.; Chicago: Ivan R. Dee Inc., 1990.
Flint, Kate, *The Woman Reader, 1837–1914*, Oxford: Clarendon Press, 1993.
Jordan, Ellen, "The Christening of the New Woman: May 1894," *Victorian Newsletter*, 48 (Spring 1983), 19–21.
Knapp, Shoshana Milgram, "Real Passion and the Reverence for Life: Sexuality and Antivivisection in the Fiction of Victoria Cross," in Angela Ingram

and Daphne Patai, (eds.), *Rediscovering Forgotten Radicals: British Women Writers, 1889–1939*, Chapel Hill and London: University of North Carolina Press, 1993.

Moore, George, *Literature at Nurse or Circulating Morals: A Polemic on Victorian Censorship*, edited and with an introduction by Pierre Coustillas, Brighton, Sussex: Harvester, 1976.

Poovey, Mary, *Making A Social Body: British Cultural Formation, 1830–1864*, Chicago: University of Chicago Press, 1995.

Pykett, Lyn, *The "Improper" Feminine: The Women's Sensation Novel and the New Woman Writing*, London: Routledge, 1992.

Said, Edward, *Culture and Imperialism*, New York: Vintage, 1994.

Orientalism, London: Routledge, 1978.

Schroeder, Natalie, "Feminine Sensationalism, Eroticism, and Self-Assertion: M. E. Braddon and Ouida," *Tulsa Studies in Women's Literature* 7 (1988), 87–103.

Sedgwick, Eve Kosofsky, *Between Men: English Literature and Male Homosocial Desire*, New York: Columbia University Press, 1985.

Squier, Susan, "Sexual Biopolitics in *Man's World*: The Writings of Charlotte Haldane," in Angela Ingram and Daphne Patai (eds.), *Rediscovering Forgotten Radicals: British Women Writers, 1889–1939*, Chapel Hill and London: University of North Carolina Press, 1993.

Suleri, Sara, *The Rhetoric of English India*, Chicago: University of Chicago Press, 1992.

Organizing women: New Woman writers, New Woman readers, and suffrage feminism

Ann Ardis

> I once asked a lady, who knew Thackeray intimately, whether he had any model for Becky Sharp. She told me that Becky was an invention, but that the idea of the character had been partly suggested by a governess who lived in the neighborhood of Kensington Square, and was the companion of a very selfish and rich old woman. I inquired what became of the governess, and she replied that, oddly enough, some years after the appearance of *Vanity Fair*, she ran away with the nephew of the lady with whom she was living, and for a short time made a great splash in society, quite in Mrs. Rawdon Crawley's style, and entirely by Mrs. Rawdon Crawley's methods. Ultimately she came to grief, disappeared to the Continent, and used to be occasionally seen at Monte Carlo and other gambling places.
>
> Oscar Wilde, "The Decay of Lying" (1889)[1]

In "The Decay of Lying," Oscar Wilde caricatures the woman reader by noting how she cannot distinguish between fiction and reality: reading about Thackeray's Becky Sharp, she seeks to become Becky Sharp. Like the "silly boys" who read the "adventures of Jack Sheppard and Dick Turpin" and "pillage the stalls of unfortunate apple-women, break into sweet-shops at night, and alarm old gentlemen returning home from the city by leaping out on them in suburban lanes, with black masks and unloaded revolvers," the woman reader epitomizes "life's imitative instinct," its unimaginative literalization of art's creativity.[2] Published in 1889, Wilde's witticism both glosses and glances away from the issues this chapter will address. It nicely summarizes the debate about the relationship between life and art raised in the context of controversies in the 1880s and 1890s regarding New Woman fiction and decadence; but it also glances away from these controversies through its references to early Victorian fiction rather than to *fin-de-siècle* writers.

It is not insignificant that aesthetic theory began to valorize anti-representationality at exactly the point in time when women writers with overt feminist agendas were flooding the literary marketplace with "new" novels, reaching more readers than ever before, and proselytizing for women's rights as effectively through their fiction-writing as through their political and social activism. Modernism's "rise" to aesthetic hegemony was predicated on the devaluation of women readers and women's writing; its boundaries were policed through gendered criteria of aesthetic excellence and tranhistorical universality that were first articulated in response to the perceived mass appeal of fiction written by, about, and "for" women at the *fin-de-siècle*.[3] If, however, following Wendy Mulford's lead, we set ourselves the task of assessing the "social and political force" of literature, rather than thinking about the aesthetic value of isolated "great" works, women readers and writers during this period can be evaluated quite differently.[4]

Recent criticism has (re)acquainted us with the sheer variety of *fin-de-siècle* writings about the New Woman.[5] Although most of the experimentation with this figure takes place in short stories and novels, plays and poems about New Women were also produced. Moreover, far from having "one story to tell," as Elaine Showalter once suggested, the New Woman figures in a multiplicity of stories about gender and culture.[6] Antifeminists such as Eliza Lynn Linton and Mrs. Humphry Ward were as interested in the New Woman as self-styled radicals such as Grant Allen, Mona Caird, George Egerton, and Olive Schreiner, and for a variety of reasons. Some of the sixty-odd writers discussed in *New Women, New Novels*, for example, focus on the New Woman's sexuality. Others deal mainly with her entrance into the political sphere. Still others concentrate on issues of (artistic) vocation. Some New Woman fiction is ideologically seamless, internally consistent. But much of the discourse about New Women is contradictory, heteroglossic. Radical writers were as likely as conservatives to write boomerang plots that either catapult their rebellious heroines back into conventionality or show the next generation's backlash against their mothers's feminism. And any given text is likely to pull in several directions at once.

More importantly for the purposes of this chapter, *fin-de-siècle* writings on the New Woman also need to be catalogued in terms of their cultural longevity. At one end of the spectrum lie texts such as *The Story of an African Farm* (1883) and *The Heavenly Twins*, which remained in circulation for quite some time at the turn of the century, and are once again – at least for the moment – in print. As many have noted, Schreiner's novel became the "Bible" of the suffrage movement, while Sarah Grand's novel was a "record-breaking sensation that [William Heinemann] continued to republish as late as 1923."[7] At the other end of the spectrum lie texts such as Gertrude Dix's *The Image-Breakers*, Edith Johnstone's *A Sunless Heart*, and Netta Syrett's *Nobody's Fault*. The former are Dix's and Johnstone's only publications; the latter is one of sixty books Syrett published over the course of her forty-four-year writing career.[8] None of these novels was ever in the critical limelight, none generated the kind of scandal that made Grand's *The Heavenly Twins* and George Egerton's *Keynotes* infamous bestsellers in the nineties, and only one of Syrett's novels is in print today. Interestingly enough, though, these lesser-known works by and about New Women are often more radical in many regards than the titles with which we are more familiar. As I have argued elsewhere in detail, writers such as Dix, Johnstone, and Syrett experimented much more radically with the conventions of the nineteenth-century marriage-plot than do Schreiner and Grand, though neither history nor their contemporaries credited them for this.[9]

Barbara Herrnstein Smith's work on the "economy" of literary and aesthetic value and the very complex dynamics of a text's cultural reproduction as a "classic" goes a long way toward explaining why the most radical *fin-de-siècle* New Woman writings, regardless of their aesthetic quality, were destined never to be canonized as part of the "Great Tradition." As Herrnstein Smith notes in "Contingencies of Value,"

[S]ince those with cultural power tend to be members of socially, economically, and politically established classes (or to serve them and identify their own interests with theirs), the texts that survive will tend to be those that appear to reflect and reinforce establishment ideologies. However much canonical works may be seen to "question" secular vanities such as wealth, social position, and political power, "remind" their readers of more elevated values and virtues, and oblige them to "confront" such hard truths and harsh realities as their own mortality and the hidden griefs of obscure people, they would not be found to please long and well if they were seen to undercut establishment interests *radically* or to subvert the ideologies that support them *effectively*.[10]

Given the backlash against decadence, aestheticism, and feminism that followed in the wake of the scandal surrounding Wilde's trials in 1895; given too both the ascendancy of gradualist rather than revolutionary socialism and the increasing conservatism of the British mainstream in the context of the Boer War at the very end of the century, it perhaps should come as no surprise that texts such as Jane Hume Clapperton's *Margaret Dunmore; or, A Socialist Home*, *The Image-Breakers*, Lady Florence

Dixie's *Gloriana; or, The Revolution of 1900*, and *A Sunless Heart* were not reviewed widely and disappeared quickly from cultural memory.[11] Because they undercut establishment interests *radically* and subvert liberal and domestic ideology *effectively*, they were not obvious candidates for the new curriculum in English literature that was being constructed at the turn of the century:[12] *Margaret Dunmore*'s protagonist establishes a collective home for all the misfits of a bourgeois social order; *The Image-Breakers* points up socialism's failure to speak to women's concerns; Dixie's heroine leads a people's revolution; and Johnstone's novel deals with the sexual abuse of a child. For a variety of reasons, in other words, all of these texts remained outside the mainstream reading public's interests at the turn of the century.

Herrnstein Smith's work on canon-formation does not, however, help us understand why texts such as *The Story of an African Farm* and *The Heavenly Twins* had a longer shelf life at the turn of the century than the above. Herrnstein Smith is too exclusively focused on institutionally based evaluative practices – e.g., formal reviews, influential works of literary criticism, school curricula – to explain the semi-underground economy that kept books such as *The Story of an African Farm* passing from hand to hand in the early years of the twentieth century. Her work cannot account for the way in which a feminist public sphere in Edwardian Britain operated independently of what Louis Althusser would term the ideological state apparatuses. An organization such as the Women Writers' Suffrage League, for example, published and promoted a great deal of creative writing as well as nonfictional prose. But, as Wendy Mulford has discussed at length, these materials were displayed in suffrage shops alongside texts produced by the WSPU (Women's Social and Political Union), the NUWSS (National Union of Women's Suffrage Societies), and independent publishers sympathetic to women's suffrage – not distributed through the school system or praised by reviewers in establishment periodicals. Not unlike the way in which H. D.'s poetry and fiction circulated in an activist women's community long before her work was reclaimed by academic feminism in the 1980s, suffrage poetry, essays, pamphlets, masques, farces, short fiction, and novels played a significant role "in the developing politicization of women"[13] – albeit in ways that are difficult to document, either because the networks of circulation were not institutionally based, or because feminist organizational histories have yet to be done.

Again, a great deal of work has been done recently to familiarize contemporary audiences with the range of formal and ideological experimentation undertaken in *fin-de-siècle* New Woman writings. I would like to suggest, however, that the next "stage" of research in this area should focus on reception histories. What is called for now is a full-scale investigation of the various formal and informal contexts in which Edwardian women would have encountered *fin-de-siècle* writings on the New Woman such as *The Story of an African Farm*: the networks of friendship, the informal and formal reading groups, and the suffrage organizations and rallies in which texts such as *The Story of an African Farm* were presented as utopian dystopias. Critics such as Elizabeth Long and Janice Radway have conducted ethnographic studies of romance readers, turn-of-the-century American women's book groups, and Book-of-the-Month-Club bestsellers.[14] A similarly conceptualized ethnographic study of Edwardian women's reading of *fin-de-siècle* New Woman writings would complement nicely the recovery projects of critics such as Wendy Mulford and Kate Flint – and allow us to honor the political work accomplished through women's literary production at the turn of the twentieth century.[15]

As a means of beginning this recuperative project, consider Ruth Slate's discussion of *The Story of an African Farm* in her diary entry of May 28, 1908.

Read *The Story of an African Farm* in lunch hour. Am I presumptuous in feeling that *much* of what I have been thinking and feeling so strongly is here expressed? Met Eva in the evening. Journeyed on a motor bus to Hyde Park, seeing many of the decorations put up in honour of the French President's visit on the way. Both of us feeling strongly a sudden rebellion to our old ways of living and thinking – which though expressing itself suddenly has, I think, been growing a long while; we had much to say.[16]

As literary criticism, Slate's brief reference to Olive Schreiner's *The Story of an African Farm* is hardly satisfying. For information about Schreiner herself, *The Story of an African Farm*, New Woman fiction more generally, or the relationship between *fin-de-siècle* feminist writings and the suffrage campaign, one would need to look elsewhere than the diaries and letters of this lower-middle-class early twentieth-century working woman. But as an instance of the highly selective identificatory reading practice I want to call attention to in this chapter, it is exemplary. Two things are striking about this passage: Slate is not disappointed in any regard with Schreiner's work; indeed, she is galvanized to change her life by reading it. In *A Literature of Their Own*, Elaine Showalter criticized *fin-de-siècle* feminists such as Schreiner, George Egerton, and Sarah Grand quite harshly for not offering a positive aesthetic model to the next generation of women writers. Unlike Showalter, Slate does in fact find a positive model for her own generation in Schreiner. Rather than objecting to the boomerang ending of *The Story of an African Farm*, for example, Slate seems to identify with the critique of Victorian gender ideology expressed in the middle section of the narrative, finding in it an expression of her own and her friend Eva's rebellion against "our old ways of living and thinking." In other words, in keeping with Susan Winnett's work on feminist narratology, Slate is reading against the grain of the narrative's oedipal drive to closure, reading *for* its feminist legend.[17] Or rather, to borrow Mark Amsler's phrasing, she is functioning as a "skipping reader": a women reader who defies patriarchal authority by selectively *mis*reading the text at hand. Amsler's interest lies with medieval readers such as Margery Kempe, Christine de Pisan, and the Wife of Bath, whose "countercommentary interrupts the dominant misogyny and the official interpretation of scripture in clerical discourse."[18] But his point is germane in this context as well. For Slate quite pointedly and conveniently ignores the punitive message to rebel women in *Story*'s tragic ending, focusing instead on its consciousness-raising articulation of "woman's experience."

"Woman's experience" is, admittedly, a problematic category, as recent critiques of white feminism from a number of different perspectives have shown.[19] Nonetheless, it is important to understand the role that a conceptualization of "woman's experience" played in the politicization of women such as Ruth Slate at the turn of the twentieth century, and the role that literature about New Women played as a venue for that politicization. "Experience is not a word we can do without," Joan Scott has noted, "although it is tempting, given its usage to essentialize identity and reify the subject."[20] Rather than jettisoning the term, however, she encourages us to work with it and analyze its operations by "focusing on the processes of identity production."[21] Studies of the formal and ideological experimentation of New Woman writings can lead to the impasse described in Showalter's judgment. Scott's work, by contrast, invites us to theorize the reading experience itself: the identificatory modeling of the new feminist subject that is charted through a highly selective reading of a text such as *The Story of an African Farm* by readers such as Ruth Slate and Eva Slawson. Recently, albeit for very different reasons, feminist critics have joined ranks with modernists such as Oscar Wilde in criticizing women's identificatory reading practices. But if we focus on the process of identity *construction*, as Scott suggests and as Ruth Slate's writing demonstrates, perhaps it is possible to avoid the essentialism allegedly bound up in the notion of identity and focus instead on the articulation or construction of feminist subject positions that enabled women such as Ruth Slate to change their lives – and change history in the process.

I do not mean to sound like a naive believer in the progress of history; rather, I am trying here to give credit where credit is due. Whether or not contemporary feminists can see themselves mirrored in the writings and actions of turn-of-the-twentieth-century feminists, and in spite of the fact that we can no longer ignore the orientalism of a George Egerton or the middle-class bias of a Sarah Grand, their writings changed their world – shifted the terms of their culture's discussion of the "woman question," and changed the course of history. Insofar as New Woman fiction "created and consolidated a community of women readers, who could refer to these works as proof of their psychological, social, and ideological difference from men";[22] and insofar as this community of readers viewed their reading as both an impetus for and a component of their social and political activism, identificatory claims about "woman's experience" played a crucial role in suffrage politics at the turn of the century.

A second recommendation for further work in this area emerges here: in addition to developing reception histories of New Woman writings that would explain the continued circulation of a small number of *fin-de-siècle* writings in the context of the Edwardian suffrage campaign, we need to consider the self-presentational/self-promotional strategies of *fin-de-siècle* New Woman writers who secured the longevity of their writings through their own self-display in the public arena. In other words, we need histories of the production of New Woman "authors," in a Foucaultian sense, as well as reception histories.

Sarah Grand is an interesting case in point in this regard, and Talia Schaffer's work on Alice Meynell provides a model of how to proceed. In "Writing a Public Self: Alice Meynell and the Angel in the House," Schaffer notes that Alice Meynell was the most famous female poet at the turn of the century: she was an Angel in the House admired by Coventry Patmore, an aesthete who wrote for John Lane, a fearless suffragette, a public speaker for women's causes, and a pioneer in feminist historiography. Although her arch, frivolous, pretty self-image as a female aesthete advanced her reputation at the turn of the century, it harmed her posthumous reputation, when the critical pendulum swung the other way and readers began searching the literary past for forthright feminist role models. Through detailed discussion of essays such as "The Colour of Life," Schaffer argues that Meynell's "apparently docile, domestic persona was a sophisticated literary construction, a way of marketing herself as a public icon." In this regard, Meynell's work "reveals the strategies women needed to become recognized as public intellectuals at the turn of the century." Taking refuge in obliqueness rather than the kind of obscurity Allon White has described writers practicing to protect themselves from readers' psychoanalytic scrutiny or "symptomatic readings," Meynell, Schaffer contends, produced "an artfully misleading version of herself designed to win critical plaudits."[23]

Like Meynell, Sarah Grand both carefully courted and avoided controversy at the turn of the century. Along with George Egerton's *Keynotes*, which was published some months later in 1893, *The Heavenly Twins* was a scandalous bestseller in the 1890s. It was reviewed widely and both praised and blamed for its treatment of male promiscuity, syphilis, and the impact of both on innocent wives and children. Yet, interestingly enough, in interviews published between 1894 and 1898 in periodicals such as the *Humanitarian*, *Lady's Realm*, and *Woman at Home*, Grand is very careful to distance herself from the most controversial aspects of her work and to focus instead on her mainstream, middle-of-the-road feminist concerns: the importance of education for women, the "purity" of marriage, and the essential differences between men and women. Over and over again in these interviews, she distinguishes herself from "unsexed" New Women who challenge the naturalness of gender roles; over and over again she speaks reassuringly about – or is characterized reassuringly as upholding – middle-class ideals of domesticity and femininity.

For example, interviews for, respectively, *Woman at Home* and *Woman* highlight the difference between Grand's own views and those of her characters. "So many people suppose," Grand tells the *Woman at Home*'s interviewer,

that when an author develops a character with great care and fullness, his own views may be safely identified with those expressed with that character. I have found this in the case of more than one personage in the "Heavenly Twins." The views of Evadne or Angelica, for example, are not necessarily to be accepted as my views, in fact cannot be, for they are even opposed to each other, yet people frequently write, wondering how I can possibly defend such opinions.[24]

The anonymous review featured in *Woman* plays off this same contrast even more dramatically, as the interviewer registers the shifts in his own response to her during the interview. Relieved initially by the elegance of "her pretty little blue and white drawing-room" and Grand's appearance – which "bore none of the outward signs of feminine aggressiveness" – he goes on to emphasize his own response to her first comments about *The Heavenly Twins*. "Nothing annoys me more," he reports Grand saying,

> "than the mistake made by so many in supposing that I took Colonel Colquhoun as a typical man... Only last night at a dinner party Mr.————" (naming a well-known literary character) "told me how mistaken I was in supposing that my principal male character was a fair type of the sex. Of course I only meant him to be typical of a particular type – not of the whole sex."
>
> "And you do not think us very bad?" I asked, feeling more at ease.
>
> "Oh! dear no. I am far from being a man-hater, I like and respect many men. Moreover, there is not, and never can be, any quarrel between the sexes. Women will always be women, and men always men, and marriage, in my opinion, must always be the ideal state."[25]

With increasing rapport, they then go to talk about the bachelor girl and the glorified spinster, Grand's love of domesticity and the excellence of her tea, her interest in women's emancipation from "shallowness and ignorance" (though not from "womanliness and the natural ties of wedlock"), and the inappropriateness of "affected masculinity of dress." "There is nothing unwomanly – quite the reverse – about the author of *The Heavenly Twins*," the interviewer pronounces confidently, in conclusion.[26]

Interviews published in the *Humanitarian* and *Woman at Home* also emphasize the tastefulness of Grand's personal appearance and decor. While the 1895 interview for *Woman at Home* offered great detail regarding the furnishings of her Kensington flat, the 1897 interview speaks admiringly of her love of "a free, quiet life in the country."[27] And the *Humanitarian* interviewer gives Grand an opportunity to expound at length upon political liabilities of rational dress. "Want of taste in dress on the part of many women, who advocate what are called advanced views, has thrown back the woman's cause fifty years," she tells Sarah Tooley in the *Humanitarian*.

> Everyone who takes part in the movement ought to be particularly careful in dress and manners; and I am sorry to say that the manners of some are simply disgraceful; so utterly wanting in tact and ordinary politeness... [A]ny attempt to disparage the home duties is such a mistake. While being fully in favour of

women entering the professions, speaking on public platforms, and taking their part in the movements of the time, I think they should always consider their homes and families first of all . . . The nursery is the proper place to teach the equality of the sexes.[28]

In an otherwise fascinating discussion of women writers' complex and sometimes frustrating negotiations in the literary marketplace at the end of the nineteenth century, Rita Kranidis notes the discrepancies between views expressed in Grand's short stories for *Temple Bar* and novels such as *The Heavenly Twins* and *The Beth Book*; and she blames *Temple Bar* itself for the middle-class bias informing Grand's sentimental representations of working-class women in stories such as "Janey, A Humble Administrator – A Study From Life" (1891). Grand, she suggests, was only trying to give *Temple Bar* editors and readers what they expected, as she herself struggled to "court the journal market."[29] The inconsistencies Kranidis identifies are indeed evidence of Grand's complex negotiations in the literary marketplace.[30] But instead of demanding consistency from Grand's *oeuvre* (or a feminism that meets current standards of political correctness), perhaps we should appreciate the skill with which Grand constructed a public persona that could survive in an increasingly conservative political climate – and help keep her fiction in print. In other words, we need to recognize that Grand's "apparently docile, domestic persona was" – like Alice Meynell's – "a sophisticated literary construction, a way of marketing herself as a public icon."

I do not mean to suggest that Grand's self-representations as a middle-of-the-road liberal feminist in the interviews discussed above are duplicitous. Nor do I mean to ignore or explain away Grand's middle-class bias. Rather, in attempting now to connect the two halves of my argument, I am suggesting that the ideological contradictions informing Grand's work – and that of so many other New Woman writers – are precisely what invite the skipping reader to skip: to ignore that with which she cannot identify, to fail to hear/read whatever messages miss her mark.[31] On the one hand, it is easy enough to see the line of continuity (if not influence) between Grand's self-presentation in the interviews for women's magazines of the 1890s and the properly middle-class demeanor and dress of suffrage activists in the first (non-militant) phase of the suffrage campaign (1904–07). On the other hand, it is also easy to see the line of continuity between Grand's highly controversial critique of male sexual vice in *The Heavenly Twins* and Christabel Pankhurst's even more spectacular treatment of male bodies in *The Great*

Scourge and How to End It (1913). By the time Grand began to serve as mayoress of Bath in 1922, the public had forgotten her early fame as a bestselling writer and feminist.[32] But in the context of the Edwardian suffrage campaign, this dual legacy was very much still in circulation – and available for selective appropriation through identificatory feminist reading practices.

In other words (to end by reminding my own readers of the amusing but misguided epigraph from Wilde's essay with which this chapter opened), far from epitomizing "life's imitative instinct" in the reductive way that Wilde intended this phrasing to be meant, New Woman writers were promoting both themselves and "the Cause" at the turn of the century. And New Woman readers were appropriating what they read as an expression of their *own* "experience" – with consequences far different from the tale of degeneration Vivian tells about the woman reader in "The Decay of Lying."

NOTES

1 Oscar Wilde, "The Decay of Lying," in Karl Beckson (ed.), *Aesthetes and Decadents of the 1890s* (Chicago: Academy, 1981), p. 186.
2 Ibid., pp. 186, 187.
3 For consideration of the feminization of mass culture at the turn of the twentieth century and modernism's efforts to "rise" above it, see Suzanne Clark's *Sentimental Modernism: Women Writers and the Revolution of the Word* (Bloomington: Indiana University Press, 1991); Alfred Habegger's *Henry James and the "Woman Business"* (Cambridge: Cambridge University Press, 1989); and Andreas Huyssen's *After the Great Divide: Modernism, Mass Culture, Postmodernism* (Bloomington: Indiana University Press 1986), as well as my own *New Women, New Novels: Feminism and Early Modernism* (New Brunswick, NJ: Rutgers University Press, 1990).
4 Wendy Mulford, "Socialist-Feminist Criticism: A Case Study, Women's Suffrage and Literature, 1906–14," in Peter Widdowson (ed.), *Re-Reading English* (London: Methuen, 1982), p. 182.
5 The book-length studies of New Women at the Victorian *fin-de-siècle* include: Ardis, *New Women;* Gerg Björhövde, *Rebellious Structures: Women Writers and the Crisis of the Novel, 1880–1900* (Oxford: Oxford University Press, 1987); Rita Kranidis, *Subversive Discourse: The Cultural Production of Late Victorian Feminist Novels* (New York: St. Martin's Press, 1995); Sally Ledger, *The New Woman: Fiction and Feminism at the Fin-de-Siècle* (Manchester and New York: Manchester University Press, 1997); Patricia Marks, *Bicyles, Bangs, and Bloomers: The New Woman and the Popular Press* (Lexington: University of Kentucky Press, 1990); Lyn Pykett, *The "Improper" Feminine: The Women's Sensation Novel and the New Woman Writing* (London and New York: Routledge, 1992); Elaine Showalter,

Sexual Anarchy: Gender and Culture at the Fin-de-Siècle (New York: Viking, 1990).

6 Elaine Showalter, *A Literature of Their Own: British Women Novelists from Brontë to Lessing* (Princeton, NJ: Princeton University Press, 1977), p. 215.

7 Marilyn Bonnell, "Sarah Grand," in William B. Thesing (ed.), *British Short-Fiction Writers, 1880–1914: The Realist Tradition* (Detroit, Washington, DC, London: Gale Research, 1994), p. 153.

8 Gertrude Dix, *The Image-Breakers* (London: W. Heinemann, 1900); Edith Johnstone, *A Sunless Heart* (London: Ward, Lock and Bowden, 1894); Netta Syrett, *Nobody's Fault* (London: John Lane, 1897).

9 See Ardis, *New Women*, especially pp. 83–138; "'The Journey From Fantasy to Politics': The Representation of Socialism and Feminism in *Gloriana* and *The Image-Breakers*," in Angela Ingram and Daphne Patai (eds.), *Rediscovering Forgotten Radicals: British Women Writers, 1889–1939* (Chapel Hill and London: University of North Carolina Press, 1993), pp. 43–56; and "Towards a Redefinition of 'Experimental Writing': Netta Syrett's Realism, 1908–1912," in Alison Booth (ed.), *Famous Last Words: Changes in Gender and Narrative Closure* (Charlottesville and London: University of Virginia Press, 1993), pp. 259–79.

10 Barbara Herrnstein Smith, "Contingencies of Value," in David H. Richter (ed.), *The Critical Tradition: Classic Texts and Contemporary Trends* (New York: St. Martin's Press, 1989), p. 1343.

11 Jane Hume Clapperton, *Margaret Dunmore; or, A Socialist Home* (London: Swan Sonnenschein, Lowry, 1888); Lady Florence Dixie, *Gloriana; Or, The Revolution of 1900* (London: Henry & Co., 1890).

12 For detailed discussion of changes in the curriculum for secondary and university education in Britain at the turn of the twentieth century, see Brian Doyle, *English and Englishness* (London: Routledge, 1989); Robert Colls and Philip Dodd (eds.), *Englishness: Politics and Culture, 1880–1920* (London and Dover, NH: Croom Helm, 1986); and Ivor Goodson and Peter Medway (eds.), *Bringing English to Order: The History and Politics of a School Subject* (London and New York: Falmer, 1990).

13 Mulford, "Socialist-Feminist Criticism," p. 186. See also David Rubinstein's *Before the Suffragettes: Women's Emancipation in the 1890s* (Brighton, Sussex: Harvester, 1986), in which he argues that "never before had literature and fiction contributed so much to the feminist movement as it did at the *fin-de-siècle*" (p. 24). Following Rubinstein's lead, Ledger also argues that novel-writing and feminist activism are closely associated during this period: "writing itself is seen as a liberatory activity" (*The New Woman*, p. 27).

14 Elizabeth Long, *The American Dream and the Popular Novel* (Boston: Routledge and Kegan Paul, 1985); Janice Radway, *A Feeling for Books: The Book-of-the-Month Club, Literary Taste, and Middle-Class Desire* (Chapel Hill: University of North Carolina Press, 1997).

15 Kate Flint, *The Woman Reader, 1837–1914* (Oxford: Clarendon Press, 1993).

16 Tierl Thompson (ed.), *Dear Girl: The Diaries and Letters of Two Working Women (1897–1917)* (London: The Women's Press, 1987), p. 108.

17 Susan Winnett, "Coming Unstrung: Women, Men, Narrative and Principles of Pleasure," *PMLA* 105 (1990), 505–18.

18 Mark Amsler, "Resistance and/as Reading," unpublished manuscript, p. 25.

19 See, for example, the essays collected by Chandra Mohanty in *Third World Women and the Politics of Feminism* (Bloomington: Indiana University Press, 1991).

20 Joan Scott, "Experience," in Judith Butler and Joan Scott (eds.), *Feminists Theorize the Political* (New York and London: Routledge, 1992), p. 37.

21 *Ibid.*

22 Flint, *The Woman Reader*, p. 305.

23 Talia Schaffer, "Writing a Public Self: Alice Meynell and the Angel in the House," unpublished manuscript, p. 1.

24 Jane T. Stoddart, "Sarah Grand: Illustrated Interview," *Woman at Home* 3 (1895), 248.

25 "A Chat with Mme. Sarah Grand," *Woman* 2 (1894), i.

26 *Ibid.*, ii.

27 Sarah Tooley, "Sarah Grand," *Woman at Home* 7 (1897), 178.

28 Sarah Tooley, "The Woman's Question: An Interview with Madame Sarah Grand," *Humanitarian* 8 (1896), 166.

29 Kranidis, *Subversive Discourse*, p. 51.

30 For a very different interpretation of these inconsistencies, however, see John Kucich's essay, "Curious Dualities: *The Heavenly Twins* (1893) and Sarah Grand's Belated Modernist Aesthetics," in Barbara Harman (ed.), *The New Nineteenth Century: Feminist Readings of Underread Victorian Fiction* (New York: Garland, 1996), pp. 195–204. For a more historically accurate and nuanced characterization of women's experience in the literary marketplace in the 1890s, see Margaret Stetz's work on George Egerton as well, especially: "New Grub Street and the Woman Writer of the 1890s," in Nikki Lee Manos and Meri-Jane Rochelson (eds.), *Transforming Genres: New Approaches to British Fiction of the 1890s* (New York: St. Martin's Press, 1994), pp. 21–46; and "*Keynotes*: A New Woman, Her Publisher, and Her Material," *Studies in the Literary Imagination* 30.1 (1997), 89–106.

31 In describing young women's responses to popular works such as *The Story of an African Farm*, *The Wide, Wide World*, and *Jessica's First Prayer* at the turn of the twentieth century, Sally Mitchell notes the following, which is germane to this discussion as well: "I do not therefore mean to imply any simple single theory of reading. The same material has multiple uses for different readers, for the same reader at different times, and for the same reader simultaneously when the book serves overlapping and conflicting functions. The complexity and multiplicity of interpretations make these texts interesting, even though many critics in their own day – to say nothing of the twentieth century – reject most of them as simplistic sentimental moral tales" (*The New Girl: Girls' Culture in England, 1880–1915* [New York: Columbia University Press, 1995], p. 143).

32 Carol Senf, "Introduction," Sarah Grand, *The Heavenly Twins* (Ann Arbor: University of Michigan Press, 1992), p. xxxv.

                          WORKS CITED

"A Chat with Mme. Sarah Grand," Woman (literary supplement) 2 May 1894, i–ii.
Ardis, Ann, "'The Journey From Fantasy to Politics': The Representation of Socialism and Feminism in *Gloriana* and *The Image-Breakers*," in Angela Ingram and Daphne Patai (eds.), *Rediscovering Forgotten Radicals: British Women Writers, 1889–1939*, Chapel Hill and London: University of North Carolina Press, 1993, pp. 43–56.
   New Women, New Novels: Feminism and Early Modernism, New Brunswick, NJ: Rutgers University Press, 1990.
   "Towards a Redefinition of 'Experimental Writing': Netta Syrett's Realism, 1980–1912," in Alison Booth (ed.), *Famous Last Words: Changes in Gender and Narrative Closure*, Charlottesville and London: University of Virginia Press, 1993, pp. 259–79.
Bjorhovde, Gerd, *Rebellious Structures: Women Writers and the Crisis of the Novel, 1880–1900*, Oxford: Norwegian University Press, 1987.
Bonnell, Marilyn, "Sarah Grand," in William B. Thesing (ed.), *British Short-Fiction Writers, 1880–1914: The Realist Tradition*, Detroit, Washington, DC, London: Gale Research, 1994, pp. 151–64.
Clark, Suzanne, *Sentimental Modernism: Women Writers and the Revolution of the Word*, Bloomington: Indiana University Press, 1991.
Clapperton, Jane Hume, *Margaret Dunmore; or, A Socialist Home*, London: Swan Sonnenschein, Lowry, 1888.
Colls, Robert and Philip Dodd (eds.), *Englishness: Politics and Culture, 1880–1920*, London and Dover, NH: Croom Helm, 1986.
Dix, Gertrude, *The Image-Breakers*, London: W. Heinemann, 1900.
Doyle, Brian, *English and Englishness*, London: Routledge, 1989.
Flint, Kate, *The Woman Reader, 1837–1914*, Oxford: Clarendon Press, 1993.
Goodson, Ivor and Peter Medway (eds.), *Bringing English to Order: The History and Politics of a School Subject*, London and New York: Falmer, 1990.
Habegger, Alfred, *Henry James and the "Woman Business,"* Cambridge: Cambridge University Press, 1989.
Herrnstein Smith, Barbara, "The Contingencies of Value," in David H. Richter (ed.), *The Critical Tradition: Classic Texts and Contemporary Trends*, New York: St. Martin's Press, 1989, pp. 1320–43.
Huyssen, Andreas, *After the Great Divide: Modernism, Modernity, Postmodernism*, Bloomington: Indiana University Press, 1986.
Johnstone, Edith, *A Sunless Heart*, London: Ward, Lock and Bowden, 1894.
Kranidis, Rita S., *Subversive Discourse: The Cultural Production of Late Victorian Feminist Novels*, New York: St. Martin's Press, 1995.
Kucich, John, "Curious Dualities: *The Heavenly Twins* (1893) and Sarah Grand's Belated Modernist Aesthetics," in Barbara Harman (ed.), *The New Nine-*

teenth Century: Feminist Readings of Underread Victorian Fiction, New York: Garland, 1996, pp. 195–206.

Ledger, Sally, *The New Woman: Fiction and Feminism at the Fin-de-Siècle*, Manchester and New York: Manchester University Press, 1997.

Mitchell, Sally, *The New Girl: Girls' Culture in England, 1880–1915*, New York: Columbia University Press, 1995.

Mohanty, Chandra, *Third World Women and the Politics of Feminism*, Bloomington: Indiana University Press, 1995.

Mulford, Wendy, "Socialist-Feminist Criticism: A Case Study, Women's Suffrage and Literature, 1906–14," in Peter Widdowson (ed.), *Re-Reading English*, London: Methuen, 1982, pp. 179–92.

Pykett, Lyn, *The "Improper" Feminine: The Women's Sensation Novel and the New Woman Writing*, London and New York: Routledge, 1992.

Rubinstein, David, *Before the Suffragettes: Women's Emancipation in the 1890s*, Brighton, Sussex: Harvester, 1986.

Scott, Joan, "Experience," in Judith Butler and Joan Scott (eds.), *Feminists Theorize the Political*, New York and London: Routledge, 1992, pp. 22–40.

Senf, Carol, "Introduction," Sarah Grand, *The Heavenly Twins*, Ann Arbor: University of Michigan Press, 1992, pp. vii–xxxvii.

Showalter, Elaine, *A Literature of Their Own: British Women Novelists from Brontë to Lessing*, Princeton, NJ: Princeton University Press, 1977.

Sexual Anarchy: Gender and Culture at the Fin-de-Siècle, New York: Viking, 1990.

Stetz, Margaret, "*New Grub Street* and the Woman Writer of the 1890s," in Nikki Lee Manos and Meri-Jane Rochelson (eds.), *Transforming Genres: New Approaches to British Fiction of the 1890s*, New York: St. Martin's Press, 1994, pp. 21–46.

"*Keynotes*: A New Woman, Her Publisher, and Her Material," *Studies in the Literary Imagination* 30.1 (1997), 89–106.

Stoddart, Jane T., "Sarah Grand: Illustrated Interview," *Woman at Home*, 3 (1895), 247–52.

Syrett, Netta, *Nobody's Fault*, London: John Lane, 1897.

Thompson, Tierl (ed.), *Dear Girl: The Diaries and Letters of Two Working Women (1897–1917)*, London: The Women's Press, 1987.

Tooley, Sarah A., "The Woman's Question: An Interview with Madame Sarah Grand," *Humanitarian* 8 (1896), 161–69.

"Sarah Grand," *Woman at Home* 7 (1897), 176–78.

Wilde, Oscar, "The Decay of Lying," in Karl Beckson (ed.), *Aesthetes and Decadents of the 1890s*, Chicago: Academy, 1981, pp. 167–93.

Winnett, Susan, "Coming Unstrung: Women, Men, Narrative, and Principles of Pleasure," *PMLA* 105 (1990), 505–18.

CHAPTER 12

Shot out of the canon: Mary Ward and the claims of conflicting feminisms

Beth Sutton-Ramspeck

Was the novelist Mary Ward a purveyor of outmoded ideas about womanhood? That was the widespread perception reflected in a cartoon on the cover of *Votes for Women* in July 1914. The cartoon's headline announces, "Time to Shut up Shop." Beneath these words appears a dress shop whose name we read backwards through the window: "Mrs. Humphrey [*sic*] Ward – Modiste." The lady representing Mary Ward wears a ruffled, presumably hooped skirt, representing Victorian styles; displayed behind her are a nearly identical dress, several enormous bonnets, and a cage-like set of skirt hoops. The harsh-featured Ward figure shows a large, beribboned bonnet to a pretty woman dressed in a slim-profile dress representing the latest style. The caption below reads:

WOMAN OF TO-DAY: "Surely you don't expect me to put up with any of these!"
MRS. HUMPHRY WARD: "I am sorry we have nothing newer. This style of thing gave every satisfaction – fifty years ago."

The message is clear: Ward's ideas about women are as outdated as fifty-year-old fashions.

The woman who inspired this caricature was by 1914 nearly as well known for leading the National Anti-Suffrage League as for writing novels. Upon publication, six months later, of *Delia Blanchflower*, her novel about the suffrage movement, most critics – like critics today – readily labeled the politics of the book and its author "anti-suffrage." Yet in the novel's final pages, after the suffragette heroine renounces the violence of the radical "Daughters of Revolt," she tells her future husband,

I am just as much for *women* – I am just as rebellious against their wrongs – as I ever was. I shall be a suffragist always.[1]

The unrepentant feminism of Ward's heroine challenges the dismissive assumption that Ward opposed feminism – or women's suffrage – in any simple way. It points instead to the contradictory attitudes typical of Ward's work throughout her career.

That career was a famously successful one, Ward's second novel, *Robert Elsmere* (1888), having sold more than a million copies and several subsequent novels having sold by the hundreds of thousands. Ward won critical acclaim as well, from Walter Pater and Mark Twain, Rebecca Harding Davis and William Dean Howells, Leo Tolstoy and Arthur Conan Doyle. Yet today Ward and her work are almost unknown. Ward has benefited little from two decades of interrogations of the canon, from the burgeoning interest in cultural studies, or even from the rise of feminist criticism. I will argue that Ward's gender politics were a crucial factor that stimulated hostile comments by Edwardians and modernists and have since discouraged reevaluation of her work. Ward's reputation has suffered alternately because she was a "lady novelist" interested in ideas, politics, religion, and the position of women, and because she held the "wrong" ideas. Rather than being antifeminist, Ward spent her life negotiating between competing and often contradictory feminisms; nevertheless, misunderstandings of Mary Ward's opinions about "the woman question" shaped her reputation at the turn of the century and continue to do so today.

MARY WARD AND THE WOMAN QUESTION

Ward's reputation for antifeminism stems in part from a common misunderstanding of turn-of-the-century feminism. Far from being univocal, the "first wave" of the women's movement encompassed various, often conflicting ideas and methods, the most widespread being enlightenment liberal feminism (the tradition of Mary Wollstonecraft and John Stuart Mill), and social feminism (the tradition of Hannah More and George Eliot). Liberal feminism stresses individualism, education, and equal rights; liberal feminists argue that the sexes are in all important ways alike, so women deserve the same political, economic, and educational opportunities as men. Social feminism (or "difference feminism") stresses women's family roles, celebrates what is considered distinctive to women, works to uncover a history of female accomplishments, and seeks a future with more room for "feminine values" such as nurturance and compassion. Feminists then, as now, drew ideas from both traditions, either comfortably, like most prominent suffragists, or uncomfortably, like Mary Ward.

For Ward, tensions between these conflicting feminisms led to paradoxical political positions: as a founder of Somerville College, Ward advanced the liberal feminist goal of equal educational and professional opportunities for women. Her novels sympathetically portray feisty, independent New Women in such non-traditional jobs as secretary, ambulance driver, lobbyist, and farmer. However, unlike other liberal feminists of her day, she actively opposed national women's suffrage. As a social feminist, she campaigned in support of women's political activities at the local level and women's active participation in local social welfare activities.

The ending of *Marcella* (1894) illustrates Ward's balancing act. The night before Marcella Boyce, in typical New Womanly fashion, declares her love to Aldous Raeburn and renews their engagement, she contemplates a future that balances liberal feminist self development and social feminist self-surrender:

Would marriage fetter her? It was not in the least probable that he and she, with their differing temperaments, would think alike in the future, any more than in the past. She would always be for experiments, for risks, which his critical temper, his larger brain, would of themselves be slow to enter upon. Yet she knew well enough that in her hands they would become bearable and even welcome to him ... Now, would not a wife's chief function be to reconcile him with himself and life, to cheer him forward on the lines of his own nature – to believe, understand, help? [2]

This passage represents marriage as mutually beneficial, each bringing strengths to aid the other. Granted, the differences between Marcella and Aldous reflect traditional analyses of gender difference, but his "critical temper, his larger brain" derive from his better intellectual training – of which much is made in this book that presents a strong liberal feminist protest against women's poor education and portrays the heroine's intellectual and moral development. Marcella will "cheer him forward" in his work, but she will also, on her own property, instigate her own "experiments," which he will in turn assist. Their mutual assistance in the private sphere will enhance their effectiveness in the public sphere: her "experiments" at Mellor, his work in Parliament.

The next paragraph of the passage further explores Marcella's plan for the future:

Yet always in the full liberty to make her own sacrifices, to realise her own dreamlands! She thought [of her newly-inherited estate]; she pledged herself to every man, woman and child on it so to live her life that each one of theirs should be the richer for it; she set out, so far as in her lay, to "choose equality." And beyond Mellor, in the great changing world of social speculation and endeavour, she prayed always for the open mind, the listening heart.[3]

The passage dialogically juxtaposes liberal feminist language – "liberty," "choose equality" – with a social feminist pledge to serve others. Marcella's "liberty to make her own sacrifices" will not be impaired by marriage, for marriage means not being a "fettered" "angel in the house" but pursuing an active life in "the great changing world of social speculation and endeavour."

The novel's final scene, however, suggests otherwise. Marcella unburdens her conscience to her lover about how badly she has treated him. Then, in language that seems to confirm interpretations of the novel as antifeminist, Ward ends her book:

But she had given away all rights – even the right to hate herself. Piteously, childishly, with seeking eyes, she held out her hand to him, as though mutely asking for the answering to her outpouring – the last word of it all. He caught her whisper.

"Forgive?" he said to her, scorning her for the first and only time in their history. "Does a man *forgive* the hand that sets him free, the voice that re-creates him? Choose some better word – my wife!"[4]

If Marcella momentarily gives up "even the right to hate herself," Aldous refuses her sacrifice – as she surely knew he would, or she could not love him. Instead, he reverses the positions, empowering her to set him free; together, they "choose equality." In any case, consistent with social feminist ideas, Ward advocates relationships based on mutual responsibilities, not on competing rights. So while Marcella gives up "rights," part of the point is that she has learned to be more like Aldous, who all along has thought not of rights but of responsibilities. The novel ends in a happy, but precarious, balance between liberal feminist self-development and social feminist devotion to duty.

MARY WARD AND THE "MIDDLE SUFFRAGE POLICY"

Like *Marcella* and most of her other novels, Ward's writings about women's suffrage embody tensions between liberal and social feminism. Heretofore there has been no thorough analysis of the full complexity and balance of Ward's suffrage writings. The commonsense conclusion drawn from her anti-suffrage activism is that she was virulently anti-feminist.[5] Yet close analysis of the "different ideal" that Ward proposed as an alternative to women's suffrage reveals that her intentions in opposing Parliamentary suffrage were actually to promote the women's movement.

In the suffrage controversy, Ward's social feminist ideas generally take precedence. As the Anti-Suffrage League's manifesto declares, "the spheres of men and women, owing to natural causes, are essentially different and therefore their share in the management of the State should be different."[6] It is important to recognize that, as Jane Lewis has shown, suffragists and anti-suffragists shared beliefs in sexual difference; they disagreed about the degree to which women should carry their particular gifts to a *national* arena. Suffragists believed women should reshape national government through the vote. Millicent Garrett Fawcett, leader of the National Union of Women's Suffrage Societies, wrote, "we neither deny nor minimize the differences between men and women. The claim of women to representation depends to a large extent on these differences."[7] Many feminist anti-suffragists considered women morally superior to men but feared that if women became involved in politics, their partisanship "would tend to blunt the special moral qualities of women."[8] Suffragists frequently cited women's supposed special moral and domestic qualities as a reason women should vote – to clean up politics; anti-suffragists mentioned them as potential casualties of the franchise.

Ward believed that the Parliamentary franchise would not achieve the ends that the suffragists claimed; instead, the vote would *lessen* the influence on public policy of educated and politically active women:

It is urged that the influence of women in politics would tell upon the side of morality. We believe that it does so tell already, and will do so with greater force as women by improved education fit themselves to exert it more widely and efficiently. But it may be asked, On what does this moral influence depend? We believe that it depends largely on qualities which the natural position and functions of women as they are at present tend to develop, and which might be seriously impaired by their admission to the turmoil of active political life. These qualities are, above all, sympathy and disinterestedness.[9]

The key word here is "disinterestedness," echoing Matthew Arnold, Ward's uncle. In "The Function of Criticism at the Present Time," Arnold defined criticism as "the disinterested endeavour to learn and propagate the best that is known and thought in the world," and by doing so to "create a current of true and fresh ideas."[10] He argued that criticism in this sense is the means to genuine progress, but it must maintain its disinterestedness. Granted, in commending women for "disinterested" advising on political and social issues Ward contradicts Arnold's core definition of the term, but just as his ideal "critic" or man of "culture" would stand aside from "ulterior, political, practical considerations,"[11] so would Ward's woman of "influence." Like Arnold, Ward saw education as the foundation for disinterested criticism. Here, then, we see the connection between Ward's life-long promotion of women's education and her opposition to women's suffrage.

Taken by themselves, many of Ward's arguments against women's Parliamentary suffrage do seem antifeminist, but she did not stop there. Ward campaigned for women's increased participation in local government – a program stated as a central goal in the Constitution of the Women's Anti-Suffrage League. Ward and the League put considerable energy into promoting the so-called "middle suffrage policy" – lobbying to *expand* women's eligibility to vote in local elections and even to reserve seats for women on county and borough councils. At the time, local government seemed to offer broad and expanding possibilities. Ward believed Prime Minister Asquith's prediction that many matters considered by Parliament would "ultimately be delegated to the local government councils" and liked to point out that "a woman ... may be an elected member of the London County Council, which is, in effect, the local parliament of five millions of people, and may take part in all the important affairs, including the education of eight hundred thousand children, which come under the jurisdiction of the Council." [12]

Ward thought women in local government could become a force to be reckoned with. She proposed that women delegates be elected by women on all the nation's local government bodies to form "some Statutory body ... brought into close connexion with Government and the House of Commons" to deal with factory and sanitary legislation and other matters affecting women and children.[13] Even without the proposed "Statutory body," women in local government could rectify problems identified by suffragists: they could eliminate street trading by school-age children, improve sanitation and the housing of the poor, provide for the old and for the sick and insane, "see that unemployed women were helped no less than unemployed men,"[14] and carry out projects regarding "temperance, nursing, the prevention of disease."[15]

In her study of women in local government, Patricia Hollis dismisses the Anti-Suffrage League's advocacy of women's participation in local government as mere theater – all talk and no results.[16] But the fact that Ward fought hard for the policy against bitter opposition by others in

the League shows the sincerity of her public statements. Almost as soon
as the men's and women's anti-suffrage leagues merged in 1910, the
women found themselves battling to maintain even minimal control
over policy and procedure. The group's male leaders opposed Ward's
work on the Local Government Advancement Committee, and soon
were calling her "rather a disturbing element" and "that most tiresome
woman." [17]

Despite opposition, Ward held firm, emphasizing the state's need for
women. This social feminist concept of citizenship, for both sexes –
citizenship based not on *rights* (as liberal feminists argued) but on *duties*
and responsibilities – is stated clearly in her 1889 "Appeal Against
Women's Suffrage": "While desiring the fullest possible development of
the powers, energies, and education of women, we believe that their
work for the State, and their responsibilities towards it, must always
differ essentially from those of men."[18] Both sexes have duties, though
different ones, to their families and to the nation. Ward called women's
civic duties the "enlarged housekeeping of the nation."[19] Women's
domestic skills are needed not just in a private "separate sphere" but in
the public sphere as well. Ward argued that action in the public sphere
should *reflect* differences in the private sphere. This breaking down of the
distinction between private and public is what distinguishes social feminist "civic housekeeping" from conservative "separate spheres" ideology. As her daughter observed:

It was not that she wished her sex to remain aloof from the toil and dust of the
world, as her Positivist friends would have liked; rather she felt it to be the duty
of all educated women to work themselves to the bone for the uplifting of
women and children less fortunate than themselves, and so to repay their debt
to the community; but clamour for their own "rights" was a different thing;
ugly in itself, and likely to lead, in her opinion, to a sex war of very dubious
outcome.[20]

Despite Ward's discomfort with the language of "rights," one of the
most positive characters in *Delia Blanchflower* asserts her *right* to the vote.
Sensible and witty Lady Tonbridge, who has left a brutal husband (who
still controls her property), asserts, "Here am I, with a house and a
daughter, a house-parlourmaid, a boot-boy, and rates to pay. Why
shouldn't I vote as well as you? . . . I say we ought to have it – that it is our
right..."[21] Ward spoke of "rights" in advocating that Parliament extend the local franchise to more women and that seats on local bodies be
reserved for women. "They asked what was their right," she told a
meeting of the Women's Local Government Society, "and they asked it

in no grasping or selfish spirit but in the interest of their Fatherland itself."[22] Ward claimed women's *right* to develop themselves and to control their lives, both in areas like science and art that they have in common with men, and in areas constituting the "essential" differences from men. Women must claim a right – but only the right to serve. She expected both sexes to work together for the good of all, both in public life and in private life.

FICTION AND SUFFRAGE: *DELIA BLANCHFLOWER*

Many of Ward's arguments about women's suffrage find a place in her fictional treatment of the controversy. In *Delia Blanchflower*, she portrays the shifting loyalties of the eponymous heroine, from Gertrude Marvell, leader of the Daughters of Revolt, to her guardian Mark Winnington, with whom she falls in love. Delia's disillusionment with militant suffragism arises in part from her distaste for the plot she realizes Gertrude is hatching: to destroy the historic mansion owned by an anti-suffrage cabinet minister. The novel reaches its climax when Gertrude and her collaborators burn down this symbol of the nation. The caretaker's handicapped daughter and Gertrude herself die in the fire; Delia, in an agony of grief, finally agrees to marry Winnington; and a suffrage bill is defeated by parliament. Delia remains a feminist and a suffragist, but accepts the need for slower change and constitutional methods.

Delia is an appealing character, with qualities typical of Ward's heroines: beauty, strong will, and intelligence (though, as usual, without benefit of adequate education). Ward also gives the suffragists some of the book's best lines. In one speech, for example, Gertrude proclaims, "Slaves who have no part in making the law, are not bound by the law . . . Justice – which is a very different thing from law – Justice is our mistress! – and to her we appeal."[23] Gertrude justifies violence against property as a means of calling attention to the oppression of women. After listing women's grievances, Gertrude asserts:

Now – all these things *you* may do to women, and nobody minds – nobody troubles at all. But if *we* make a bonfire of a pier, or an empty house, by way of drawing attention to your proceedings, then, you see red. Well, here we are! – do what you like – torture, imprison us! – you are only longing, I know – some of you – to pull us down now and trample on us, so that you may show us how much stronger men are than women![24]

These speeches, a fairly accurate rendering of Suffragette positions, are undeniably eloquent: their powerful language shapes the novel's discourse. As Mikhail Bakhtin has observed, "It is precisely this that defines the utterly distinctive discourse in the novel – an orientation that is contested, contestable and contesting – for this discourse cannot forget or ignore, either through naiveté or by design, the heteroglossia that surrounds it."[25] In *Delia Blanchflower*, the discourse of suffragism cannot be ignored.

I suspect that on some level Ward herself was persuaded by militant arguments about sex war and men's role in it. Take for example Gertrude's feminist theory of history, which Ward summarizes in a typically double-voiced passage – with almost as much approval as objection and certainly with no specific refutation:

The age-long monopoly of all the higher forces of civilisation by men; the cruel and insulting insistence upon the sexual and maternal functions of women, as covering the whole of her destiny; the hideous depreciation of her as an inferior and unclean creature, to which Christianity, poisoned by the story of Eve, and a score of barbarous beliefs and superstitions more primitive still, had largely contributed, while hypocritically professing to enfranchise and exalt her; the unfailing doom to "obey," and to bring forth, that has crushed her; the labours and shames heaped upon her by men in the pursuit of their own selfish devices; and the denial to her, also by men, of all the higher and spiritual activities, except those allowed by a man-made religion: – this feminist gospel, in some respects so bitterly true, in others so vindictively false, was gradually and unsparingly pressed upon Delia's quick intelligence.[26]

This bleak analysis of masculine behavior is not applied only to history, for the novel offers plenty of fodder for feminist scrutiny. Delia seems justified in arguing that "It is simply and solely because I am a woman" that her father's will appoints a male trustee and conditions Delia's inheritance upon her choosing the right opinions and husband. Gertrude Marvell's feminism derives from life-long experience of masculine brutality, notably in her alcoholic father, a "small-minded domestic tyrant," and in her brother-in-law, "a canting hypocrite, who would spend his day in devising petty torments for his wife, and begin and end it with family prayers."[27] In addition to Madeleine Tonbridge's abusive husband and the men understood to be in the background of another character's rescue work, we learn of an unscrupulous employer who impregnated the feeble-minded daughter of one of Delia's tenants. It is a depressing catalogue. Indeed, Ward's fiction is full of overbearing and sexually threatening men, for she had a rather bleak vision of masculinity. In *The Coryston Family* she notes the "secret contempt for women, inbred in all but a minority of men" and describes an upper-class young man's tone in speaking to his sister as having "the peremptory ring natural to many young men of his stamp in dealing with their inferiors, or – until love has tamed them – with women."[28] Misogyny is "natural" and "inbred," biological language typical of the evolutionary metaphors Ward frequently applied in her discussions of violence and unrestrained sexuality. She used such language to criticize militant suffragists who she believed to be at war with "that long effort of humanity to realize the Divine in itself – as against the 'ape and tiger' of the flesh."[29] Ward more often associated the ape and tiger with men, as in *Delia Blanchflower*, when Miss Dempsey, rescuer of prostitutes, uses Tennyson's phrase: "men are what their mothers make them!... And when women are what God intended them to be, they will have killed the ape and the tiger in men."[30] According to this classic social feminist argument, women have the capacity and responsibility to help society evolve, to raise its moral tone.

Caryn McTighe Musil has criticized Ward for understating or even justifying male violence against suffragists, and in light of the well-documented injustices against suffrage demonstrators, some of Ward's handling of the issue seems questionable. A disillusioned suffragist in the novel, appalled by "young women beating men's faces" during a demonstration, observes that "The police were rough too!... But you couldn't wonder at it, Miss Blanchflower, could you?"[31] While this remark blames the victims, it also reflects Ward's dim view of masculinity. Tigers and apes are wild animals and must be handled accordingly. We don't blame a tiger for attacking a handler who teases it. Men's brutality can only be counteracted by the influence of good women – "until love has *tamed* them."

The danger from suffrage, as Ward saw it, was that it fostered not "taming" but "sex rivalry." Ward, like more recent analysts, believed that men become violent when they feel threatened by women's achievements in traditionally masculine fields. Gertrude Marvell in *Delia Blanchflower* not only recollects that less qualified men had more opportunities and higher salaries than she, but also recalls "the development of that new and ugly temper in men – men now hard-pressed themselves – who must now see in women no longer playthings or sweethearts, but rivals and supplanters."[32] Certainly Ward did not advocate that women like Gertrude relinquish their intellectual or professional ambitions to become "playthings" or that working-class women ignore their economic needs. But given the inevitability (and desirability) of women's progress in many formerly male spheres, it was that much more important that women learn to work cooperatively with men. The suffragists, she believed, did precisely the opposite.

Without a doubt, suffragists brought to the fore the misogynist responses of many men. A case in point is a letter to the editor of the *Times* about suffragist "hysteria," written by Sir Almroth Wright and endorsed by Ward's male colleagues in the Anti-suffrage League but angrily and publicly repudiated by Ward. Wright gleefully asserted that militant suffragists had invited retaliation; Ward rejoined that "The violence of men towards women due to their superior physical strength is a dismal chapter, far from closed; Sir A. Wright would have done far better to admit it."[33]

Thus, Ward's own experiences help explain the convincing tone of her militants' denunciations of male "tyranny" and sexual threat, but she also denies that it is the whole truth, and disagrees with the suffragist response. After a street speaker finishes describing "the hungry and sensual appetites of men," Winnington, who has listened attentively, gallantly guides her out of the hostile crowd, carrying the stool she had been standing on, then politely advises her to look up her facts. Gentle, chivalrous, disinterested Mark Winnington stands as Ward's ideal man, answer to militant suffragist misandry.

In the end, Delia rejects sex war. Her opinions are altered by an independent confrontation with reality – the arson plot and Gertrude's callous treatment of her – and by recognition that not all men are as Gertrude has characterized them but that some are like Mark. She has learned to make up her own mind. In *Marcella* and *Helbeck of Bannisdale*, the capacity and willingness of both partners to think for themselves is vital to an ideal marriage; *Delia Blanchflower* promises that the Winningtons will enjoy just such a marriage. When Mark proposes, he insists that he does not wish to control Delia's mind: "Do you imagine I should want to dictate to you – or tyrannise over you? Do you imagine I don't sympathise with your faiths, your ideals . . . ? Delia, we'd work together! – it mightn't always be in the same way – nor always with the same opinion – but we'd teach – we'd help each other."[34] Delia influences Mark as well: he begins with no opinion, even "indifference" about women's suffrage; knowing Delia forces him to recognize that "Englishmen – all Englishmen – had now got to face" "this wide-spread claim of women . . . to share the public powers and responsibilities of men."[35] Significantly, the feminism Winnington discovers is a social feminist claim of responsibilities.

Delia's love of Winnington "bring[s] her face to face with the deeper loves and duties and sorrows which she in her headstrong youth knew so little about, while they entered so profoundly into his own upright and humane character"[36] – by which Ward means the community service she advocated as the alternative to suffrage. In Delia's future life we anticipate that she will join Mark in charitable and educational projects and in local government – a social feminist adaptation of domestic values to the public sphere.

Although Delia rejects violent methods to win the vote, she emphatically distinguishes strategy from substance, insisting, "I am just as much for *women* – I am just as rebellious against their wrongs – as I ever was. I shall be a suffragist always." Ward thus explicitly posits a multivocal feminism, in which being "for women" means different things to such different people as Delia, Gertrude, Miss Dempsey, Lady Tonbridge, and Mark Winnington. Despite the novel's structural closure – ending as it does with Gertrude's arson death, the defeat of the suffrage bill, and the marriage of Delia and Mark – the "internal open-endedness of the characters and the dialogue" disrupts ideological closure.[37]

This ideological open-endedness was ignored by most British reviewers – who assumed they knew Ward's views about women's suffrage – but recognized by an American reviewer of *Delia Blanchflower*, H. W. Boynton, who obviously did not follow the British suffrage debate: "That [Ward] believes in suffrage as apart from militancy is clear, but her closing paragraph shows how little, with her serious intelligence, she relies upon such remedies as 'the vote' for the final settling of the woman's problem."[38] That a reader unaware of Ward's anti-suffrage reputation could read the novel in this way provides remarkable evidence of the novel's genuine balance.

GENDER POLITICS AND WARD'S REPUTATION

Nevertheless, Boynton's response was the exception. Her daughter reported that Ward "always believed that her Anti-suffrage activities, culminating in the writing of [*Delia Blanchflower*], had a markedly bad effect on the circulation of her books."[39] Indeed, analysis of contemporary reviews confirms that gender politics shaped Ward's reception and reputation, from the very beginning. One reason for her early popularity was her effective articulation of women readers' struggles with changing gender ideology, though some male critics disliked her "radicalism." In the years before she (reluctantly) became active in the anti-suffrage movement, Ward was considered feminist (though the

word itself had not yet gained wide currency) and endured misogynist
and antifeminist criticism. Some critics' reviews of Ward's books became opportunities to attack feminism. A reviewer of *Marcella* describes
the title character as "the new woman to the life" – that is, "crude and
chaotic; self-centered and self-exaggerated" and "an intrepid young
Amazon"; he then complains that "Mrs. Ward has not a quick eye for
absurdity" – that is, she admires her New Woman too much.[40] Still
another review derides "what is so ludicrously miscalled the higher
education among women, itself a part of that foolish misconception of a
woman's true place in the world which goes under the name of
Woman's Rights."[41] Clearly the problem for these reviewers is that
Ward has stepped outside her "true place."

Years passed, and the suffrage campaign became increasingly central
to public perceptions of feminism. Ward's prominence made her a
convenient lightning rod in the stormy ideological battles among early
twentieth-century feminists. That Ward's opinions about suffrage ir-
revocably discredited her, undermining respect for her career as a
whole, is evidenced in a comment in Vera Brittain's remarkable mem-
oir, *Testament of Youth*. As a teenager, Brittain recalls, she was deeply
influenced by Ward's *Robert Elsmere*, but Brittain admits, "Had I realized
when I read it that its author was even then portentously engaged in
rallying the anti-suffrage forces, it might have influenced me less, but I
remained ignorant until some years later of Mrs. Ward's political
machinations, and her book converted me."[42] Presumably the thousands of pro-suffrage women who did know of Ward's anti-suffrage
activities chose, as Brittain later did, to reject Ward and no longer
respect her books. In fact, a suffrage organization proposed a boycott of
Ward's novels.[43]

Men also mention Ward's suffrage position in attacks that mix aesthetic and political judgments. Their comments frequently become
outright misogynist, suggesting that Ward's unpopular suffrage stance
merely provided a convenient excuse to deny credibility to this woman
of undeniable influence. Arnold Bennett's criticism of her writing seems
inseparable from his mockery of her continuing popularity and her
anti-suffrage "agitating." His "review" culminates in an imagined gang
rape:

I have invented a destiny for Mrs. Humphry Ward's heroines. It is terrible, and
just. They ought to be caught, with their lawful male protectors, in the siege of a
great city by a foreign army. Their lawful male protectors ought, before sallying

forth on a forlorn hope, to provide them with a revolver as a last refuge from a brutal and licentious soldiery. And when things come to a crisis, in order to be concluded in our next, the revolvers ought to prove to be unloaded.[44]

This fantasy contrasts oddly with Bennett's condemnation of Ward's anti-suffragism, a discrepancy which suggests that one gender-based criticism conceals another. Such sexually charged responses, coming from men who, arguably, are Ward's direct literary descendants, strongly suggest an anxiety of influence, as described by Harold Bloom, and, more specifically, seem to participate in the sometimes vicious twentieth-century battle of the sexes described by Sandra Gilbert and Susan Gubar in *No Man's Land.*

In their analysis of "the futile rage with which men of letters greeted female literary achievement," Gilbert and Gubar describe many powerful reactions, such as a story in which the male protagonist enacts "a cross between a ritual rape and a sacrificial burning at the stake" to destroy a woman-authored text.[45] The story, while not directly responding to Ward, holds an uncanny resemblance to reactions by Ward's real-life detractors. Bennett having supplied the ritual rape of Ward's heroines, H. G. Wells provided the flames. Wells, who liked to think of himself as a feminist but whose feminism often seems more about women's sexual availability than about their social power, describes in his autobiography a response to one of Mary Ward's anti-suffrage editorials (whose content he misrepresents):

One day we found in a copy of *The Times* we had brought with us, a letter from Mrs. Humphrey [*sic*] Ward denouncing the moral tone of the younger generation . . . and, having read it aloud, we decided we had to do something about it. So we stripped ourselves under the trees as though there was no one in the world but ourselves, and made love all over Mrs. Humphrey Ward. And when we had dressed again we lit a match and burnt her. *The Times* flared indignantly and subsided and wriggled burning and went black and brittle and broke into fragments that flew away.[46]

And so, too, has flown away Mary Ward's reputation. In seizing on her gender politics as the fuel with which to destroy her, Ward's detractors succeeded brilliantly. Even today, Ward, who was condemned as a radical early in her career, and whose opinions changed little as she aged, is perceived as a conservative reactionary. When all feminism is defined by the terms of liberal feminism – wanting for women exactly the same privileges men have – then it is easy to make this mistake. In *A Literature of Their Own,* Elaine Showalter dismisses Ward's ideas about

women as "awkwardly outdated."[47] Recent studies of novels about the
New Woman or the suffrage movement echo Showalter's views or fail to
mention Ward at all.[48] The rediscovered women's novels now back in
circulation tend to be by women whose feminist credentials are more
readily identifiable.[49] Too often, it seems, feminist criticism listens only
to those suppressed voices from the past that speak a feminist language
most like our own.

Mary Ward's turn-of-the-century bestseller status shows that, far
from being "outdated" in her time, she in fact spoke powerfully to her
original readers. To be sure, by the time she published *Delia Blanchflower*,
she had gained the reputation – strengthened, certainly, by her anti-
suffrage stance – for holding opinions as outmoded as Victorian crino-
lines. Yet Ward remained open-minded. In the ensuing years, visiting
munitions plants and military hospitals as a war reporter, she was
impressed by women's competence at some of the very endeavors –
agriculture, heavy industry, finance – she had listed in 1889 as perma-
nently belonging to men's sphere. She privately admitted that "the war
has changed so many things" and that to concede the vote would be far
less dangerous in 1918 than it would have been before.[50]

As her daughter observed, "Service, not 'rights,' was in effect her
watchword... Perhaps it was too austere a gospel for our day, and in the
end she watched her country choose the opposite path without bitter-
ness, and even with some degree of hope. At any rate she had done her
part in laying before her countrywomen a different ideal."[51] If Mary
Ward's ideal for women is not exactly our own ideal, it likewise is not as
repressive as her detractors have claimed. To ignore Ward and to deny
her feminism are not only to distort and oversimplify the culture and
gender politics of her time but to silence one of its most prominent and
interesting voices.

NOTES

1 Mary Ward, *Delia Blanchflower* (New York: Hearst, 1914), p. 356.
2 Mary Ward, *Marcella* (London: Smith, Elder, 1894), p. 555.
3 *Ibid.*, p. 555.
4 *Ibid.*, p. 560; emphasis Ward's.
5 For example, Elaine Showalter describes Ward and her heroines as "hostile
   ... to the methods and theories of the suffragettes" (*A Literature of Their Own:
   British Women Novelists From Brontë to Lessing* [Princeton, NJ: Princeton University Press, 1977], p. 231). Laura Stempel Mumford describes Ward's position
   as "vocal antifeminism" ("Virile Mothers, Militant Sisters: British Feminist
   Theory and Novels, 1880–1920" [dissertation, University of Iowa, 1983],

p. 7). Jane Eldridge Miller, deriding the social feminist assumptions of gender difference that Ward shared with suffragists, asserts that they "demonstrate ... how antagonistic that ideology is to feminism" (*Rebel Women: Feminism, Modernism and the Edwardian Novel* [London: Virago, 1994], p. 157).

6 Mary Ward, "The Women's Anti-Suffrage Movement," *The Nineteenth Century and After* 64 (1908), 345.

7 Millicent Garrett Fawcett, "The Appeal Against Female Suffrage: a Reply," *The Nineteenth Century* 26 (1889), 96.

8 Mary Ward, "An Appeal Against Female Suffrage," *The Nineteenth Century* 25 (1889), 783.

9 *Ibid.*

10 Matthew Arnold, "The Function of Criticism at the Present Time," in *Essays in Criticism* (1865; London: Macmillan, 1907), pp. 38, 18–19.

11 *Ibid.*, p. 18.

12 Mary Ward, "Why I Do Not Believe In Woman Suffrage," *Ladies' Home Journal* (November 1908), 15.

13 Mary Ward, "Let Women Say! An Appeal to the House of Lords," *The Nineteenth Century and After* 83 (1918), 54.

14 Quoted in "Women on Borough Councils," *Times* (October 21, 1909), 4e.

15 Mary Ward, "Rhetoric and Revolution: Mrs. Ward's Reply to Mr. Lloyd George," letter, *Times* (November 27, 1911), 9f.

16 Patricia Hollis, *Ladies Elect: Women in English Local Government, 1865–1914* (New York: Oxford University Press, 1987), pp. 471–72.

17 Quoted in Brian Harrison, *Separate Spheres: The Opposition to Women's Suffrage in Britain* (London: Croom Helm, 1978), p. 131.

18 Ward, "Appeal," 781.

19 Quoted in "The Anti-Suffrage Demonstration," *Times* (July 14, 1910), 9f.

20 Janet Penrose Trevelyan, *The Life of Mrs. Humphry Ward* (New York: Dodd, 1923), p. 225.

21 Ward, *Delia*, p. 105.

22 Quoted in "The Needs of Local Government," *Times* (November 2, 1910), 12d.

23 Ward, *Delia*, p. 167.

24 *Ibid.*, p. 166.

25 Mikhail M. Bakhtin, "Discourse in the Novel," in *The Dialogic Imagination: Four Essays*, trans. Caryl Emerson and Michael Holquist, ed. Michael Holquist (Austin: University of Texas Press, 1981), p. 332.

26 Ward, *Delia*, p. 62.

27 *Ibid.*, p. 245.

28 Mary Ward, *The Coryston Family* (New York: Harper, 1913), pp. 100, 286.

29 Mary Ward, "Religion and the Suffrage: Protest by Mrs. Humphry Ward," letter, *Times* (June 19, 1912), 14b.

30 Ward, *Delia*, p. 332.

31 *Ibid.*, p. 370.

32 *Ibid.*, p. 246.

33 Mary Ward, "Mrs. Ward and Sir A. Wright," letter, *Times* (April 12, 1912), 15a.
34 Ward, *Delia*, p. 300.
35 *Ibid.*, pp. 35, 34.
36 *Ibid.*, p. 268.
37 Mikhail M. Bakhtin, *Problems of Dostoevsky's Poetics*, trans. Caryl Emerson, Theory and History of Literature 8 (Minneapolis University of Minnesota Press, 1984), p. 39.
38 H. W. Boynton, "Some Novels from Abroad," review of *Delia Blanchflower*, *The Nation* 99 (October 15, 1914), 462.
39 Trevelyan, *Life*, p. 239.
40 "Fiction New and Old," *Atlantic Monthly* 87 (January 1901), 128.
41 "Culture and Anarchy," review of *The History of David Grieve*, *Quarterly Review* 174 (April 1892), 341.
42 Vera Brittain, *Testament of Youth: An Autobiographical Study of the Years 1900–1925* (New York: Macmillan, 1934), p. 41.
43 "Britain's Premier for Woman Suffrage," *Current Literature* 45 (July 1908), 20.
44 Arnold Bennett, "Mrs. Humphry Ward's Heroines" *New Age* 3 (October 1908). Reprinted in *Books and Persons: Being Comments on a Past Epoch, 1908–1911* (New York: Doran, 1917), p. 52.
45 Sandra M. Gilbert and Susan Gubar, *No Man's Land: The Place of the Woman Writer in the Twentieth Century*, 3 vols. (New Haven: CT: Yale University Press, 1987–94), vol. I, p. 127.
46 H. G. Wells, *H. G. Wells In Love: Postscript to an Experiment in Autobiography*, ed. G. P. Wells (London: Faber, 1984), p. 89.
47 Showalter, *A Literature of Their Own*, p. 227.
48 *Marcella* and its sequel *Sir George Tressady* are listed among New Woman novels but described as books that "delegitimize" new womanly ambitions in Ann Ardis, *New Women, New Novels* (New Brunswick, NJ: Rutgers University Press, 1990). There is no mention of Ward in Gail Cunningham, *The New Woman and the Victorian Novel* (London: Macmillan, 1978) or Lyn Pykett, *The "Improper" Feminine: The Women's Sensation Novel and the New Woman Writing* (London and New York: Routledge, 1992). Nor does Showalter reexamine her earlier assessment in her chapter on the new woman in *Sexual Anarchy: Gender and Culture at the Fin-de-Siècle* (New York: Viking, 1990).
49 The most dramatic reversals from complete obscurity to canonization have been with authors like Kate Chopin, Charlotte Perkins Gilman, and Olive Schreiner. Series like the Feminist Press suffrage series include books like Elizabeth Robins' *The Convert*, overlooking Ward's more ambiguous *Delia Blanchflower*. The Virago series, though it has included Charlotte Mary Yonge and Margaret Oliphant, runs toward the most liberal feminist texts by those authors. More typical Virago authors are Rebecca West, Sarah Grand, and Winifred Holtby.
50 Quoted in Harrison, *Separate Spheres*, p. 205.
51 Trevelyan, *Life*, p. 245.

WORKS CITED

"The Anti-Suffrage Demonstration," *Times* (July 14, 1910), 9f.
Ardis, Ann, *New Women, New Novels*, New Brunswick, NJ: Rutgers University Press, 1990.
Arnold, Matthew, "The Function of Criticism at the Present Time," in *Essays in Criticism*, 1865; London: Macmillan, 1907, pp. 1–41.
Bakhtin, Mikhail M., "Discourse in the Novel," in *The Dialogic Imagination: Four Essays*, trans. Caryl Emerson and Michael Holquist, ed. Michael Holquist, Austin: University of Texas Press, 1981, pp. 259–422.
    Problems of Dostoevsky's Poetics, trans. Caryl Emerson, Theory and History of Literature 8, Minneapolis: University of Minnesota Press, 1984.
Banks, Olive. *Faces of Feminism: A Study of Feminism as a Social Movement*, New York: St. Martin's Press, 1981.
Bennett, Arnold, "Mrs. Humphry Ward's Heroines," *New Age* 3 (October 1908), rpt. in *Books and Persons: Being Comments on a Past Epoch, 1908–1911*, New York: Doran, 1917, pp. 47–52.
Black, Naomi, *Social Feminism*, Ithaca: Cornell University Press, 1989.
Boynton, H. W., "Some Novels from Abroad," review of *Delia Blanchflower*, *The Nation* 99 (October 15, 1914), 461–62.
"Britain's Premier for Woman Suffrage," *Current Literature* 45 (July 1908), 18–20.
Brittain, Vera, *Testament of Youth: An Autobiographical Study of the Years 1900–1925*, New York: Macmillan, 1934.
"Culture and Anarchy," review of *The History of David Grieve*, *Quarterly Review* 174 (April 1892), 317–44.
Cunningham, Gail, *The New Woman and the Victorian Novel*, London: Macmillan, 1978.
Fawcett, Millicent Garrett, "The Appeal Against Female Suffrage: a Reply," *The Nineteenth Century* 26 (1889), 86–96.
"Fiction New and Old," *Atlantic Monthly* 87 (January 1901), 127–32.
Gilbert, Sandra M., and Susan Gubar, *The War of The Words*, vol. 1 of *No Man's Land: The Place of the Woman Writer in the Twentieth Century*, 3 vols., New Haven, CT: Yale University Press, 1987–94.
Harrison, Brian, *Separate Spheres: The Opposition to Women's Suffrage in Britain*, London: Croom Helm, 1978.
Hollis, Patricia. *Ladies Elect: Women in English Local Government, 1865–1914*, New York: Oxford University Press, 1987.
Lewis, Jane, *Women and Social Action in Victorian and Edwardian England*, Edward Elgar, 1991.
Miller, Jane Eldridge, *Rebel Women: Feminism, Modernism and the Edwardian Novel*, London: Virago, 1994.
Mumford, Laura Stempel, "Virile Mothers, Militant Sisters: British Feminist Theory and Novels, 1880–1920," dissertation, University of Iowa, 1983.
Musil, Caryn McTighe, "Art and Ideology: The Novels and Times of Mrs. Humphry Ward," dissertation, Northwestern University, 1974.
"The Needs of Local Government," *Times* (November 1910), 12d.

Offen, Karen, "Defining Feminism: A Comparative Historical Approach," *Signs: The Journal of Women in Culture and Society* 14 (1988), 119–57.

Pykett, Lyn, *The "Improper" Feminine: The Women's Sensation Novel and the New Woman Writing*, London and New York: Routledge, 1992.

Rendall, Jane, *The Origins of Modern Feminism: Women in Britain, France and the United States, 1780–1860*, New York: Schocken, 1984.

Showalter, Elaine, *A Literature of Their Own: British Women Novelists From Brontë to Lessing*, Princeton, NJ: Princeton University Press, 1977.

Sexual Anarchy: Gender and Culture at the Fin-de-Siècle, New York: Viking, 1990.

Trevelyan, Janet Penrose, *The Life of Mrs. Humphry Ward*, New York: Dodd, 1923.

Ward, Mary A. (Mrs. Humphry), "An Appeal Against Female Suffrage," *The Nineteenth Century* 25 (1889): 781–88.

The Coryston Family, London: Smith, Elder, 1913. New York: Harper, 1913.

Delia Blanchflower, New York: Hearst, 1914. London: Ward, Lock, 1915.

Helbeck of Bannisdale, London: Smith, Elder, 1898. New York: Macmillan, 1898.

"Let Women Say! An Appeal to the House of Lords," *The Nineteenth Century and After* 83 (1918), 47–59.

Marcella, London: Smith, Elder, 1894. New York: Macmillan, 1894.

"Mrs. Ward and Sir A. Wright," letter, *Times* (April 12, 1912), 15a.

"Religion and the Suffrage: Protest by Mrs. Humphry Ward," letter, *Times* (June 19, 1912), 14a–b.

"Rhetoric and Revolution: Mrs. Ward's Reply to Mr. Lloyd George," letter, *Times* (November 27, 1911).

"Why I Do Not Believe In Woman Suffrage," *Ladies' Home Journal* (November 1908), 15ff.

"The Women's Anti-Suffrage Movement," *The Nineteenth Century and After* 64 (1908), 343–52.

Wells, H. G. *H. G. Wells In Love: Postscript to an Experiment in Autobiography*, ed. G. P. Wells, London: Faber, 1984.

"Women on Borough Councils," *Times* (October 21, 1909), 4e.

Wright, Almroth E., "Suffrage Fallacies: Sir Almroth Wright on Militant Hysteria," letter, *Times* (March 28, 1912), 7–8.

CHAPTER 13

E. Nesbit and the woman question

Amelia A. Rutledge

In E. Nesbit's fantasy, *The Magic City* (1910), two children, Philip and Lucy, travel to a realm governed by an edict decreeing that "Girls are expected to be brave and the boys, kind."[1] The children are followed by Philip's nursemaid, who becomes the "Pretenderette" to the city-kingdom's throne. In this character (her title is derisively similar to "suffragette"), Nesbit satirizes both working-class resentment and the New Woman's political ambition.[2] After the children defeat the Pretenderette, her crimes are symbolically chastised by enforced "proper" female activity – learning to feel affection for others (nurturing) and reforming the allegorical dragon Sloth (the maintaining of moral standards). Although Lucy has successfully insisted that Philip obey the ruling precept and accept her agency on several occasions, her self-enforced emancipation is countered by the Pretenderette's fate, a strategy typical of Nesbit's ambivalence toward, if not compromise with, her contrary impulses toward sustaining and undermining the hegemony of conventional female roles.

Nesbit, born in 1858, did not begin her career as a novelist until she was nearly forty; thus her first novel, *The Secret of Kyriels* (1899), was written at the end of the period normally assigned to the New Woman novels; Nesbit is clearly a late entry into the field, but perhaps the currently stylish term "retro" best describes her adult fiction. An innovator in defining the children's time fantasy – although F. Anstey's *The Brass Bottle* (1900) preceded her stories, her work has influenced writers from C. S. Lewis to Edward Eager – her fiction for adults resembles what had been available to her in her twenties and thirties and is recognizably a holdover from the heyday of the New Woman novels. Children's fantasies inspired her most creative efforts; there was little that was original in her adult fiction. In form and content, *The Secret of Kyriels* most closely resembles the sensation novel, and shares with it an unusually agressive heroine of the type that was to become characteristic for Nesbit – the girl just out of school. It focuses more on enigmas surrounding maternity and marriage, complete with an imprisoned madwoman than on broader women's issues.[3] By the time she produced her later novels, the use of the emancipated female protagonist had lost much of its polemical edge. I wish to argue that Nesbit thus represents the appropriation by the dominant fictional discourse of material whose subversive force could now be contained by aligning it with non-threatening "entertainment" in which the shocking is denatured to the mildly naughty – a "normalized" version of the "new" or "eman-cipated" woman. The novels, not reprinted in her lifetime, perhaps because of her being "type cast" as a children's writer and a producer of light verse, merit reexamination not only as documents of her expressive constructions of issues but in themselves, as complex, albeit not wholly successful, literary artifacts.

Nesbit's work resembles what Ann Ardis calls "boomerang" novels, i.e., those that present New Woman elements but then subvert them by a reversion to the marriage-plot at the end.[4] That there was a market for such stories in Nesbit's day argues for the persistent appeal of these more conservative works long after the initial flurry of New Woman novels. Nesbit's heroines submit gladly to matrimony; there is only minimal struggle to assert independence, and the unmarried state is merely a brief transitional period. These women can be free temporarily from some social constraints, yet completely acceptable to any but the most censorious conservatives. Thus, Nesbit's novels transmute the polemic of New Woman fiction into popular romance by means of a brief fling (a job and independence) that is resolved if not by marriage, then at least by the strong suggestion that that, too, will come.

If the first reviewers' alarm or vituperation catch the eyes of twenti-eth-century critics as they recuperate New Woman fiction, and most studies suggest this, then the superficial attention to Nesbit's fiction in its own day easily accounts for today's neglect. A perusal of newspaper reviews for her later novels shows that with the exception of *The Red House* (1902) and *Salome and the Head* (hereafter *Salome*, 1909), her later novels received only brief notice in the reviews of a month's crop of light fiction. To reviewers, some of her heroines – notably Daphne Car-michael of *Daphne in Fitzroy Street* (1909) – resemble the flighty schoolgirl more than the pioneers or martyrs of woman question fiction, but even when the content of her work might be viewed as controversial or scandalous, as was the case with *Salome*, the reviewers criticized surface features – gruesome details or a reference to a contemporary figure that the reviewer considered ill advised – while paying little attention to the gender issues in the novel except as they were related to the "love interest." These reviewers certainly did not address any potentially subversive content of the novels. Although Nesbit's reviewers will be discussed at the end of this study, it suffices to note here that they tended to be perplexed by her forays into serious adult fiction and tended to suggest that light comedy and children's literature were her true fields of endeavor.[5] Before examining her children's fiction, it will be helpful to consider both the social and literary contexts that fostered Nesbit's ambivalences toward feminist issues and dictated her choices in the writing of fiction.

As one of the founding members of the Fabian Society, Nesbit was a member of the "Old Gang," the part of the membership that consistently evaded consideration of women's issues despite their advocacy of the rights of the (male) working class. In *The Magic City*, for example, Nesbit the Fabian socialist and "liberated" woman becomes an advocate of acquiescence to hierarchical social relationships who severely narrows the scope of the bravery she has mandated by edict. Bravery, it seems, is acceptable for little girls in resolving fantastic dilemmas; otherwise, along with self-assertion, it is a destabilizing impulse that must be ridiculed out of existence – especially when exhibited by a member of an underclass.

Nesbit was aware of all of the controversies subsumed under the woman question, but she refrained from active participation beyond her membership in the Fabian Society and her limited association with its Women's Group. On the other hand, she admired militant advocates such as Olive Schreiner, who offered a sincere tribute to Nesbit's personal warmth and kindness.[6] Her allegiances were consistently personal instead of ideological; on the other hand, she could use one ideology, socialism, as a defense against another, woman suffrage, as I will discuss below. In all of her writing, Nesbit employed strategies of displacement and distancing with regard to feminist issues, whether by adoption of the fantastic mode, as in her children's fiction and occasionally in her adult work, or by substituting for polemic the compensatory fantasy characteristic of popular romance.

While Nesbit's narrative strategies rendered her works non-controversial – she constructed an implied author and addressed an implied audience both of which were acceptable to the less radical, non-militant readership – these same strategies have left the adult fiction outside the serious critical attention that her children's fiction has received. In fact, the novels that most directly address women's social issues show Nesbit negotiating her conflicting and conflicted views of the place of women in society and the novels demonstrate the ways in which the pressure of a writing public inflected those views.

In her personal life, Nesbit was enmeshed in multiple quandaries; whatever her sentiments with regard to women's roles, she lived with the realities of patriarchal practice and sentiments, and she never resolved these many conflicts with any explicit act or statement. Nesbit had demonstrated her own essentially willful character by marrying Hubert Bland despite her mother's suspicious disapproval; she had already flouted convention, being seven months pregnant when she married. Bland, as all accounts indicate, was keeping a mistress at the time, and later had several affairs during his married life, fathering the two children born to his wife's housekeeper-companion, Alice Hoatson. Nesbit adopted both children as her own, and they long remained ignorant of their true parentage. Nesbit, bound in and to this marriage by social custom as well as by her expressed deep love for Bland, compensated by having several affairs of her own; these were of varying degrees of involvment, and included an extended, unconsummated affair with George Bernard Shaw. Further, it is quite likely that her reticence on suffrage issues is, in part, grounded in her deference to Bland's anti-suffrage views.[7]

Bland, for all of his socialist leanings, expressed in numerous articles and reviews after he established himself as a writer, was a touchstone of patriarchal ideology and male sexual privilege, considering women as ideally ornaments. His essay "If I Were a Woman" would seem a caricature of male chauvinism if its content were not repeated in various guises throughout his writings: "Woman's realm is the realm of the heart and the afternoon tea-table, not of the brain and the intelligence. It is hers to bewitch man, not to convince him."[8] He also declared, on the subject of women's franchise, "Votes for women? Votes for children! Votes for dogs!"[9] The most scathing criticism of Bland's hypocrisies is to be found in the autobiography of H. G. Wells, although the latter's commentary requires measured consideration since his unsuccessful attempt to elope with Bland's daughter, Rosamund, effectively ended what had been friendship between Wells, Bland, and Nesbit .[10]

More often than not the primary breadwinner of her household, Nesbit in no way conformed to the image of the "Angel in the House." Her Fabian allegiances do not necessarily contradict her conservatism, since the group was itself characterized by a limited, narrow set of radical impulses. Although she had written and published poetry prior to her marriage, Nesbit had not defined herself in any way as a professional writer. Nor had she, until becoming involved along with her husband in the newly formed Fabian Society, expressed any particular political opinions. In the Fabian ambience, she adopted the visible attributes of the "advanced" woman – bobbed hair, cigarette smoking, loose-fitting "aesthetic" clothing, knickers for cycling – but consistently demurred at any opportunity to become a public advocate for suffrage, at one point stating that she considered it a potential distraction from the advance of socialism.[11] In the May 29, 1908 meeting of the newly formed Fabian Women's Group, she astonished the audience when she announced that the subject of her invited address would be the "natural disabilities of woman." She had received the invitation to speak on "women and work" because of her success both as a wife and mother and as a published writer of some renown. She spoke instead in her persona as the wife of Hubert Bland. Dismayed, the Women's Group responded with a series of lectures, the first by a woman physician, that were clearly mounted to counter this reversal of expectations.[12] The Women's Group episode epitomizes Nesbit's fundamental ambivalence toward gender issues. The division between public acclaim and painful private compromises was never bridged in real life.

Nesbit did not participate when the Fabian Women's Group supported the women's suffrage movement, nor was there explicit engagement with feminist issues in her adult fiction. She did, however, allow herself some narrative liberties in the depiction of female characters, especially in her fairy tales; the use of the fantastic mode in the children's fiction allowed a "space" for non-traditional configurations.[13] Alison Lurie suggests that Nesbit's children's fiction presents elements of covert and explicit protest against the reinforcement of intellectual and social subjection of women in patriarchal culture by literature intended for the socialization of children.[14] When her children's stories were set in contemporary England, she used ironic depictions of male characters' investments in patriarchal practice as strategic displacements of feminist impulses; even a fictionalized contemporary setting exerted powerful constraints on her subversive impulses. In her fairy tales she could more explicitly counter gender stereotypes.

The fairy tale offered Nesbit a socially acceptable (and profitable) venue for publication and a flexible structure that would admit of variations in plot and even departures from convention, but the development of fairy tales from evening adult entertainment to vehicles for the socialization of children, especially girls, had long carried with it a diminution of female agency. The shift in the characterization of Red Riding Hood, signaled by Jack Zipes, from a successful trickster to a dead victim is an extreme case, but a similar sequence can be traced for other tales as well.[15] Many of Nesbit's earliest efforts do not depart from conventional depictions of male and female gender roles, but she profited from the "new tradition" in fairy tale writing that followed the publication of work by Lewis Carroll, George MacDonald, Juliana Horatia Ewing, and others. Lurie and U. C. Knoepflmacher have both pointed out that something of the original vigor of the female characters began to be recaptured in the nineteenth century, as women writers, Nesbit among them, published the increasingly popular fantastic tale.[16] Knoepflmacher has also suggested that although Nesbit is one of the writers who recaptures the children's story for women after an extended period of appropriation by male editors and authors such as Perrault and the brothers Grimm, thereby regaining "space" for active female characters, she does not depart in any marked fashion from the "patriarchal patterns," and "pronounced moralism" of nineteenth-century children's fiction; in this she is similar to George Eliot, whose work also manifests internalized gender ideology.[17]

Most discussions of Nesbit's fiction focus on her series books (the adventures of the Bastables or of the "Five Children"), although Lurie's text and the collection edited by Auerbach and Knoepflmacher discuss the short tales as well. When Nesbit does rework the fairy tale, the depictions of female characters are vital and intense, and suggest a response to what the public expected of a woman writing fairy tales operating concurrently with a desire for a break with convention. Since many folk tales and fairy tales focus on a single heroine, and present, in their earliest versions, examples of strong female agents, they offer a structure conceivably suited to weakening the force of convention.[18] The stories set in Nesbit's "present day" (even the fantasies of the "Five Children" begin in this world) were too firmly linked to mimesis to allow much freedom. The "carnivalesque" space she opens for her creative activity in the formal structures of the fairy tale demonstrates that Nesbit was able to "write out," but not necessarily to resolve in her own life, some of those tensions inherent in her ambivalence; her writing is thus a series of complex negotiations, complicated by her own vexed relationship to female roles, between transcending convention and marketing her work.

The term "carnivalesque" is used advisedly, since the experience of

fantasy creates "nested" carnivalesque structures: first, the act of reading fantasy creates an interval of "freedom" in daily life that might be
likened to the sanctioned break with customary activities and conventions that, according to Mikhail Bakhtin, characterizes the carnival.[19]
Secondly, the fantastic narrative encloses another carnivalesque structure, since within it a brief period of reversal occurs that acts out its own
precepts and then yields to its dissolution. It is within that carnivalesque
story-space that Nesbit finds a controlled yet liberating freedom. On the
other hand, this ludic "freedom" is carefully circumscribed, existing
only within the limits of the narrative just as carnival exists within the
dominant social structure, so that Nesbit cannot be said here, any more
than in her own life, directly to confront or to challenge convention.[20]

The primary public manifestation of carnival is the temporary unsettling of hierarchical distinctions and "natural" oppositions. One such
binary, and one that Nesbit addressed most frequently in her children's
stories, was male active agency and aggression in opposition to female
passivity and altruism. Nesbit's conservative tendencies are most evident
in those stories – the greater percentage of her major fiction – in which
the protagonists operate as a group.[21] In her stories of the "Five
Children," the female characters, especially Anthea, the elder of the two
girls, are the nurturing exemplars of empathy.[22] She also tended to select
male characters as her narrators and protagonists – most notably
Oswald Bastable, but also Dickie Harding of *The House of Arden* (1908)
and *Harding's Luck* (1909), a practice that carried over into her adult
fiction; even when the protagonist is a female, the action tends to be
focalized through the principal male. These male narrators are transparently unreliable and their egotistical self-presentation ironically
undermines their pretentiousness. For example, Gerald, in *The Enchanted
Castle*, constantly narrativizes his own actions – he seems incapable of
referring to himself except as a pseudo-literary adventure hero:

"The young explorers ... could see nothing. But their dauntless leader, whose
eyes had grown used to the dark while the clumsy forms of the others were
bungling up the entrance, had made a discovery."
"Oh, what!" both the others were used to Gerald's way of telling a story
while he acted it, but they did sometimes wish that he didn't talk quite so long
and so like a book in moments of excitement.[23]

Although Nesbit sustains this ironic depiction of spurious male superiority throughout the story, her treatment of male arrogance loses force
because the children's effective power succumbs to the generally disas-

trous results attendant on all their escapades; her ironies cannot even begin to undercut the powerful presence of gender conventions when the adventures themselves are self-canceling.

John Stephens suggests that Nesbit employs the *conventions*, but not the spirit or the subversive potential, of the carnivalesque, in ways that reinforce the subjected status of her child protagonists and reaffirm the social codes governing adult–child relationships.[24] Thus adults' authority is never seriously (if at all) undermined. Stephens' strictures are valid, but when one examines Nesbit's *fairy tales*, I think it necessary to qualify these observations since Nesbit's use of a series of strategies ranging from arbitrary whimsy to complex and self-reflexive intertextuality enable her to reclaim not only the appropriated genre of the fairy tale, but also a subversive "voice." Nesbit self-reflexively reveals her manipulations of plots as well-known to the reader as to herself, explicitly calling attention to the "rules" of the fairy tale while simultaneously bending many of them, thus drawing her implied audience into her intertextual web and insuring that the shared humor retains its subversive force. A similar, although more constrained exploitation of carnivalesque freedom characterizes her adult novels, this time sanctioned by the relatively permissive "entertainment" environment of popular romance for women.

At this point, it is useful to examine the apparent sources of Nesbit's sense of freedom within the limits of the fairy tale by considering the dynamics of one of her lesser-known short stories, "The Twopenny Spell," from *Oswald Bastable and Others* (1905). In this story, paired protagonists make the simplest gender subversion, role-reversal, both workable and acceptable, judging from the frequency with which she employed the device here and elsewhere.

In "The Twopenny Spell," the prankish Harry is subjected to the vengeance of his sister, Lucy (not the heroine of *The Magic City*); she purchases a "twopenny" spell that preserves outward appearances but reverses the siblings' personality traits. The boy, one of the leaders among his schoolfellows, becomes pathetically timid and is repeatedly trounced, the girl plays malicious tricks on *her* schoolfellows and foments several quarrels. Even here, however, Nesbit cannot resolve the plot without a conventional gesture. Lucy regrets her act upon learning of Harry's humiliation: Lucy "[s]uddenly ... was really sorry. She had done this, she had degraded her happy brother to a mere milksop ... Remorse suddenly gripped her with tooth and claw."[25] On the other hand, she then proposes that Harry disguise himself as a girl and attend *her* school under her protection. His affectionate response and her apology cancel the spell (which, it must be admitted, had already done its punitive and reforming work), providing a moral fillip that reads almost apologetically after the obvious relish with which the girl's mischief has been narrated.

The passage is a study in shifting constructions; just at the moment that an affirmation of Lucy's independent agency seems to occur, we see instead that the spell has had no effect on Lucy's true, "innate" impulses. Despite the tendency to cancel any moves she makes toward alternative depiction, Nesbit does show that gender rivalry has been shifted toward androgyny and teamwork.[26] The siblings, especially Harry, have both gained more balanced personalities, integrating both altruism and self-assertion. Lucy apologizes, and Harry "thrashed Simpkins Minor thoroughly and scientifically on the first opportunity; but he did not thrash him extravagantly: he tempered pluck with mercy."[27]

This story illustrates Nesbit's tactics in negotiating the boundary between outright advocacy of female agency and an ultimate rejection of it in favor of domesticity. The same carnivalesque interval of the children's fantasy was also Nesbit's choice when she turned to her adult fiction; but the results are less impressive with her grown-up "princesses." In his study *Secret Gardens*, Humphrey Carpenter criticizes the absence of real risk in Nesbit's children's stories, and that same "safety net" is present in the protectors with whom she surrounds her heroines.[28] Carpenter's criticisms are valid, although harsh, when applied to Nesbit's children's stories; his reading is, however, an accurate assessment of Nesbit's practices in her *adult* fiction. Once the romantic dilemma of these novels has been resolved, the courtship structure is restored and the brief non-traditional episode of female power is ensconced in a "safe" narrative framework. The surviving remnant of her fantasy – the unlikely rescues of her heroines from amorous scrapes – deprives her mimetic heroines, in most cases, of the opportunities to demonstrate the real bravery available to the least significant of her fairy tale heroines.

Katherine, the heroine of *The Incredible Honeymoon* (1916) most fully embodies Nesbit's game of adult wish-fulfillment. Unwilling to marry Edward Basingstoke, with whom she flees an confining family life, Katherine consents to a "mock marriage" (at a London registry!). Here the seriousness of free choice in love as presented by novelists such as Olive Schreiner and Mona Caird approaches bedroom farce. Likewise, Nesbit evades full affirmation of a woman's self-worth when Daphne

Carmichael, the heroine of *Daphne of Fitzroy Street*, rejects suitors who value her for the artist who has exploited her as a model, brutally expressed his valuation of his work over any woman, and reneged after proposing marriage. Although the outcome of their relationship is less clear than Nesbit's reviewers and her biographers Doris Langley Moore and Julia Briggs suggest – there is no explicit acceptance of his final proposal – Daphne is the ethical opposite of the New Woman despite her bohemian career as an art student. Nesbit exploits the escapist potential of the now-old New Woman novel, but the underlying model of the fairy tale undercuts, without completely eliminating, elements of feminist polemic.

Nesbit's tendency to update by romanticizing the dilemmas of the New Woman continues in the novels that most resemble her children's fiction: *Daphne in Fitzroy Street*, *The Red House*, *The Incomplete Amorist* (1906) and *The Incredible Honeymoon*. In these works, Nesbit's most effective New Women are the independent spinsters who double as fairy godmothers; only *The Incredible Honeymoon* lacks such a character. These figures present female agency firmly domesticated as brusque nurturant behavior. The marginalized female rescuer was Nesbit's best effort at the New Woman, and this depiction is problematized only in Cecily, Lady Blair, of *Dormant* (1911).

Katherine, Daphne, and Betty are all variations on the "New Girl" story, directed to adolescents and young working women, which began to flourish between the years 1880 and 1915;[29] Nesbit was a contributor to *The Girl's Own Paper*, one of the most influential periodicals. These heroines, safely and unremittingly modest but not homebound, often act out a public version of angelic domesticity. Nesbit's adult fiction seems to represent an astute, but not necessarily cynical, market-awareness and an ability to translate the adventurous children for whom she is justly famous into callow but mildly pleasing young women who threaten no conservative mores. Such is not the case in her adult fantasy novels, sometimes called "sensational" by her reviewers – a dubious designation, since Nesbit's heroines are quite tame when contrasted with the Lady Audleys or even the Herminia Bartons of traditional sensational fiction. At the same time, however, Nesbit involves Sandra Mundy of *Salome and the Head* and Rose Royal of *Dormant* in serious confrontations with issues of female resistance to and subversion of gender stereotypes.

Salome is the story of Sandra, a young woman in flight from an impulsive and imprudent marriage; in fact, the marriage is a hoax to gain her money, but she is unaware of this for at least half of the novel. She establishes herself in London as an interpretive dancer, successfully maintaining her privacy and reputation; the "house" of the American title refers to the faceless house, lacking an address and any visible means of entry, in which she resides. When her "husband" is murdered and Sandra finds that the stage-prop head of her "Salome" dance is that of his corpse, her new lover, accepted in the belief that her husband had already died, deserts her, and she is rescued by an admirer who falsely claims the murder as his own.

Sandra finds the resolve at the end to reject, resoundingly, her vacillating lover in favor of the man who truly sacrifices for her; she does not yield to the importunities of an unworthy potential mate. Sandra embodies Nesbit's own contrary impulses – she is both "risky" and "safe" – and she is Nesbit's most sustained portait of self-determination in an adult female protagonist.

On the other hand, there is little focus on the risks – especially that of becoming *déclassée* – that Sandra takes in establishing her career; every element of notoriety is carefully removed from her life. Her career, clearly modeled on that of Maude Allan and her dance to music from Richard Strauss's *Salome*, also stands as a model of the careful cultivation of respectability by professional performers outlined by Mary Jane Corbett in *Representing Femininity*.[30] Without writing a fantastic narrative, Nesbit nevertheless idealizes Sandra's charmed life. Potentially serious consequences remain *in potentia*, and self-sacrificing male rescuers abound.

Dormant, a "Theosophical" romance of reincarnation, is Nesbit's most ambitious and most complex narrative, with the exception of the inter-connected children's novels *Harding's Luck* and *The House of Arden*. Fur-ther, it is her darkest view of the "emancipated" heroine, one who is not only displaced from the center of her own narrative, but who is also rendered ineffectual by supernatural forces that ultimately destroy her lover, a "Frankenstein" in nature and activity. The "exploded" science of Paracelsus returns, becoming the Theosophy of Helena Blavatsky and Annie Besant – the latter a close friend of Nesbit and Bland. Nesbit had used the Frankenstein motif in some of her gothic tales; in *Dormant*, it is interwoven with the Sleeping Beauty motif in a confrontation of male with female power that can have no positive resolution.

Nesbit at first seems to place women's issues in the foreground, when Rose Royal, transparently the young Nesbit in appearance and outlook, resolves to live alone in a slum property that is the source of her income.

Rose's agency is diminished as the novel increasingly focuses on her lover, Anthony Drelincourt, ostensibly a chemist and anatomist, but also a secret adept in "ancient wisdom" and the Paracelsian quest for the elixir of life. Anthony, if anything even more self-absorbed and narcissistic than Victor Frankenstein, falls in love with Eugenia, the woman whom he discovers and "resurrects," unaware that she is the lover of his namesake uncle who attempted to render her immortal; he perishes with Eugenia as a result of his attempts to render himself as immortal as she.

If Rose and Eugenia share between them the Sleeping Beauty role, then Cecily, Lady Blair, Eugenia's past rival and Anthony's mentor, is cast, and indeed named on many occasions, as the fairy godmother. In this role, she is pathetically lacking, especially in the ruses by which she tries to recall her long-vanished youth. Yet it is Lady Blair who supports Eugenia – with mixed motives, one is sure – in her resistance to Anthony's schemes, and she is consistently Rose's advocate as well.

Eugenia resembles the Sleeping Beauty who awakens in power even if her male counterpart seems to hold patriarchal mastery over her fate.[31] Her passage through "death" has given her both the will and the intellect to resist Anthony's plan; there is, even in her consent to his desire to undergo the ritual, a suggestion that she knows and welcomes the inevitable failure. The resistance to Anthony mounted by all three women, who are dispersed aspects of Nesbit herself both as young and as aging lover, represents Nesbit's critique of his blindness and arrogance. Her persistent focalization via Anthony renders the female characters a passive "Greek chorus," however; it seems that patriarchy can be punished, but not dethroned. It is a significant index of Nesbit's characteristic ambivalence that Rose, the contemporary and more mimetic character, is locked into a set of conventional behaviors – her rueful meditations accepting second place to Anthony's work affirm female acquiescence in the *status quo* – while the "magical" Eugenia, like the girl-heroines of her fairy tales, is able to act effectively, even though it means her destruction.

Nesbit was dismayed that she was marginalized as a writer of children's fiction.[32] Her first desire was to become a poet, and even after she won critical and public acclaim with her "Bastable" books and the "Five Children" series, she longed to be recognized as a "serious" writer, even to the point of attempting short stories, clearly imitative of Henry James, in *The Literary Sense* (1903). Nesbit seems to have been caught in a double bind that was partly of her own making and partly that of society's. In evading any real confrontation with New Woman issues in her fiction, she was unlikely to receive much critical notice, and the critics' general tendency to dismiss women's fiction insured that little notice was taken of her work.[33] When *Dormant*, for example, was mentioned at all by the critics, the novel's serious issues were passed over in silence, and the whole was treated as a comic episode – one critic emphasized the difficulties of transporting a catatonic body by rail to London.[34] Her critics met each of her adult novels with the same response, either praising her "light" or "humorous" touch, or expressing dismay that she had, in the words of one critic of her first novel, *The Secret of Kyriels*:

done violence to her delicate imagination by challenging comparisons with Miss Florence Warden and Mrs. Williamson. *The Secret of Kyriels* is a clever *tour de force*, but it affords the author little scope for indulging in her sense of humor. Romantic comedy rather than melodrama is the domain in which she ought to achieve genuine success.[35]

This assessment, almost the first review of her fiction, was to be repeated throughout her career, either as praise or as blame. Even where possibilities for irony existed, such as the male-narrated *The Red House*, the critic for *The Academy* was uneasy at her "gender-bending":

most people will agree that for a woman-writer to tell a story in the guise of a man is a distinct risk, and a risk not worth taking. And E. Nesbit is a particularly feminine woman-writer; that is the secret of her charm. So we feel resentful when she cheats us of what she has taught us to expect from her, for the sake of masquerading in doublet and hose . . . We wish very heartily that [the narrator] had been the person called Chloe, for by letting her husband tell the tale she has left us to form the impression of a most effeminate and rather tiresome young man.[36]

For a woman to satirize male unreliability and foibles as she had done when speaking in the voice of the boy Oswald Bastable will not do, it seems, when she speaks through the grown-up, Len.

In her life, Nesbit avoided public involvement with feminist issues; privately she raged and acquiesced to the impositions of her married life. By reducing the New Woman to an iconic "new" romantic heroine, Nesbit sidestepped engagement with the serious potential of such characters and lost desirable critical attention. It is necessary to read Nesbit selectively if one's agenda is to recuperate her for feminism, but in the interests of a "thick description" of the *feminisms* of the late nineteenth and early twentieth centuries, she remains a figure who provides a valuable middle term between equally adamant feminists and anti-feminists. Imaginative release from socially constituted repressions is the true license of fantasy. It has been attested, for Nesbit and others, many times, and it is the hallmark of nineteenth-century fantasy. The demands of writing purely mimetic fiction effectively repressed much protest in Nesbit's work. It is perhaps inevitable that the most forthright and independent females Nesbit ever depicted are a dancer, one who is outside the pale or nearly so, and a woman magically recalled from the dead.

NOTES

1 *The Magic City* (London: Ernest Benn, 1910; New York: MacMillan, 1910), p. 164.
2 Julia Briggs discusses the topicality of *The Magic City* in her biography of Nesbit, *A Woman of Passion: the Life of E. Nesbit, 1858–1924* (London: Hutchinson; New York: New Amsterdam Books, 1987), pp. 333–35. Nesbit is generally sympathetic to the hardships of working people, but, on occasion, the assumptions of her class are inscribed quite harshly.
3 *Ibid.*, pp. 193–95.
4 Ann Ardis, *New Women, New Novels* (New Brunswick, NJ: Rutgers University Press, 1990), p. 140.
5 Nesbit also produced a small number of competent gothic short stories, collected as *E. Nesbit's Tales of Terror* (London: Methuen, 1983), although only a few, most notably "Man-Sized in Marble," effectively exploit gender issues.
6 Doris Langley Moore, *E. Nesbit: A Biography*, revised edition (New York: Chilton Books, 1966). Langley Moore quotes from a letter of October 22, 1888 Olive Schreiner wrote to Havelock Ellis: "Mrs. Bland ... was so kind to me before I left London. I don't think I should have got away without her. She came the last morning to finish packing my things and see me off. Do you know, she's one of the noblest women? I can't tell you about her life, because I mustn't, but it's grand ..." (p. 110). Schreiner is obviously referring to the open secret of Hubert Bland's infidelities.
7 Briggs, *A Woman of Passion*, p. 333.
8 Hubert Bland, *Essays By Hubert*, ed. E. Nesbit (London: M. Goschen, 1914), p. 209. Ironically, Nesbit edited this and similar essays after Bland's death, dedicating them to "The readers who loved Hubert."
9 Quoted in Briggs, *A Woman of Passion*, p. 333.
10 Wells described Bland as one who lived an imagined persona of "a great Man of the World, a Business Man (he had no gleam of business ability)" (quoted in Ruth Braddon, *The New Women and the Old Men* [New York: Norton, 1990], p. 174).
11 Briggs, *A Woman of Passion*, p. 335.

12 This episode is attested to in the Fabian treatise *Three Years' Work* in Sally Alexander (ed.), *Women's Fabian Tracts* (New York, London: Routledge, 1988), p. 154. Nesbit is generally supposed to have been anti-suffrage, but the relevant documents suggest that her opposition may have developed over time.

13 Edith Lazaros Honig, *Breaking the Angelic Image: Woman Power in Victorian Children's Fiction* (New York: Greenwood Press: 1988). Honig states that "In humorous fantasy . . . an independent heroine could be readily dismissed as part of the delightful reversal of reality, all the while insidiously presenting a subversive feminist message that was there for the reader to note or to disregard" (p. 71).

14 Alison Lurie, *Don't Tell the Grownups* (New York: Avon, 1990), p. 105.

15 Jack Zipes, *Fairy Tales and the Art of Subversion* (New York: Routledge, 1983), pp. 28–30.

16 Lurie, *Don't Tell the Grownups*, p. 117, and U. C. Knoepflmacher, "Of Baby-lands and Babylons: E. Nesbit and the Reclamation of the Fairy Tale," *Tulsa Studies in Women's Literature* 6.2 (Fall 1987), 299–325. See also Nina Auerbach and Knoepflmacher (eds.), *Forbidden Journeys: Fairy Tales and Fantasies by Victorian Women Writers* (Chicago and London: University of Chicago Press, 1992). The introductions to the divisions of this anthology also emphasize the increasing prominence of women writers of fairy tales.

17 Knoepflmacher, "Of Babylands and Babylons," 302.

18 Lurie, *Don't Tell the Grownups*, p. 21.

19 Mikhail Bakhtin, *Rabelais and His World*, trans. Hélène Iswolsky (Bloomington: University of Indiana Press, 1984). Bahktin's theories have been exhaustively analyzed. William Touponce has indicated their applicability to some aspects of young readers' literature in his study "Laughter and Freedom in Ray Bradbury's *Something Wicked This Way Comes*," *Children's Literature Association Quarterly* 13.1 (Spring 1988), 17–21.

20 Karen A. Hohne and Helen Wussow, *A Dialogue of Voices: Feminist Theory and Bakhtin* (Minneapolis: University of Minnesota Press, 1994). As the editors to this volume indicate, "It must be stressed that in Bakhtin's definition, carnival continues to exists within authority's framework . . . Instead of smashing social frameworks, carnival reinscribes them by being contained within them" (p. xii).

21 In addition to Elmar Schenkel's article "Utopie und Phantasktik in den Kinderbüchern von E. Nesbit," *Inklings: Jahrbuch für Literatur und Aesthetik* 8 (1990), 107, in *Long Ago When I Was Young*, Noel Streatfeild, ed., (London: Ronald Whiting and Wheaton, 1966), the editor has also pointed out that Nesbit's most positive experiences are grounded in the escapades with her brothers, in which, as the indulged youngest sibling, she was allowed to participate (pp. 14, 19).

22 One exception, however, is Elfrida in Nesbit's *The House of Arden* (London: Ernest Benn, 1908; New York: Coward, McCann, 1908), who is consistently depicted as being more courageous than Edred, her brother.

23 Nesbit, *The Enchanted Castle* (London: T. Fisher Unwin, 1907; New York: Harper, 1908), p. 15.
24 John Stephens,*Language and Ideology in Children's Fiction* (New York and London: Longman, 1992), pp. 125–32.
25 Nesbit, "The Twopenny Spell," in *Oswald Bastable and Others* (London: Wells, Gardner, Darton, and Co., 1905; New York: Coward, McCann, 1960), p. 177.
26 Claudia Nelson discusses the question of the tensions between the angelic and the virile ideals in representing masculinity in her book *Boys Will Be Girls: The Feminine Ethic and British Children's Fiction, 1857–1917* (New Brunswick, NJ: Rutgers University Press, 1991). Alan Richardson also discusses the representation of masculinity in "Reluctant Lords and Lame Princes: Engendering the Male Child in Nineteenth-Century Juvenile Fiction," *Children's Literature* 21 (1993), 3–19.
27 Nesbit, "The Twopenny Spell," p. 178.
28 Humphrey Carpenter, *Secret Gardens* (Boston: Houghton Mifflin), 1985, pp. 133–37.
29 Sally Mitchell, *The New Girl: Girls' Culture in England, 1880–1915* (New York: Columbia University Press, 1995), p. 3.
30 Mary Jane Corbett, *Representing Femininity: Middle-Class Subjectivity in Victorian and Edwardian Women's Autobiographies* (New York: Oxford University Press, 1992), pp. 107–29.
31 Nina Auerbach, *Woman and the Demon* (Cambridge, MA: Harvard University Press, 1982). Citing H. Rider Haggard's Ayesha in *She* as only one of several examples (p. 42), Auerbach suggests that the passivity of Sleeping Beauty is a matter more of societal wish-fulfillment, a way of containing female potential, rather than an emblem of female subjection.
32 Briggs, *A Woman of Passion*, pp. 399–401.
33 See Nicola Diane Thompson, *Reviewing Sex: Gender and the Reception of Victorian Novels* (London: Macmillan: New York: New York University Press, 1996) for a fuller discussion of these issues.
34 *The Saturday Review* (December 23, 1911), 805.
35 *The Spectator*, 81 (December 10, 1898), 873. One reviewer, in *The Literary World*, 31 (March 31, 1900), did praise Nesbit's control over her involved, suspense-filled plot, noting, however, that it was "not a study of character, but a tale of incident" (71).
36 Review of *The Red House*, *The Academy* (March 7, 1903), 225–26.

WORKS CITED

Alexander, Sally (ed.), *Women's Fabian Tracts*, New York, London: Routledge, 1988.
Anderson, Nancy Fix, "Eliza Lynn Linton: *The Rebel of the Family* (1880) and Other Novels," in Barbara L. Harman and Susan Meyer (eds.), *The New Nineteenth Century: Feminist Readings of Underread Victorian Fiction*, New York and London: Garland, 1996.

Ardis, Ann, *New Women, New Novels*, New Brunswick, NJ: Rutgers University Press, 1990.

Auerbach, Nina and U. C. Knoepflmacher (eds.), *Forbidden Journeys: Fairy Tales and Fantasies by Victorian Women Writers*, Chicago and London: University of Chicago Press, 1992.

Auerbach, Nina, *Woman and the Demon*, Cambridge, MA: Harvard University Press, 1982.

Bakhtin, Mikhail, *Rabelais and His World*, trans. Hélène Iswolsky, Bloomington: University of Indiana Press, 1984.

Bland, Hubert, *Essays by Hubert*, ed. E. Nesbit, London: M. Goschen, 1914.

Braddon, Ruth, *The New Women and the Old Men*, New York: Norton, 1990.

Briggs, Julia, *A Woman of Passion: the Life of E. Nesbit, 1858–1924*, London: Hutchinson; New York: New Amsterdam Books, 1987.

Carpenter, Humphrey, *Secret Gardens*, Boston: Houghton Mifflin, 1985.

Corbett, Mary Jane, "'Artificial Natures': Class, Gender, and the Subjectivities of Victorian Actresses," in *Representing Femininity: Middle-Class Subjectivity in Victorian and Edwardian Women's Autobiographies*, New York: Oxford University Press, 1992.

Hohne, Karen A. and Helen Wussow, *A Dialogue of Voices: Feminist Theory and Bakhtin*, Minneapolis: University of Minnesota Press, 1994.

Edith Lazaros Honig, *Breaking the Angelic Image: Woman Power in Victorian Children's Fiction*, New York: Greenwood Press: 1988.

Knoepflmacher, U.C., "Of Babylands and Babylons: E. Nesbit and the Reclamation of the Fairy Tale," *Tulsa Studies in Women's Literature* 6.2 (Fall 1987), 299–325.

Lurie, Alison, *Don't Tell the Grownups*, New York: Avon, 1990.

Mitchell, Sally, *The New Girl: Girls' Culture in England, 1880–1915*, New York: Columbia University Press, 1995.

Moore, Doris Langley, *E. Nesbit: A Biography*, revised edn., New York: Chilton Books, 1966.

Nelson, Claudia, *Boys Will Be Girls: The Feminine Ethic and British Children's Fiction, 1857–1917*, New Brunswick, NJ: Rutgers University Press, 1991.

Nesbit, E. *Dormant*, London: Methuen, 1911; published as *Rose Royal*, New York: Dodd, Mead, 1912.

Daphne in Fitzroy Street, London: George Allen and Sons, 1909; New York: Doubleday, Page, and Co., 1909.

The Enchanted Castle, London: T. Fisher Unwin, 1907; New York: Harper, 1908.

Five Children and It, London: Ernest Nister, 1902; New York: Dodd, Mead, 1905.

The House of Arden, London: Ernest Benn, 1908; New York: Coward, McCann, 1908.

Harding's Luck, London: Ernest Benn, 1909; New York: Fredrick Stokes, 1910.

The Incomplete Amorist, London: Constable and Co., 1906; New York: Doubleday, Page, and Co., 1906.

The Incredible Honeymoon, New York: Harper and Brothers, 1916; London: Hutchinson and Co., 1921.

The Book of Dragons, London: Harper, 1899; New York: Harper, 1900.

"My School Days," in *The Girl's Own Paper* (October 1896–September 1897); rpt. in *Long Ago When I Was Young*, ed. Noel Streatfeild, London: Ronald Whiting and Wheaton, 1966.

The Literary Sense, London: Methuen, 1903; New York: MacMillan, 1903.

The Magic City, London: Ernest Benn, 1910; New York: MacMillan, 1910.

The New Treasure-Seekers, London: T. Fisher Unwin, 1904; New York: Fredrick Stokes, 1904.

Oswald Bastable and Others, London: Wells, Gardner, Darton, and Co., 1905; New York: Coward, McCann, 1960.

The Red House, London: Methuen 1902; New York: Harper, 1902.

Salome and the Head, London: Doubleday, Page, and Co., 1909; published as *The House with No Address*, New York: Doubleday, Page, and Co., 1909.

The Secret of Kyriels, London: Hurst and Blackett, 1898; Philadelphia: Lippincott, 1899.

The Story of the Treasure-Seekers, being the Adventures of the Bastable Children in Search of a Fortune, London: T. Fisher Unwin, 1899; New York: Frederick Stokes, 1899.

E. Nesbit's Tales of Terror, London: Methuen, 1983.

Review of *Dormant*, *The Saturday Review*, 23 December 1911.

Review of *The Red House*, *The Academy* (March 7, 1903), 225–26.

Review of *The Secret of Kyriels*, *The Spectator* 81 (December 10, 1898), 873.

Review of *The Secret of Kyriels*, *The Literary World* 31 (March 31, 1900), 71.

Reynolds, Kimberley, *Girls Only? Gender and Popular Culture in Britain*, Philadelphia: Temple University Press, 1990.

Richardson, Alan, "Reluctant Lords and Lame Princes: Engendering the Male Child in Nineteenth-Century Juvenile Fiction," *Children's Literature*, 21 (1993), 3–19.

Schenkel, Elmar, "Utopie und Phantasktik in den Kinderbüchern von E. Nesbit," *Inklings: Jahrbuch für Literatur und Aesthetik*, 8 (1990), 103–24.

Stephens, John, *Language and Ideology in Children's Fiction*, New York and London: Longman, 1992.

Thompson, Nicola Diane, *Reviewing Sex: Gender and the Reception of Victorian Novels*, London: Macmillan; New York: New York University Press, 1996.

Touponce, William, "Laughter and Freedom in Ray Bradbury's *Something Wicked This Way Comes*," *Children's Literature Association Quarterly* 13.1 (Spring 1988), 17–21.

Zipes, Jack, *Fairy Tales and the Art of Subversion*, New York: Routledge, 1983.

CHAPTER 14

"An 'old-fashioned' young woman": Marie Corelli and the New Woman

Annette R. Federico

Although she wrote at a time when feminist agitation was at its peak, Marie Corelli (1855–1924) was not exactly on the vanguard of feminism's first wave. She opposed women's suffrage and detested the New Woman, and she was able to speak directly to a discontented audience who felt alienated from the tenets of emerging feminists and practitioners of the New Fiction. At the same time, Corelli believed in the intellectual equality of women, supported women's economic independence as an indispensable right, and loudly opposed sexism within the male literary establishment. This apparent contradiction has invited recent examinations of Marie Corelli as a cultural phenomenon. Her conspicuous place in late-Victorian society has become a way of entering discussions of feminism, decadence, class ideology, and Victorian and early modern literary culture.

And she *is* conspicuous: in 1886, Corelli began an unparalleled publication record. At the turn of the century, sales of her novels averaged 175,000 copies, and *Temporal Power* (1902) achieved a first day record of 120,000.[1] Her fall in popularity was sudden and total after World War I, and Corelli's reputation today as a low-status author of "bestsellers" has hardly been disputed, despite the fact that her success had a lasting impact both on the publishing industry and on generations of readers, who found her narrative energy and moral assertiveness irresistible.

Several critics have worked within a feminist framework under the assumption that Corelli's huge popularity and splintered feminism may provide us with information about women and culture at the turn of the century.[2] Although extremely important for nineteenth-century studies, the historical and demographic focus of these works tend to dispense with any sustained or formal reading of Corelli's novels. And yet aesthetic considerations are essential to an understanding of Marie Corelli's strain of feminism. Corelli feared the androgynous leanings of New Women and male aesthetes, and in her novels and essays she frequently inserts denunciations of the New Woman as "sexless" and insists on the innate differences between men and women. Yet the specificity of her fictional works, often generic blends of the society novel, the gothic, literary decadence, and the historical romance, do not artlessly articulate the categorical assumptions behind them. Also, like many New Women novels, Corelli's texts are dialogic or polyphonic, refusing to "conform to traditional expectations for realistic and formalistic fiction,"[3] allowing Corelli to give voice to opposing arguments which are often unsatisfactorily resolved. Her novels maneuver conventions of form, perspective, realism, *and* gender, and many of them fully participate in the sexual questions which were being canvassed and debated in the works of "erotomaniacs" and New Women – indeed, almost surpass those novels in their provocations and suggestions of "sexual anarchy."

In a brilliant chapter on Corelli in *The Gender of Modernity*, Rita Felski points out the emotional ambivalence in Corelli's representations of gender, explaining that Corelli oscillates "between recurring expressions of anger, frustration, and resentment toward the male sex," and yet yearns "for oceanic dissolution of the self in an ecstatic merging of souls."[4] Corelli's reliance on feminine stereotypes and her disapproval of the New Woman notwithstanding, she was able to envision a blissful utopia of sexual democracy – in *The Soul of Lilith* (1892), for example, a mystic claims that God has both feminine and masculine attributes and that the "marvellous Evolution which resulted in Humanity" originates in the two governing vital forces of the male and the female "reigning together."[5] But Corelli's mystical utopia is very different from that of the New Woman, whose pragmatic dissections of social and sexual relations undermined romantic bliss.[6] Her dreams of sexual equality are not located in politics and praxis, but in culture, especially in her faith in the emotional power of literature, and a female aesthetic which involves typical feminine attributes, such as outward grace, inward purity, gentleness, and beauty. Marie Corelli is – as she herself would have declared – too "old fashioned" to be included under our definitions of the "New Woman," a creature Gail Cunningham says must be "in conflict with social convention [as] *a matter of principle*" and, according to Ann Ardis, must challenge "the naturalness of sex, gender, and class distinctions."[7] The New Woman's pragmatism, combined with her association with the realist school of sexually explicit New Fiction, provokes an antithetical stance in Marie Corelli, whose emotional defenses of women's special nature and unique contributions to art and literature resemble cultural feminism more than they do conservative backlash.[8] As Silvia Boven-schen argues, the supposed dominance of "gentleness" in the feminine repertoire is inherently ambivalent: on the one hand, it is an emblem of female subjugation and passivity, but on the other hand, it "contains utopian moments and lends us an idea of human behaviour beyond oppression, competition, and compulsory achievement."[9]

In this chapter I would like to explore the ways Corelli attempts to assert a feminine aesthetic which ostensibly relies upon "the radical incompatibility of masculine and feminine spheres"[10] by privileging her 1895 bestseller *The Sorrows of Satan* with a somewhat close reading. Although I want to keep culture and history emphatically in the fore-front (and would not dream of trying to rescue Marie Corelli for feminism), I do think the imaginative peculiarity of her protestations deserves some reflection, especially if we bear in mind the ambivalence evoked by Bovenschen. Marie Corelli repeatedly locates her resistance within the realm of art, a fluid and ambiguous territory. Furthermore, her vision of sexual equality is tied to her reliance upon artistic expres-sion, especially the extravagances of romance, for there her anger at male privilege *and* her desires for sexual fulfillment can be given free play. The masculine publishing world was insensitive to Corelli's liber-atory notions and her idealism, and she felt forced into an attitude of unwomanly aggression. The "Authoress," she wrote, must learn to take part in the "rough-and-tumble" of the literary arena and "fight with the rest unless she prefers to lie down and be walked over."[11] Corelli's articulations of feminist resistance are almost always in relation to her situation as a writer, and indeed just about every novel published after 1886 includes an offhand comment about men's prejudice against women writers, whether relevant to the plot or not. Significantly, Corelli's conservative belief in sexual difference is weighed against an equally strong faith in the transforming powers of literature. Her obses-sion with aesthetic issues over social or political ones makes her appear comparatively uninterested in female emancipation: women do not need art as much as art needs women. Caught between her opposition to the New Woman and her ongoing battles with male critics, Corelli ends up relying on the "free space" of art as the means to universal truth, and the power of literature to give humanity "the thoughts that live – the words that burn."[12] But conflicting discourses of value in late-Victorian culture make such a retreat untenable. In the 1890s, the aesthetic is not *really* a free space, but a sexually contested territory.

Corelli's assertion of the liberatory value of the aesthetic is not an unfamiliar reaction to the encroachments of politics on the "literary." Her insistence on the centrality of the imagination and her almost religious devotion to "Literature" is part of a conservative tradition which claims the aesthetic for its own purposes. As Terry Eagleton explains,

> From Burke and Coleridge to Matthew Arnold and T. S. Eliot, the aesthetic in Britain is effectively captured by the political right. The autonomy of culture, society as expressive or organized totality, the intuitive dogmatism of the imagination, the priority of local affections and unarguable allegiances, the intimidatory majesty of the sublime, the incontrovertible character of the "immediate" experience, history as a spontaneous growth impervious to rational analysis: these are some of the forms in which the aesthetic becomes a weapon in the hands of political reaction.[13]

Eagleton's list of absolutes describes Marie Corelli's beliefs and motives perfectly. Her faith in "the intuitive dogmatism of the imagination" and "the priority of local affections and unarguable allegiances" is expressed in many statements about "the dignity of Literature" and the magical powers of the imagination, "the first element in artistic greatness."[14] Woman's beauty, purity, and innate selflessness lay special moral claims upon her when she picks up the pen, for the imaginative is, for Corelli, a place for "beauty and harmony ... poetry and prophecy."[15] Women writers should be committed to an ideal: beautifying life. Thus Ouida is Corelli's favorite woman writer because she is "a *romancer*" who writes against an age of "Prose and Positivism."[16] But the New Woman writer has shifted attention away from the true and the beautiful, and even her "mannish" appearance is an affront to Corelli's aesthetic faith, since feminine beauty is itself a means to moral reform. In this sense, what Corelli chiefly objects to in the New Woman is her *unloveliness*, and this extends to the sordid realism of New Woman fiction.

But for all her striving after romance and the ideal, Corelli was accused by male critics of being impossibly coarse and "uncurtained." "Has not the 'World' called *me* 'Oudia-and-Onions' and have I done aught but *wonder* at the extraordinary bad taste of the masculine mind that so attacked me?" she wrote to her publisher in 1892.[17] W. T. Stead, in a review of *The Sorrows of Satan*, invited readers to imagine *Paradise Lost* served up with smokey chimneys, draughty lodgings, and tasteless porridge.[18] A Corelli novel can be remarkably slippery, the meeting place of romance and vulgarity, epic and melodrama, sentimental trash and high-minded art.

These paradoxical evaluations come up against Corelli's apparent ignorance of the contradictions her novels embodied. Her confidence in her art was absolute. Corelli romanticizes woman's essential nature and particular knowledge, and she sees the politics and poses of the New Woman as dangerous because *these* women are romanticizing masculinity. It is not so much the New Woman's politics that Corelli objects to – she believes in women's equality and when she sees sexism she names it – but she views the New Woman's apparent betrayal of feminine culture and a female aesthetic as a misguided allegiance with men rather than a commitment to women. For Corelli, sexual equality must not erase sexual difference, for women possess special gifts which she fears are disappearing into the dominant sphere of the masculine. Thus in a letter written in 1889 declining an invitation to contribute to a new magazine called *Woman*, Corelli doubts the direction the women's movement is taking: "Again, though I wish to admire 'progressive womanhood' – the 'progress' is assuming disastrously masculine forms which I shall never consent to approve or uphold, my theory being that woman is never seen to better advantage than when in her own naturally ordained sphere of action and influence."[19]

Corelli's repulsion of "masculine forms" on the political front seems pretty staunch, and it is partly based upon her suspicion that masculine culture – including the results of science, technology, and industrial capitalism – tramples upon feminine gifts. She even says she would not want to see women in Parliament because the sex "pre-eminent for grace and beauty" would be degraded by having to participate in "'scenes' of heated and undignified disputations."[20] In "The Advance of Woman," Corelli writes:

In claiming and securing her intellectual equality with Man, she should ever bear in mind that such a position is only to be held by always maintaining and preserving as great an Unlikeness to him as possible in her life and surroundings. Let her imitate him in nothing but independence and individuality. Let her eschew his fashions in dress, his talk, and his manners. A woman who wears "mannish" clothes, smokes cigars, rattles out slang, gambles at cards, and drinks brandy and soda on the slightest provocation, is lost altogether, both as woman and man, and becomes sexless.[21]

This is a clear statement of Corelli's limited concession to feminism: equality is asserted on the level of intellectual and economic independence, but the New Woman's masculine attitude makes her sexually neuter – and neutralizes her power, for a woman cannot combat patriarchal oppression if she longs to be a patriarch herself. But "neutrality" is exactly what is most valued in the male literary establishment. Writing in 1904 on *The Feminine Note in Fiction*, William Courtney says, "[M]ore and more in our modern age novels are written by women for women... It is the neutrality of the artistic mind which the female novelist seems to find it difficult to realize."[22] As Ann Ardis has explained, Courtney ensures the marginality of New Woman fiction by "feminizing" this literature: "'femaleness'... is a synonym for aesthetic second-rateness."[23] Thus Corelli's heroic rejection of masculine style is complicated by the cultural authority of the masculine and the practical value of male approval, especially for a writer. Her scepticism of male-identified New Women inevitably conflicts with the social prestige of so-called "masculine" writing. Although she defends her feminine aesthetic by repeatedly asserting the value of romance over realism and by criticizing the prejudices of male critics, Corelli appreciates that in literature to be "manly" is not without its advantages. In a letter to her publisher, George Bentley, Corelli says,

And here we come to your allusion to my "sister authors"! Do I not know them? Have they not hurt me, while I was yet weak enough to *be* hurt? Have they not taken my hand and kissed my lips, and then gone away to write abuse of me afterwards? Yes, indeed – over and over again, and I have never paid them back in their own coin – I *could* not do so. I have never had a moment's jealousy of any other living writer, male or female. The principal thing my "sisters" grudge me is the "man's pen" that one amiable critic allowed I possessed; I do not write in a "ladylike" or effeminate way, and for that they hate me.[24]

This is not the only place where Corelli faults literary women for their jealous backbiting. The New Woman's sisterhood with other women writers is dubious, to say the least. But given Corelli's advertisement of "ladylike" attributes in her own person and the fact that just about everything that was understood culturally as masculine received her loud disapproval, her pride in writing like a man is incongruous.

In fact, there was no consensus among reviewers about the gendered qualities of Corelli's writing. She boasts to Bentley that the Prince of Wales admires her books for the "fearless courage" of her opinions. "He said, 'There is no namby-pamby nonsense about you – you write with a man's pen, and I should think you would fight your enemies like a man!' These words delighted me, for to be 'namby-pamby' would be a *horror* to me," she writes.[25] But plenty of critics slighted her novels for being *very* "namby-pamby" and effeminate, and they used typical sexist epithets:

"the hysterical vapourings of a mind without balance," "feminine redundancy of adjectives," "extravagant flights of fancy," "the littleness of the woman thrust in every chapter."[26] Corelli's perceptions of the unwomanly New Woman (and her mistaken allegiance to masculine models) interferes with the cultural value of writing with a "man's pen" – a value which did not hold with Corelli's feminine and moral aesthetic. For she detested what was called "virile" writing. "Anything written in this fashion is at once pronounced 'virile' and commands wide admiration ... particularly if it be a story in which women are depicted at the lowest kickable depth of drabism to which men can drag them, while men are represented as the suffering victims of their wickedness," she writes. "'Virility'... means ... men's proper scorn for the sex of their mothers, and an egotistical delight in themselves, united to a barbarous rejoicing in bad language and abandoned morals. It does not mean this in decent every-day life, of course; but it does in books."[27] In social life, virility is not necessarily pejorative – Corelli even says, "I cannot abide the 'flabby-minded' of my sex, who show no fight."[28] But virility in books is another thing: it is an unacceptable aesthetic. Corelli admiringly quotes an MA who asserts, "'Art ... if it be genuine and sincere, tends ever to the lofty and the beautiful. There is no rule of art more important than the sense of modesty.'"[29] The mannish, cigar-smoking woman in Corelli's novella "My Wonderful Wife," for example, dashes off a novel which the male narrator (her husband) describes as "not rubbish," having "no silly idyllic-sublime stuff in it," being rather sporting, "full of slap-dash vigour and stable slang; a really jolly, go-ahead, over-hill-and-dale, cross-country sort of book."[30] Later, he comments – and surely this is Corelli's view – "[I]t is just the subtle charm of her finer sex that should give the superiority to her work – not the stripping herself of all those delicate and sensitive qualities bestowed on her by Nature, and the striving to ape that masculine roughness which is precisely what we want eliminated from all high ideals of art."[31]

Corelli repeatedly inserts aesthetic judgments in her protests against patriarchal assumptions, and yet as we have seen, opinion was divided whether Marie Corelli herself wrote with a "man's pen" or with womanly delicacy. It is clear, though, that Corelli was trying to articulate a specifically feminine aesthetic in opposition to both patriarchal literary values and to the New Woman novel. *The Sorrows of Satan* interestingly plays out this fissured aesthetic in its coincidental treatment of a corrupt masculine literary world, New Woman novels, and wholesome popular literature. Corelli's opinions on these literary matters are unmistakable, if not glaring. Stead wrote a twelve-page review of the novel where he not only suggested that the character of the writer Mavis Clare is an idealized portrait of Corelli herself, but that half of the novel is about "the sorrows of Marie Corelli" as she "goes for her adversaries" in the literary market.[32] There is plenty of personal axe-grinding in the book, to be sure. But, interestingly, *The Sorrows of Satan* also exploits the more titillating characteristics of literary decadence, and by connection the New Woman novel, since the two were often conflated in the Victorian imagination.[33] It accommodates sexually transgressive attitudes with startling suggestiveness. As Stead says, "it is very much uncurtained indeed, nor would it be surprising if an unthinking reader mistook 'The Sorrows of Satan' for what its author describes as 'the loathliest of the prurient novels that have been lately written by women to degrade and shame their sex.'"[34] The novel irresistibly challenges apparently immutable and antithetical genres, styles, and audiences. Also, male aesthetes, with their associations of homosexuality, and "unwomanly" New Women were equally accused "of threatening the survival of the human race" with their sexual and social demands.[35] On the surface, Corelli's bestseller may seek to deflate these fears and reassure readers of the essential functions of men and women sexually and socially. But it may also encode sexual dissidence as enthusiastically as more self-consciously political texts. In fact, its exploitation of sexual dissidence may be partly responsible for its status as a bestseller.

The Sorrows of Satan is a melodrama set in modern London "swagger" society, where Satan, the wealthy, handsome, and charming Prince Lucio Rimanez, pulls strings in the publishing world and throws lavish parties for the English upper crust. The hero and narrator is Geoffrey Tempest, a struggling novelist, who suddenly inherits five million pounds at the same time he receives a letter of introduction to the Prince. Tempest finds Lucio fascinating, if somewhat cynical, and the two become close companions as Lucio introduces Tempest into fashionable London society, and helps him to "boom" his novel, which succeeds in making him famous, though sales remain low. Lucio, a savage misogynist, arranges Tempest's marriage to an heiress, the beautiful but cold Lady Sibyl Elton, who has been corrupted by reading New Woman novels. Again with Lucio's help, Tempest buys Willowsmere in Warwickshire, the childhood home of Lady Sibyl. Their neighbor in "Lily Cottage" is Mavis Clare, a sweetly feminine popular novelist, who writes wholesome books and is much loved by the masses, though she is always "slashed" by reviewers. (The doves in her dovecote are named "The Westminster Gazette," "The Pall Mall," etc., and she cheerfully feeds her reviews to her dog.) In the novel's most designedly melodramatic scene, Lady Sibyl declares her passion for Lucio and offers herself to him. When he brutally scorns her she swallows poison. In her sensational autobiographical suicide note, which takes two chapters and is partly a posthumous composition, Sibyl explains that her training for the marriage market, combined with reading New Fiction and too much Swinburne at an impressionable age, blackened her soul and chilled her heart: "Between their strained aestheticism and unbridled sensualism, my spirit has been stretched on the rack and broken on the wheel."[36] Distraught, Tempest agrees to travel to the East with Lucio. They are on his yacht (*The Flame*) when, in the book's wildest and most overwritten chapters, Lucio reveals his identity and demands Tempest's allegiance; he chooses God instead and is abandoned in the mid-Atlantic. He is picked up by an English steamer, and learns that his bankers have absconded with his millions. Back in London, Tempest is again poor but chastened, doing "battle with the monster, Egotism, that presented itself in a thousand disguises" (p. 468). A venomous critic digs out his book from Mudie's underground cellar and "slashes" it, but the capricious public suddenly find it worthwhile and buy it by the thousands. Mavis Clare's new book is also abused in the reviews, but it is "borne along to fame by a great wave of honest public praise and enthusiasm" (p. 468). The novel ends at the Houses of Parliament, with Satan walking arm in arm with a well-known Cabinet minister.

The Sorrows of Satan was an immediate bestseller, a fact which some critics felt portended the end of good taste among literate British subjects. H. G. Wells, for example, referred to it, along with *The Heavenly Twins* and *A Superfluous Woman*, as a book which points to the "debasing influence of the female" in modern fiction.[37] Corelli, of course, would have been appalled to find her novel grouped with New Woman fiction. *The Sorrows of Satan* is a self-righteous corrective to feminist trends and the "debasing" literature Wells and other male critics so disliked – indeed, Corelli distinctly implies that her "strong-minded" literary competitors are directly responsible for the woman reader's damnation. At the same time, the novel is a passionate defense of women's place in the literary world, exemplified in the redemptive Mavis Clare, whose "delicate attractiveness," "golden halo" (p. 222), and "tender, wistful, wonderfully innocent eyes" (p. 252) refute sexist stereotypes about literary women and give femininity an esteemed place in the book wars.

Marie Corelli appears untroubled by these conflicting views of women: her disdain for the strong-minded woman does not preclude her insistence on the independence of the literary woman. In a similar way, *The Sorrows of Satan* resists assignment to a single genre. H. G. Wells groups it with New Woman novels not necessarily because Corelli's text belongs to that category of fiction, but because it participates in the vogue for inferior books "whose relation to life is of the slightest, and whose connection with Art is purely accidental."[38] In this case, Corelli's indulgence of the late-Victorian taste for the strange and the sinful is excoriated as lurid and effeminate trash, opposed to "strong" realists (such as Zola who, says Corelli, "prostituted his powers to the lowest grade of thought").[39]

Though certainly anti-realist, *The Sorrows of Satan* is in curious collusion with decadence, a movement dominated almost entirely by young men. One aspect of decadent literature, according to Max Beerbohm, is "a love of horror and all unusual things."[40] Corelli's book certainly qualifies here, and incorporates many other *fin-de-siècle* tendencies: the exotic, mysticism, dream sequences, Egyptology, French verse and phrases, strange music, eroticism (including homoeroticism), two suicides, and, not least, purple prose. The topicality of the novel is another feature which makes it like New Woman fiction. It indulges the bourgeois reader's curiosity about London high society with its operas, dinners, and gambling dens, makes references to recognizable literary and dramatic people, and is very up-to-date in references to the current slang.

Still, *The Sorrows of Satan* strains after a bourgeois ethic as opposed to decadence and strains to accept Victorian constructions of gender. But the implicit homoeroticism in the friendship of Lucio and Tempest, the many references to women who are "unsexed" and of men who are "effeminate," and Corelli's use of a male narrator, undermine the novel's attempt at sexual stratification.

The relationship of Lucio and Tempest recalls the friendship of Lord Henry and Dorian in *The Picture of Dorian Gray*, and there are similar overtones of homoeroticism. From the first, Tempest is fascinated by Lucio's beauty, especially his "eyes . . . large and lustrous as the eyes of a beautiful woman" (*The Sorrows of Satan*, p. 82). I could cite dozens of examples: "He clapped me on the shoulder cordially and looked straight into my face, – those wonderful eyes of his . . . fixed me with a clear masterful gaze that completely dominated me. I made no attempt to resist the singular attraction which now possessed me for this man whom I had but just met, – the sensation was too strong and too pleasant to be combated" (p. 29). One scene is particularly illustrative of Tempest's submerged desire for Lucio, and it is incidentally a good example of the decadent fashion Corelli exploits. When Lucio plays a "piercing sword-like tune" on the piano, Tempest's reaction is unmistakably sexual: "My breath failed me, – my senses swam, – I felt that I must move, speak, cry out, and implore this music, this horribly insidious music should cease ere I swooned with the voluptuous poison of it . . ." When the music finally ends, Tempest feels, "Something . . . had instilled itself into my blood, or so I fancied, and the clinging subtle sweetness of [the music], moved me to strange emotions that were neither wise nor worthy of a man" (p. 151). To him the music suggests "Crime! You have roused in me evil thoughts of which I am ashamed." Lucio smilingly replies, "If you discover evil suggestions in my music, the evil, I fear, must be in your own nature." Tempest gazes at Lucio and "For one moment his great personal beauty appeared hateful to me, though I know not why" (p. 151). The contemporary reader thinks she does. The reference to an unspecified crime and Tempest's feeling of humiliation for "unworthy" emotions resonate in a novel published just six months after the notorious trials of Oscar Wilde. (Corelli, in fact, was worried that the public would be distracted from her latest book because of the trials.) The oblique allusion is highlighted a page later when Lord Elton dismisses modern poets as "effeminate, puling, unmanly humbugs!" (p. 153). As Alan Sinfield has explained, the Wilde trials circulated an image not only of homosexuality, but of aestheticism as effeminate, degenerate, and aristocratic.[41] Corelli's suddenly aristocratic hero appears to battle not only his own homosexual desires, but also Victorian culture's incipient link, in 1895, between wealthy, university-educated literary men and homosexual tendencies. This is mitigated in several ways: one is obviously the "purchase" of a beautiful and highly sexed heiress whom Tempest displays as testimony to his virility. He also makes many misogynist statements, such as "A man is always a man, – a woman is only a man's appendage, and without beauty she can not put forth any just claim to his admiration or support" (*The Sorrows of Satan*, p. 42). He is most virulent when it comes to successful literary women, such as Mavis Clare, and he takes delight in "slashing" her new book, significantly titled *Differences* (of which more later). He, by comparison, is a sell-out and a literary whore: "My book . . . haunted my days and nights with its lustful presence" (p. 177). In order to prove his masculinity he joins "in every sort of dissipation common to men of the day" (p. 151), which is Corelli's critique of upper-class vice, but also exposes the constraints of Victorian gender ideology. Tempest gambles "solely for the reason that gambling was considered ... indicative of 'manliness' and 'showing *grit*'" (p. 175). He frequents low houses with "half-nude brandy-soaked dancers" "because this kind of thing was called 'seeing life' and was deemed part of a 'gentleman's' diversion" (p. 175). His exaggerated efforts to appear manly suggest a fear of sexual inadequacy. He compares himself to "a fidgety woman," and later, after his marriage, admits that he gives way to his "brute passions" because he fears his lustful wife would sneer at him for an "effeminate milksop" were he to suggest they "reform."

Suggestions of the hero's effeminacy – of a man who must prove his heterosexuality and conform to social codes of masculinity – are counterparts to suggestions of the progressive woman's "sexlessness." Corelli here engages the ongoing conversation about women's changing roles, and while she clearly disapproves of assertions about women's intellectual and biological inferiority, she still deplores the sexual entrepreneurship of the New Woman, which is responsible for the erosion of Christian idealism and the degeneration of true womanly virtues. This is Satan's brand of misogyny:

And why I especially abominate them is, that they have been gifted with an enormous power for doing good, and that they let this power run to waste and will not use it. Their deliberate enjoyment of the repulsive, vulgar and commonplace side of life disgusts me. They are much less sensitive than men, and infinitely more heartless. They are the mothers of the human race, and the faults of the race are chiefly due to them. That is another reason for my hatred. (p. 84)

Corelli's critique of the New Woman's beastliness is a mainstay of her antifeminist position, and Sibyl Elton, who is in *this* novel, is a product of *that* literature. Importantly, New Woman fiction creates a continuum between exclusive heterosexuality and exclusive homosexuality which suggests a threatening indeterminacy, an inability to align with either sexuality. Sibyl declares, "I despise men, – I despise my own sex, – I loathe myself for being a woman!"(p. 198). Her friends recommend books that are "so dreadfully *queer*" and which describe "outcasts" and "the secret vices of men"(p. 197). Sibyl's intense admiration for Mavis Clare – she has an ecstatic vision of the writer's face before she dies – and her desire for men point to Sibyl's sexual confusion. She suffers no moral pangs when she throws herself at the charismatic Lucio because in these days "nobody can decide as to what *is* vice, or what *is* virtue"

(p. 39). This deplorable relativism is largely due to "all the 'new' writers of profitable pruriency" (p. 361). We should keep in mind that this "new" literature was chiefly a critique of the double standard, and therefore was interpreted as a subversive attack on Victorian gender ideology. Nineteenth-century political and social stability relied to a large extent on maintaining the doctrine of separate spheres. Satan sees the biological consequences for the race in this disintegration of gender identities: "As for the tom-boy tennis players and giantesses of the era, I do not consider them women at all," says Lucio. "They are merely the unnatural embryos of a new sex which will be neither male nor female" (p. 82).

Advanced women, like aesthete men, crossed ideological gender lines, and sometimes the two types became blurred in the figuration of another freak of nature: the woman writer. One hundred and fifty pages later, Lucio and Tempest return to the subject:

> "Literary women are my abhorrence, – they are always more or less unsexed."
> "You are thinking of the 'New' women, I suppose, – but you flatter them, – they never had any sex to lose. The self-degrading creatures who delineate their fictional heroines as wallowing in unchastity, and who write freely on subjects which men would hesitate to name, are unnatural hybrids of no-sex." (p. 216)

The exception to these hybrid literary creatures is the exaggeratedly feminine Mavis Clare: she is the "'old-fashioned' young woman," a paradoxical description Corelli would no doubt apply to herself. But the name of Mavis Clare's latest bestseller, as I have mentioned, is *Differences*, which strikes me as far from old-fashioned – it is a very nineties title (e.g., *Cameos, Keynotes, Discords, Silverpoints, Caprices*). We are never told what her novel is about, though we receive broad hints of its uplifting nature: "Clearness of thought, brilliancy of style, beauty of diction, all these were hers, united to consummate ease of expression and artistic skill" (p. 170). The title, however, suggests a contribution to the discourse on the collapse of gender differences initiated by New Women and dandies, as well as the visibility given to homosexuality after Wilde's trials. Mavis Clare's *Differences*, and Marie Corelli's blatant insinuation that her novel is "different" from degenerate New Fiction, rely upon the simmering tensions in the late-Victorian literary world, with its categorical opposi-tions of high and low fiction, of the intellectually pure male writer and the "debasing" yet popular female muse. Corelli attempts in this novel to reverse these stereotypes in an effort to reclaim a feminine aesthetic,

but as we have seen, the novel reacts against Corelli's polemical intentions. Although the text is unquestionably a conservative reaction to the
prevailing ideological confusion about gender, Corelli is concerned that
men and women are not preserving their "unlikeness" as polar opposites and whatever is sliding between these categories is "unnatural."
The Sorrows of Satan is not simply a novel of gender retrenchment, nor a
simple repudiation of masculine aesthetics and the New Woman's
immorality. It is, in fact, deeply incriminated in the debates about sexual
"differences"; in the context of these observations, Corelli's choice of a
male narrator deserves some attention.

It is not uncommon for New Women and decadent female writers to
choose the male point of view, either to comment ironically on the male
perspective or to explore the male experience.[42] Rita Felski, for instance,
argues that Corelli's frequent choice of a male narrator allows her
"greater narrative license to explore the erotically thrilling dimensions
of feminine beauty than would otherwise have been possible."[43] This
suggests that the male narrator permits an expression of homoerotic
fantasies for women readers. But because the grammatical gender of the
narrator in a Victorian novel is ideologically constructed, Corelli's
masculine, objectifying, frequently misogynistic voice itself embodies a
critique of masculinity. Although Tempest's egotism, materialism, and
moral cowardice are linked to his suddenly becoming a millionaire
(Corellian moral: wealth corrupts), his fierce competitiveness in the
literary world, especially his absolute hatred for women writers, raises
questions about cultural authority. "I never paid any attention to the
names of women who chose to associate themselves with the Arts," says
Tempest, "as I had the usual masculine notion that all they did, whether
in painting, music, or writing, must be necessarily trash, and unworthy
of comment. Women, I loftily considered, were created to amuse men, –
not to instruct them." (*The Sorrows of Satan*, p. 137). Corelli, of course,
inserts Mavis Clare as a rejoinder to this sexism. But if the portrait of
Mavis Clare is a conspicuous and idealized self-dramatization and yet
the voice of the novel is male, one could say "Marie Corelli" appears in
this novel discursively as both a man and a woman (and given the long
first-person suicide note from Sybil, even as a degenerate New
Woman!). Thus instead of constituting sexual binarisms, the fluidity and
constructedness of these identities ride out the indeterminacies the novel
ostensibly fears.

As W. T. Stead pointed out, Corelli's novels dwell upon displays of
heterosexual passion to the point of erotic frenzy. It is interesting, then,

to learn that Corelli lived intimately with another woman, Bertha Vyver, her entire life (and dedicated several books to her).[44] Again, it is worth keeping in mind that Wilde was sentenced for "gross indecency" on May 25, 1895, just four months before the publication of *The Sorrows of Satan* on October 21. Suggestive readers of *The Picture of Dorian Gray* may have found hints of homoeroticism in *The Sorrows of Satan*, especially given Corelli's personal and domestic arrangements. Though far from "mannish" in her personal appearance, the fact that Corelli never married made her vulnerable to attacks every bit as fearful and cruel as those leveled against sexually independent New Women. One of the most blatant accusations of Corelli's "unnatural" sexuality appeared in the *Westminster Review* in 1906, under the title "A Note Upon Marie Corelli By Another Writer of Less Repute":

> She is an erotic degenerate of the subtlest type. Had she been domesticated she might have been as harmless as her foreign contemporaries. As it is she stands alone, and the woman who has lost her womanliness is diseased. We may have in her case the body, the methods, and the talents of a woman, but there are unmistakably demonstrated also the arrogance and the intense prejudices of a man. Despite her photograph, and the sentimental interviews that she has caused to be published concerning her home-life, the only term which can be honestly applied to Marie Corelli is a "man-woman." So soon as a woman begins to concern herself passionately and discontentedly with problems which are not within the normal sphere of experience she loses the most charming asset of her sex. It is only on degenerate subjects that hysterical people can make effect. A strong and healthy man looks for a woman who is above all things else womanly and kind. Marie Corelli's celibacy is a fact of wonderful psychological value.[45]

It is disconcerting to find Brian Masters more than seventy years later saying, "Women without men usually have overweening ambition, coupled with a ruthless determination to satisfy it. Deprived of the primitive function which is their right, they spend their lives trying to show the world that they too can achieve something . . . The phenomenon of Marie Corelli is less a case for the literary critic than for the psychiatrist."[46] Not knowing what to do with Marie Corelli's popular success and her disregard of male critical standards, her campy femininity and her self-reliance and financial freedom, her high moral tone and her barely suppressed eroticism, there is always female neurosis to fall back upon. But I do not want to oversimplify these judgments. By reducing Corelli to an hysteric or a "man-woman," these critics submit to her complex and mysterious attraction for so many readers.

"Is there a feminine aesthetic?" asks Bovenschen."There is, thank heaven, no premeditated strategy which can predict what happens when female sensuality is freed... Art should become feminised, and women's participation ... would do it a lot of good."[47] Marie Corelli certainly had no premeditated strategy, but she shares the self-consciousness of modernist women writers, such as Virginia Woolf, Dorothy Richardson, and Djuna Barnes, who *were* strategically concerned about avoiding masculine literary habits. In 1890, she wrote triumphantly to George Bentley, "my puzzled critics will consider me a sort of literary *chameleon!*"[48] Indeed, the proliferation of sexual identities, competing aesthetics, and multiple political positions in the nineties were used by Corelli as cultural camouflage for her own ventures in the literary world as well as for her appropriations of feminism. In 1898 Oscar Wilde could joke, "the public like an open secret. Half of the success of Marie Corelli is due to the no doubt unfounded rumour that she is a woman."[49] Corelli's movement artistically between New Women novels, decadence, and popular melodrama, along with her equivocal sexuality, inconsistent feminism, and apparently inexplicable celebrity exemplify the problem of attaching a single cultural interpretation to a writer whose fame partly relied on her uneven management of broader cultural obsessions about women, men, sexuality, and aesthetics – a few of the "open secrets" of late-Victorian and early modern England.

NOTES

1 I am relying on Corelli's most recent biographer, Brian Masters, for these figures. Hall Caine was Corelli's nearest rival in sales: Corelli's books sold 100,000 a year on average; Caine's 45,000; Wells' only 15,000. See Masters, *Now Barabbas Was a Rotter: The Extraordinary Life of Marie Corelli* (London: Hamish Hamilton, 1974), pp. 6–7.

2 See Janet Galligani Casey, "Marie Corelli and *Fin-de-Siècle* Feminism," *English Literature in Transition* 35:2 (1992), 163–78; Rita S. Kranidis, *Subversive Discourse: The Cultural Production of Late Victorian Feminist Novels* (New York: St. Martin's Press, 1995); and N. N. Feltes, *Literary Capital and the Late Victorian Novel* (Madison: University of Wisconsin Press, 1993).

3 Carolyn Christenson Nelson, *British Women Fiction Writers of the 1890s* (New York: Twayne, 1996), p. 5. Despite the title, Nelson's book focuses on New Women writers and does not mention Corelli. Similarly, Elaine Showalter's anthology of short fiction, *Daughters of Decadence: Women Writers of the Fin-de-Siècle* (New Brunswick, NJ: Rutgers University Press, 1993) includes works of New Women almost exclusively.

4 Rita Felski, *The Gender of Modernity* (Cambridge, MA: Harvard University Press, 1995), p. 130.
5 Corelli, *The Soul of Lilith* (New York: The American News Company, 1892), p. 136.
6 Corelli's books would not by any means belong to the category of utopian feminist fiction, but they do cling to a belief in an ideal world. For discussions of feminist utopias at the turn of the century see Ann Ardis, *New Women, New Novels* (New Brunswick, NJ: Rutgers University Press, 1990), pp. 118–22, and Elaine Showalter, *Sexual Anarchy: Gender and Culture at the Fin-de-Siècle* (New York: Viking, 1990), pp. 50–51.
7 Gail Cunningham, *The New Woman and the Victorian Novel* (London: Macmillan, 1978), p. 10; Ardis, *New Women*, p. 17.
8 I am using "cultural feminism" (or "radical feminism") as analyzed by Alice Echols, and described in Linda Alcoff's "Cultural Feminism Versus Poststructuralism" in Nancy Tuana and Rosemarie Tong (eds.), *Feminism and Philosophy* (Boulder, CO: Westview, 1995), pp. 435–56. Alcoff states: "Echols identifies cultural feminist writings by their denigration of masculinity rather than male roles or practices, by their valorization of female traits, and by their commitment to preserve rather than diminish gender differences" (p. 437).
9 Silvia Bovenschen, "Is There a Feminine Aesthetic?" trans. Beth Weckmueller, in Gisela Ecker (ed.), *Feminist Aesthetics* (Boston: Beacon Press, 1985), p. 35.
10 Felski, *Gender of Modernity*, p. 128.
11 Corelli, "The Happy Life," *Strand* 28:163 (1904), 74.
12 Corelli, *Free Opinions* (New York: Dodd, Mead, 1905), p. 325.
13 Terry Eagleton, *The Ideology of the Aesthetic* (London: Blackwell, 1990), p. 60.
14 Corelli, *Free Opinions*, p. 309.
15 *Ibid.*, pp. 320–21.
16 Corelli, "A Word About 'Ouida'," *Belgravia* 71 (March 1890), 370–71.
17 *Corelli–George Bentley Correspondence*, Beinecke Rare Book and Manuscript Library (Yale University, New Haven, CT), February 4, 1892.
18 W. T. Stead, "'The Sorrows of Satan' – and of Marie Corelli," *The Review of Reviews* 12 (July–December 1895), 453.
19 *Corelli–George Bentley Correspondence*, December 6, 1889.
20 Corelli, *Free Opinions*, p. 202.
21 *Ibid.*, p. 203.
22 Quoted in Ardis, *New Women*, p. 54.
23 *Ibid.*
24 *Corelli–George Bentley Correspondence*, September 8, 1890.
25 *Ibid.*, September 15, 1892.
26 These quotations are from *The Daily Mail* (August 2, 1906), *The Times* (quoted in Masters, *Now Barabbas Was a Rotter*, p. 102), *The Academy* (December 30, 1893 [583]), and Stead, "Sorrows," 453.
27 Corelli, *Free Opinions*, pp. 275–76.

28 *Corelli–George Bentley Correspondence*, September 5, 1892.

29 Corelli, *Free Opinions*, p. 274.

30 Corelli, *Cameos* (Freeport, NY: Books for Libraries, 1895; 1970), p. 181.

31 *Ibid.*, p. 203.

32 Stead, "Sorrows," 453.

33 An interesting and informative article about this cross-identification is Teresa Mangum, "Style Wars of the 1890s: The New Woman and the Decadent," in Nikki Lee Manos and Mari-Jane Rochelson (eds.), *Transforming Genres: New Approaches to British Fiction of the 1890s* (New York: St. Martin's Press, 1994), pp. 47–66. See also Showalter, *Sexual Anarchy*, especially ch. 38.

34 Stead, "Sorrows," 454.

35 Mangum, "Style Wars," p. 50.

36 Corelli, *The Sorrows of Satan* (Philadelphia: Lippincott, 1896), p. 404. Subsequent references will appear in the text.

37 H.G. Wells, *The Literary Criticism of H.G. Wells*, eds. Patrick Parrinder and Robert Philmus (Brighton, Sussex: Harvester, 1980), p. 74.

38 *Ibid.*

39 Corelli, *Free Opinions*, p. 277.

40 This is from a letter of May 1894, quoted in *Aesthetes and Decadents of the 1890s*, ed. Karl Beckson (Chicago: Academy Chicago, 1993), p. 66.

41 See Alan Sinfield, *The Wilde Century: Effeminacy, Oscar Wilde, and the Queer Moment* (New York: Columbia University Press, 1994), especially ch. 4.

42 Nelson, *British Women*, p. 3.

43 Felski, *Gender of Modernity*, p. 131.

44 According to Lillian Faderman in *Surpassing the Love of Men* (New York: QPBK, 1981; 1994), Bertha Vyver is an example of a woman who fashioned her life around a beloved friend, and although there is no evidence that Marie and Bertha were lesbian lovers (Faderman calls such bonds "romantic friends"), both women were stigmatized as frustrated spinsters. See Faderman, *Surpassing the Love of Men*, pp. 213–15.

45 J. M. Stuart-Young ("Peril"). "A Note Upon Marie Corelli by Another Writer of Less Repute," *Westminster Review* 167 (1906), 691.

46 Masters, *Barabbas Was a Rotter*, p. 240.

47 Bovenschen, "Feminine Aesthetic," 49–50.

48 *Corelli–George Bentley Correspondence*, August 10, 1890.

49 *The Letters of Oscar Wilde*, ed. Rupert Hart-Davis (London: Harcourt Brace, 1962), January 8, 1898.

WORKS CITED

Ardis, Ann, *New Women, New Novels*. New Brunswick, NJ: Rutgers University Press, 1990.

Bovenschen, Silvia, "Is There a Feminine Aesthetic?" trans. Beth Weckmueller, in Gisela Ecker (ed.), *Feminist Aesthetics*, Boston: Beacon Press, 1985.

Corelli, Marie, *The Soul of Lilith*, New York: The American News Company, 1892.

The Sorrows of Satan, Philadelphia: Lippincott, 1896.

"My First Book," *Idler* 4 (1893), 239–52.

"The Happy Life," *Strand* 28:163 (1904), 72–6.

Free Opinions, New York: Dodd, Mead, 1905.

"A Word About 'Ouida'," *Belgravia* 71 (March 1890), 362–71.

Cameos, 1895. Freeport, NY: Books for Libraries, 1970.

Corelli–George Bentley Correspondence, Beinecke Rare Book and Manuscript Library, Yale University.

Cunningham, Gail, *The New Woman and the Victorian Novel*, London: Macmillan, 1978.

Eagleton, Terry, *The Ideology of the Aesthetic*, London: Blackwell, 1990.

Felski, Rita, *The Gender of Modernity*, Cambridge, MA: Harvard University Press, 1995.

Mangum, Teresa, "Style Wars of the 1890s: The New Woman and the Decadent," in Nikki Lee Manos and Mari-Jane Rochelson (eds.), *Transforming Genres: New Approaches to British Fiction of the 1890s*, New York: St. Martin's Press, 1994, pp. 47–66.

Masters, Brian, *Now Barabbas Was a Rotter: The Extraordinary Life of Marie Corelli*, London: Hamish Hamilton, 1974.

Nelson, Carolyn Christenson, *British Women Fiction Writers of the 1890s*, New York: Twayne, 1996.

Sinfield, Alan, *The Wilde Century: Effeminacy, Oscar Wilde, and the Queer Moment*, New York: Columbia University Press, 1994.

Stead, W. T., "'The Sorrows of Satan' – and of Marie Corelli," *The Review of Reviews* 12 (July–December 1895), 453–55.

Stuart-Young, J. M. ("Peril"), "A Note Upon Marie Corelli by Another Writer of Less Repute," *Westminster Review* 167 (1906), 680–92.

Wells, H. G., *The Literary Criticism of H.G. Wells*, eds. Patrick Parrinder and Robert Philmus, Brighton, Sussex: Harvester, 1980.

Wilde, Oscar, *The Letters of Oscar Wilde*, ed. Rupert Hart-Davis, London: Harcourt Brace, 1962.

CAMBRIDGE STUDIES IN NINETEENTH-CENTURY LITERATURE AND CULTURE

General editor
Gillian Beer, *University of Cambridge*

Titles published

Lightning Source UK Ltd.
Milton Keynes UK
UKOW052150140512

192557UK00002B/20/P